Challenging women

Challenging women
Psychology's exclusions, feminist possibilities

Erica Burman
Pam Alldred
Catherine Bewley
Brenda Goldberg
Colleen Heenan
Deborah Marks
Jane Marshall
Karen Taylor
Robina Ullah
Sam Warner

Open University Press
Buckingham · Philadelphia

Open University Press
Celtic Court
22 Ballmoor
Buckingham
MK18 1XW

and
1900 Frost Road, Suite 101
Bristol, PA 19007, USA

First Published 1996

A catalogue record of this book is available from the British Library

ISBN 0 335 19510 5 (pb)   0 335 19511 3 (hb)

Library of Congress Cataloging-in-Publication Data

Challenging women: psychology's exclusions, feminist possibilities /
Erica Burman . . . [et al.].
p. cm.
Includes bibliographical references and index.
ISBN 0–335–19511–3 (hb.)   ISBN 0–335–19510–5 (pb.)
1. Women—Psychology. 2. Feminist psychology. I. Burman, Erica.
HQ1206.C397 1995
305.42—dc20   95–30473
CIP

Typeset by Dorwyn Ltd, Rowlands Castle, Hants
Printed in Great Britain by Biddles Ltd, Guildford and Kings Lynn

Contents

Authors

Pam Alldred completed a psychology degree at Leicester University, then worked for three years as a researcher interviewing children about their families and 'families in general', and is now teaching part-time in the Department of Sociology, University of East London. She is currently working on her PhD thesis which is about developmental psychology, recent British social policy debates, approaches to discourse, and popular representations of children and parents. She is also affiliated to the Discourse Unit at the Manchester Metropolitan University.

Catherine Bewley is currently policy officer at the Centre for Policy on Ageing in London. She has a background in social policy research and community development in voluntary organisations. The feminist research upon which her chapter is based was part of an MSc in Occupational Psychology undertaken in 1990 at the University of Sheffield.

Erica Burman lectures in developmental psychology and women's studies at the Department of Psychology and Speech Pathology, Manchester Metropolitan University. Her previous publications include *Feminists and Psychological Practice* (edited, 1990), *Discourse Analytic Research* (co-edited, 1993) and *Deconstructing Developmental Psychology* (1994). She is co-convener of the Discourse Unit at Manchester Metropolitan University, is currently on the editorial board of *Feminism and Psychology*, and writes on feminist critiques of psychology and development, and the politics of contemporary forms of subjectivity.

Brenda Goldberg is a research assistant at the Discourse Unit, Department of Psychology and Speech Pathology, Manchester Metropolitan University.

Colleen Heenan was a founder member of the Leeds Women's Counselling and Psychotherapy Service. She is a feminist psychotherapist in private practice in Bradford, West Yorkshire and a part-time lecturer at Birkbeck College, London. She is also currently completing a PhD at the Discourse Unit, Department of Psychology and Speech Pathology, Manchester Metropolitan University on the relations between feminist therapy and discourse analysis.

Deborah Marks came to do a PhD in psychology at the Discourse Unit, Manchester Metropolitan University, after first and second degrees in sociology and social anthropology. She teaches in the Centre for Psychotherapeutic Studies, Department of Psychiatry at Sheffield University where she directs an MSc in Disability Studies.

Jane Marshall works for Wirral Community Healthcare Trust, Merseyside, as a consultant clinical psychologist specialising in women's health. As well as her therapeutic work with women, she is engaged in research into menorrhagia and is a research student at the Discourse Unit, Department of Psychology and Speech Pathology, Manchester Metropolitan University.

Karen Taylor is currently completing an MPhil at the Department of Psychology and Speech Pathology, Manchester Metropolitan University.

Robina Ullah completed her psychology degree in 1993 from Manchester Metropolitan University and now teaches in further education on access courses at MANCAT, Manchester.

Sam Warner is a principal clinical psychologist with special responsibility for therapeutic psychological services for sexually abused children and young people at the Royal Liverpool Children's Hospital, Alder Hey, Liverpool. She conducts in-service training and has written and given conference papers on sexual abuse. She is also a research student at the Discourse Unit, Department of Psychology and Speech Pathology, Manchester Metropolitan University.

Acknowledgements

This is a co-authored book. We have all been important to the production and elaboration of this work in multiple ways, and we each owe much to each other in managing to do this. So our first thanks go to each other. In addition, we would like to thank particular people for their help and support in relation to individual chapters, for:

Chapter 1, we thank Miriam Zukas, Carol Sherrard, Ann Hobbis and Sue Hyatt, and especially Colleen's psychotherapy clients.
Chapter 2, thanks to Thelma Lidster, Geoff Lidster and Adrian Levy.
Chapter 7, thanks to Angel Gordo Lopez.
Chapter 9, thanks to Louise Carolin, Rosie Garland, Rose Hughes, Fiona Measham, Helen Molloy and Debi Roker.
Thanks to the psychology technicians, especially Gareth Preston, at MMU for finding and eliminating the virus and helping Erica and Brenda assemble it all.

Erica Burman, Pam Alldred, Catherine Bewley, Brenda Goldberg, Colleen Heenan, Deborah Marks, Jane Marshall, Karen Taylor, Robina Ullah and Sam Warner

Introduction: Contexts, contests and interventions

Erica Burman

This book is by and for women struggling to maintain feminist identities and activities around psychology. We write as women researchers and practitioners, professional and academic psychologists; some of us have already left psychology for more congenial political and disciplinary climates. This book arises out of our conviction that the analytical and practical questions which engage us are part of the shared landscape of the contemporary feminist practice of psychology. By psychology we mean not only theories and models, but also the full gambit of technical, professional and everyday practices that psychology informs. Thus, given psychology's role as a key technical and cultural resource that particularly affects women's lives, we use our shifting positions as feminists, as psychologists and as principled dissidents in/from psychology. The issues that we address in this book are not just specific to psychology. They are central to feminist struggles around education, health, mental health and social policy as well as the more academic preoccupations of feminist theory and research processes. In writing this book we claim our place within the landscape of feminist debates, as offering a vital vantage point on psychology as a crucial arena for feminist intervention.

But the challenges we pose in this book are not only directed to psychology. As feminists, we argue that not only should we intervene in psychology, but, using our specific and multiple locations within academic and professional psychology, we also intervene in discussions of feminist theory, methods and practices. The subtitle of this book, 'Psychology's Exclusions, Feminist Possibilities', reflects the spirit of questioning brought about by the mutual engagement of feminist thinking with post-structuralist and social constructionist ideas (especially their Foucauldian varieties, see e.g. Bell, 1993). We challenge psychology by highlighting the gendered agendas that structure the shape of the discipline and are performed by its academic, clinical, educational and research practices. As Hekman suggests:

> The gaps, silences and ambiguities of discourse provide the possibility for a resistance, for a questioning of the dominant discourse, its revision or mutation. Within these silences and gaps new discourses can be formulated that challenge the dominant discourse. This theory of discourse and their mutability provides an accurate understanding of the task of feminism.
>
> (Hekman, 1990: 189–90)

Like feminists elsewhere, we see the absences and silences within current conceptualisations in psychology, not as innocent omissions, but rather as structural indices of the rules that govern and maintain the discipline. We challenge the truths about women produced by psychology, and take issue with its knowledge-producing practices.

Equally, in the same spirit of political commitment we extend this critical stance to feminist approaches in the conviction that feminist analyses can only emerge strengthened and better-informed from such scrutiny. It is in these two senses that, as authors, we are 'challenging women'. As women we challenge psychology, exploring the significance of its exclusions (of topics of study, of research processes, of practical–political effects) as collusive of the maintenance of inequalities. But we also demonstrate how we need to put into question the cultural, class and heterosexual presuppositions of contemporary feminist analyses. In very direct practical ways this book reflects our joint and separate engagement with the question of the grounds on which 'we' can presume to speak and write in a collective voice.

This book therefore expresses a critical and mutual engagement between our feminist commitment and psychological practices. In the rest of this introduction we map out our view of the current state of feminist discussions in psychology, and how these reflect and inform more general feminist discussions. The key themes of difference, power and reflexivity form the threads of continuity not only through the three Parts of this book, but also link our work in producing this text with yours in reading it.

Feminism and psychology

Feminist issues now have some public presence in psychology. But there is a constraint on the varieties of feminist interventions tolerated or even encouraged by the discipline. Feminists take as axiomatic that women's experiences and positions are produced by and through the positions we have been accorded within patriarchal relations. Thus the qualities, attributes and stereotypes associated with women gain what truth they have, not through any necessary or essential 'femininity', but as a result of the historical positions women have been accorded and have correspondingly (if unwillingly) occupied. Femininity is thus a construct, the contours of which reflect the intersections of a variety of institutional power relations. These are organised not only around gender, but also 'race', class and sexuality. For example, that representations of white women as mothers and as sexual prey are central to the maintenance of colonial authority highlights how definitions of womanhood are inextricably interwoven with other discourses of heterosexuality, 'race', class and imperialism (see Ware, 1992).

By contrast, psychology has tended to abstract and contain the 'woman question' (cf. Evans, 1994). In doing so, it suppresses the dynamic relations between definitions of femininity and masculinity, and the cultural, national and historical contexts which produce and modulate them. While women's studies now debates the coherence and value of the category 'woman' (e.g. Riley, 1988; Butler, 1990a; Spelman, 1988), psychology has tended to fix women in this category by focusing on the outcome rather than the process of engenderment. The relevance of these discussions for psychology is not to call for more developmental research on gender socialisation, but rather to comment on the institutional forms and fora which allow expression of gender issues. In psychology, gender issues tend to be seen as women's problems. Women carry the burden of gender, in relation to the normalised, and therefore invisible, masculinity that permeates the disciplinary models and methods.

An important strand of feminist and critical intervention in psychology has therefore been to highlight the deep structure of gender that underlies psychological theory and practice. Accounts such as those of Gilligan (1982), Broughton (1988) and Ussher (1989) all testify to the ignorance and devaluation of women's experiences in psychology. Within clinical work, the controversial Broverman *et al.* (1970) study put on to the agenda the suggestion that psychology's model of the thinking, knowing, reasoning individual was in fact a model of *man*. The corresponding implication for the evaluation of women was that we are inherently abnormal since we are evaluated in relation to male-defined criteria.

There are at least two sets of interpretations of the consequences of such critical work for the status of psychology. Some feminist work in psychology has taken a corrective form, retaining some commitment to existing standards of evaluation, claiming that adjusting and supplementing the models to include women or limit the male bias results in better psychological theory. While we should be wary of making simplistic judgements, titles of textbooks, courses and even organisations that connect 'women' with a topic in psychology by the preposition 'and' can suggest that women should be added into the discipline, rather than transforming it. (We return to the particular work achieved by the title 'Women and Psychology' see pp. 6–7). Such research exemplifies the feminist empiricist position discussed by Harding (1986).

Other work, connected with radical feminist traditions, rejects existing psychological categories, seeing these as inadequate to describe women's positions. Instead they call for the production of models that take women as central, rather than merely as additions, to existing theories. This corresponds to Harding's feminist standpoint position. Examples here include 'women-centred' models of psychological development (Baker Miller, 1976), some readings of Gilligan (1982), and discussions of women's therapy (Ernst and Maguire, 1987). Research expressions of this strand can be seen in work that addresses experiences that are specific to women, often focusing on reproduction and menstruation (e.g. Ussher, 1989; Choi and Nicolson, 1994; Chapter 6 of this book). Revaluing women's experiences in their/our own terms, and placing women's issues on the agenda for psychology, has been a significant intervention in extending and commenting on the boundaries of what counts as psychology.

However, the cost of separatism for feminist psychology is marginalisation. Like the general criticisms of feminist theories that assume the primacy of commonalities between women based on shared experiences of embodiment, feminist psychological approaches are vulnerable to the charge of essentialism, whether of the biological or cultural varieties (see Squire, 1989). In these, differences between women are subordinated to presumed core common features of women's experiences, as determined either by our biology, or by institutional interpretations of, and responses to, women's biological differences. Such approaches are now being contested in the light of black (e.g. Carby, 1987), Third World (e.g. Spivak, 1988) and lesbian critiques (e.g. Wilton, 1993) that question the unity of women's positions and demonstrate how women are divided by class, 'race', culture and sexuality. Thus a unitary view of 'woman', or of 'feminism' for that matter, reflects and maintains the white middle-class heterosexual privilege of those who have formulated the dominant models.

In terms of the reverberations of these debates in psychology, the project of revaluing women's experiences is cast in relation to its previous devaluation, and as such is an important strategy. However, where this has become an end rather than a means, it threatens to feed into existing disciplinary defences of ghettoisation and containment. Since periods and post-natal depression do not directly affect men, we as women are accorded uncontested expertise and legitimacy to address these issues without too much disturbance to the boundaries and topology of the discipline. And while there are ways of warding off the essentialist tendencies of feminist standpoint (which treat gender as a fixed, unchanging and common experience flowing from a predetermined biology) (Griffin *et al.*, in press), we need to be wary of allowing a cosy collusion between feminist and psychological practices with traditionally gendered divisions of labour. This division between mental vs manual, and detached vs interpersonal labour is reproduced through the gendered distribution of academic and applied psychology, with more women, and more women achieving higher status positions, in 'applied' – clinical, educational – contexts.

In addition, one of our agendas for this book is to take seriously the implications of differences between women for the varieties of feminist interventions in psychology. Notwithstanding the difficulties, we retain a commitment to a notion of feminism that may sometimes be plural (as feminisms) and at other times assumes a more unitary voice. In this sense, we see feminism as naming a potential, if not current, collectivity, and we take recent forms of expression of this in psychology (as in the journal *Feminism & Psychology*, see e.g. Kitzinger and Wilkinson, 1992; Bhavnani and Phoenix, 1994) as welcome. With these considerations in mind we turn now to reflections of these debates in psychology, as mediated through the arena of 'the psychology of women'.

Psychology of women?

The main place in which gender figures in undergraduate psychology courses is in Psychology of Women courses (which may also be the place where you have encountered this book). Now sanctioned by the British Psychological Society as part of every undergraduate degree (British Psychological Society Scientific Affairs Board, 1988) and reflected in the structure of professional psychological organisations (such as Division 35 in the USA), the presence of such courses often provides a much needed space for students to reflect on their gendered experience of psychology. Nevertheless, they also often function to let the remainder of degree schemes carry on unchanged in their wilful gender-blindness and corresponding male-privilege. The very title, 'Psychology of Women', betrays how gender relations are treated as properties of women, a tendency exacerbated by its prefacing with 'Psychology of' which powerfully delineates the topics mobilised around 'Women' as internal, general and unchanging.

It is this static, universalised understanding of women's experiences that we seek to challenge here. Just as outside psychology feminists have contested the category 'woman' as suppressing both the diversity of women's positions and the power relations between women, so too we start this book by questioning the adequacy of 'the' 'psychology of women' in its singular form. This maintains an ahistorical and culture-free representation of women which threatens to elaborate a model of Everywoman that can be as oppressive as that of the Everyman of contemporary main/malestream psychology. While the arena of 'the psychology of women' stands in strategic opposition to a psychology which has been the psychology of men, it is in danger of reproducing a similar structural dynamic of homogenisation and privilege. In this book we take up questions of 'difference' as not mere variations or diversities to be celebrated, but as structural power relations between men and women, and between women. This fractures 'the psychology' of women into multiple psychologies. Moreover, we do not take it as given that gender is the only, or primary, power relationship. This imports current discussions of queer theory to disrupt the binary male–female divisions (McIntosh, 1993), and discussions of the articulation of race and gender (Anthias and Yuval-Davis, 1992; Afshar and Maynard, 1994). Hence the ways in which the psychologies of men are different from those of women become a topic rather than a tenet.

Returning this discussion to the current political possibilities in psychology, the struggles around the formation of the Psychology of Women Section of the British Psychological Society (documented in Burns and Wilkinson, 1990) demonstrate how politically charged such formulations as the 'Psychology of Women' are. This organisation could not be called a Women's Section, since that implied gendered identity (specifically a women-only organisation) and activity (specifically political activity) and was correspondingly designated as 'not scientific', as if 'science' is not gendered and political. The epithet 'Psychology of Women' thus performs the double work of describing an area of study as well as (covertly) an arena for intervention and organisation. It is significant that the British Women and Psychology annual conference can only function as a forum for women to address the relations between feminist discussions and psychological models and practices by virtue of being sponsored jointly by both the Psychology of Women Section of the British Psychological Society and by an organisation formerly called Women in Psychology (from which the Section originally developed) which, after some transformations (from WIPS to WAPS – Women and Psychology), is now reconstituted as the Alliance of Women in Psychology (AWP).[1] We highlight these institutional and organisational histories here as key indicators of the delimited positions available to 'women' organising within psychology.

But moving from a focus on 'women' to 'gender' does not solve these problems. As Evans (1990) and Kremer (1990) have cogently argued, attention to gender can work to treat gender relations as symmetrical, rather than as unequal power relations. Here the incipient dangers of the individualisation of social relations are apparent within the psychological discourse of 'roles'. Subscription to a 'gender roles' model can imply that roles can be unproblematically assumed or exchanged, or, worse still, that we 'choose' them (here importing the discourse of the market) (Carrigan *et al.*, 1987; Moore, 1988). This thoroughly asocial representation of free-floating genderless subjects portrays gendered identities and positions as attributes that we can combine, don or slough off. It thus fails to engage with the deeply gendered structure of our experiences. More than this, it decontextualises and flattens out the power relations that are organised around gender such that it affords a victim-blaming account of women's positions. Thus, as a parallel to discussions of strategic essentialism which treat gender as a political position around which to organise rather than a common category or experience to be assumed (Spivak, 1990), we would argue that there is a rhetorical value in retaining the label 'women' both as forum and voice.

In terms of its relevance for the project and the teaching of 'Psychology of Women', this book offers a critique of psychology through a juxtaposition with feminist analyses at the level of theory, research and practice. We adopt a women-centred approach in our selection of topics central to feminist engagement and intervention. But, like much feminist psychology in the UK (British Psychological Society Scientific Affairs Board, 1994), we avoid a commitment to a particular psychological model, such as a lifespan approach to women's lives. In our view this not only offers too constrained a structure for our feminist purposes, but also produces too individualised an account of women's lives. As such it reproduces the potential, and produces an apparatus, for normalising the diversity of women's experiences and positions.

Our issue-based and polemical approach aims to stimulate debate rather than offer tidy answers or programmatic activities. As feminists in/around psychology we tread an insecure but exciting path. On one hand we expose the exclusive (elitist) basis and functioning of psychology, thus highlighting its corresponding ignorance of what it excludes. On the other, we maintain a vision both of the fruitfulness of feminist analyses to critique psychology, and also the possibility that we might selectively appropriate some features of psychology for our own ends.

Challenging psychology

Turning now to the specific forms these discussions take in this book, the challenges we pose for psychology relate to its theoretical models, research methods and institutional practices. These form the structure of this book, although the distribution of these issues is not absolutely confined to each section. Each chapter poses challenges at the level of theory, method and practice, both for psychology and for feminism. We adopt this tripartite structure to identify the primary focus of intervention for each Part, but we do not want to be read as presuming an absolute separation of these areas. Such a position runs counter to discussions in feminist research which claim a necessary link between experience and knowledge, and correspondingly, between theory and practice (Stanley, 1990). Yet this compromise of form may facilitate clarity of reading and engagement with the practices we comment upon. As Grosz (1992) points out, strategic interventions mean that we necessarily participate in those structures we seek to change. We write here as participants in psychology as well as feminists. In the next sections we review the main critiques of psychology elaborated in this book.

Theoretical challenges

Feminist research has done much to highlight the gendered definitions that implicitly inform the formulation of research questions. In terms of theories put forward to explain women's experiences, we begin by questioning the assumptions about women's relations with our bodies in Chapter 1. This examines the meanings of consumption and refusal underlying aetiologies of women's problems around food, showing how these recycle and professionalise popular notions of femininity. Developing this, Chapter 2 highlights how stereotypical definitions of femininity inform approaches to the study of child sexual abuse and vice versa. Here the focus on the characteristics of 'victims' and 'abusers' as internal stable properties works to produce the very identities that they then regulate. In both these arenas, then, the focus on woman as patient, or as recipient of service interventions, can so remove the women's experiences from the contexts in which they arise that analyses lapse into victim-blaming. General questions about sexed and gendered identities thus gain acute significance through being traced out in these practical arenas.

In Chapter 3 our challenge to psychology takes a further theoretical turn, moving beyond the critique of existing models to explore new resources to express women's relationships within the discipline of psychology. In a provocative analysis, we juxtapose psychoanalytic theories of humour with the treatment of gender in psychology. As with jokes, psychological views of 'sex differences' and 'race differences' are structured around fantasies of fear and hatred, and the compulsion to ward off the anxiety that fears of women and black people promote. In this chapter we not only counter the stereotype of feminists as humourless, but take humour itself as a key resource to understand, transgress and subvert disciplinary rules. While the earlier two chapters of this Part are concerned with important areas of professional practice, then, this third chapter speaks to all students of psychology.

Reflecting on research

It is perhaps in the area of methods that feminists have made the most impact in psychology, both in their critiques of positivist approaches and in sharpening up the analysis of power relations in qualitative research (see e.g. Wilkinson, 1988, and review in Banister *et al.*, 1994). Although questions of research practices have formed the backdrop for the theoretical critiques discussed in Part One, these are taken up as a topic in Part Two. Here we take up and extend current debates on feminist research to explore not only exclusions and suppressions of research practices, but also the compromises, challenges and opportunities of engaging with orthodox research agendas. Through an analysis of specific research experiences, we focus on the key issues of the conceptualisation and distribution of power in research. We argue for the need to analyse institutional locations both as determinants of, and as constraints upon, research agendas, and for the importance of interpreting absences and silences in the research material.

The starting point for Chapter 4 is the question of selection and self-censorship to attract funding and be acceptable in a medical setting. Here we trace the transformation that took place of a research project intended to explore the benefits to women of hearing about their experiences and concerns around menstruation. While intended as a counter to the medical trivialisation of women's experiences and to cavalier attitudes to the womb, the imperative to write the proposal in fundable terms threatened to become a collusion with stereotypical perceptions of women as unreasonable, mistaken (and even psychiatric) cases clamouring for hysterectomies. Juxtaposing the range of meanings women accord their heavy periods with the version they are accorded in medical literature powerfully highlights the rhythm of compromise, appropriation, empowerment and advocacy that is present in all research to some degree.

The importance of theorising the intersections of 'race' and gender positions forms the topic for Chapter 5, which focuses on the experience of conducting a study itself devoted to the question of the representation of black people in institutions (in this case in schools). Significantly, the experience of conducting this research reproduced the issues it attempted to investigate, in that the obstacles faced by the black woman student and parent doing the research mirrored those of other mothers (and fathers) in their marginalisation from parent governor positions and meetings. The range of institutional forms of gatekeeping governing the performance of this research illuminates very general features of the process of research production. In particular, this exposes the processes by which certain topics get addressed, and others remain silenced. Developing this, we can begin to consider what other suppressed research agendas we fail to document as significant commentaries on the structure of psychology and its institutional allies.

Chapter 6 demonstrates the dangers of taking a naïve empowerment model which, combined with a positivist legacy, treats the researcher as a mere extension of the research instrument. This approach fails to theorise the research encounter as a social relationship. We analyse a particular situation in which (self-)censorship of researcher subjectivity rendered the researcher vulnerable to sexual harassment. This is an important intervention in discussions of research, since women – due to our supposedly 'rapport'-inducing abilities – are frequently employed as interviewers and visit interviewees in their homes in out of work hours. The failure to theorise the research relationship as a human, gendered and sexed encounter highlights both the theoretical limits of models of research, and the need to extend current policies on women's safety to protect women researchers and professionals. By documenting their difficulties with, and departure from, dominant research processes, the three chapters in Part Two provide important reflections on key aspects of them.

Interventions

The feminist project is one of active transformation rather than contemplative critique. In Part Three, institutions, interventions and difference, we further address the practical arenas that psychology informs, showing how attention to gender and sexuality affords new ways of conceptualising, and acting within, these. In Chapter 7 we explore the gendered dynamics of 'care' that permeate multidisciplinary education case conferences. We show how these dynamics work to form alliances and mask power relations not just between professionals, but also between professionals and parents. The prevailing ethos of democratic consensus functions to sanitise conflict and maintains professional privilege. Crucial to this is how the gendered identity of the women professionals and the mothers and children they advise, assess and 'help', constrains all parties to avoid expression of negative feelings either in relation to other participants or to the child who is the (usually absent) subject of the meeting. Decisions are therefore arrived at in indirect ways, are deferred or ultimately resolved outside the meetings. This analysis is of clear relevance to professionals working in interdisciplinary teams or engaged with work with parents and young people. It exemplifies how treating gender as a structural relation between women provides important additional means of understanding professional activity.

Moving to the relations between psychology and social policy, Chapter 8 explores the consequences of psychological theory's privileging of the nuclear heterosexual family for the evaluation of single parents, particularly mothers. We develop this analysis in relation to three key instances, themselves topics of contemporary moral panics and policy regulation: eligibility to fertility services, selection for foster parenting and adoption, and finally the custodial vulnerability of lesbian mothers. In all three areas psychological theory is mobilised – explicitly in legitimating heterosexist and discriminatory practices, and implicitly in the recycling of common-sense norms about family forms, gender development and sexual relationships. This chapter highlights how psychology's claims to be neutral and value-free in its commitment to a scientific model works as a dangerous disguise for its bolstering of oppressive institutional practices. We therefore call upon all those who develop and apply such theories to scrutinise the ideological assumptions underlying them and revise them accordingly.

Chapter 9, our final chapter, marks a shift from an area of over-representation of issues of gender and sexuality, to one of significant silence within psychology. Organisational theory is based on the analysis of large hierarchical male institutions. We show it to have little relevance for small feminist organisations, where forms and relations of power are different. There is a challenge here for psychology both to address the functioning of organisations such as these, and, further, to reflect upon the significance of its failure to theorise these structures. Psychology's exclusions both indicate and reflect the radical alternatives feminist activity offers. Coordinating these provides a powerful critique of, and important opportunities for, psychology.

Challenging feminism

The separation between 'women' and 'psychology' (marked, for example, by the annual Women and Psychology conference held in the UK) is helpful in making a space for critical reflection upon psychological practices from the vantage point of women and feminists, rather than from within the discipline. But in relation to feminist debates and women's studies, we would want to emphasise that these are not separate spheres; they share common cultural and intellectual resources. What we, as feminists familiar with psychology, can offer is a vigilance and commentary on the permeation of psychology into everyday discourses on gender, relationships, life events. In this sense, feminism and psychology may be antithetical, with as Squire (1990) puts it, 'feminism as antipsychology'.

This book aims to develop feminist analyses, as well as fuel critiques of psychology. It extends feminist theorising and opportunities for intervention around key areas of feminist academic and practical activity. We deal with the limits of clinical and theoretical models for addressing the needs of women with 'eating disorders' (Chapter 1), women who have been sexually abused (Chapter 2), whose reproductive cycles are medicalised and robbed of meaning (Chapter 4), and who are subject to the legally inscribed normative power of psychology in childbearing and caring (Chapter 8). We develop new analyses of relationships between women for the conduct of particular professional situations (Chapter 7), and of feminist organisations generally (Chapter 9). We offer contributions to current discussions of feminist methodology by highlighting the dangers of a naïve empowerment model of research as producing the researcher's position as powerless and physically vulnerable (Chapter 4). We document the limits of taking a static view of our multiple 'raced', classed, gendered positions to comprehending the gatekeeping of research (Chapter 4), the production and selection of the material available for analysis, and the political and interpretive importance of exploring absent presences in the racialisation and gendering of research processes (Chapter 5).

But we also go beyond this to challenge feminist analyses as well as psychology. This book develops conceptual tools for a more rigorous engagement with the institutional practices we function and intervene within. We identify unhelpful residues of stereotypical gender norms in models of feminist therapy (Chapter 1) as informing the paradigms of explanation of child sexual abuse (Chapter 2). We develop an understanding of power relations based on feminist engagement with post-structuralist ideas (especially Foucault, see e.g. Henriques *et al.*, 1984; McNay, 1992; Ramazanoglu, 1993) that is not monolithic. This multi-dimensional approach to power demands vigilance in research as well as practice contexts (Chapter 4), and offers new sites for feminist subversion and the transgression of dominant structures (discussed here in Chapter 3 in terms of psychological theory and pedagogy). We follow through an anti-essentialist analysis to critique the romanticisation of relations between women in mainstream professional contexts (Chapters 5 and 7) and also in the vital feminist alternatives to these such as Women's Aid and Rape Crisis Centres (Chapter 9).

Reflexivity

Thus this book is an expression of our feminist anger with injustice. Feminists have challenged claims that emotion is absent from academic work. While emotion is usually counterposed to rationality, feminists have deconstructed this opposition to show how such rationality is merely a culturally privileged form of emotional experience (Hollway, 1989), and one that is celebrated within psychology and research processes only at the cost of denying the subjective reality of the researched, and often of the researcher too. Not only does this fuel the exploitative potential of academic psychological research, but it also denies a rich research resource. Acknowledging subjectivity does not mean dispensing with rigorous and systematic analysis. Feminist attention to reflexive issues in research has shown not only how these are inevitable, but how they are also vital for a better account (Wilkinson, 1988). Nor, once the objective–subjective dimension is disrupted, does this necessarily mean surrendering objectivity. Rather we could argue that feminist reflexive work is more objective, in the sense of being better informed of, and more accountable for, the subjective resources that structure our research relations and reports (Stanley, 1990; Burman, 1992a, b; Bhavnani, 1993).

In this book we highlight problems with the official proscription of emotion in research, not least because this denies or pathologises the political commitment of our work, and abstracts our activity from the material conditions that prompted our topics. In addition, as we elaborate in Chapter 6, the proscription against attending to emotional reactions prevented the use of strategies for personal protection that in other contexts would have been spontaneously adopted. We extend the reflexive work in Chapter 5 to interpret the hostile gaps and silences in research material as informative of structural and exclusionary practices governing access to forms of political representation. Similarly, Chapter 7 illustrates how drawing on emotion as a research resource allows insight into the links between institutional exclusions and personal defences. The identifications and anxieties mobilised around professionals' needs to contain their frustration and sense of helplessness are shown to be enacted through the gendered discourse of 'care'. This account highlights how attending to unconscious dynamics can inform the analysis of institutional relations, and can help explain how oppressive practices are maintained despite our conscious opposition and commitment to change.

But in asserting the importance of emotional responses and reactions for research topics, relations and analysis, we are not advocating their simple celebration or indulgence. In Chapter 3 we treat emotion not as converse to cognition or rationality, but, like the unconscious, as the domain of the repressed that betrays the structure of regulation. Foucault (1976) exposed the myth of the repressed Victorians, showing that not only were they preoccupied with sex and sexuality, but that the structures of suppression and exclusion themselves constituted the desires they sought to hide. Similarly, we do not take emotion as a necessary site of liberation (although acknowledging emotional investments and reactions in our disciplinary climate can be a relief). Rather, that which is treated as apparently trivial informs us about the serious. Thus in wry and playful style, Chapter 3 draws parallels between joking relations and the regulatory functions of psychology.

In the final section of this volume we provide a reflexive account of the process of the production of this book. But we finish here by pointing out that we write to express, share and reflect on our experiences. Rendering our physical and mental activity into text such as this is an intervention of both form and content (for psychology at least), and of political and therapeutic value. In the process of accounting for what we have done in this joint forum, we validate our own experiences by discovering that they are not only ours, and, thus empowered, we can create new vistas and strategies for action. The topics in this book arise from deeply felt and long-standing commitments. We write them here with the aim of engaging others who can identify with, or otherwise relate to, the injustices and exclusions we document.

Locations and resources

In this book we aim to extend feminist, as well as psychological, analyses by subjecting both to critique. We do not take our commitment to feminism as inviolable or beyond criticism. Nor do we consider that feminist analyses are undermined by making clear their multiple and contested status. The theoretical correlate of this political choice to go public in our criticisms is that we are committed to challenging approaches which mystify what women are and do, whether in relation to our supposed natures (discussed in Chapters 1 and 4), nurturing qualities (Chapter 7), sexualities (Chapter 9) or our supposed cooperative conviviality (Chapter 9).

We draw here upon a potent cocktail of theoretical resources – both inside and outside psychology – to inform this project, ranging from psychoanalysis to queer theory and organisational theory. But this is more a strategic appropriation than uncritical subscription (e.g. Burman, 1990; Kitzinger and Wilkinson, 1995). We position ourselves outside the academy such that part of our intervention is to acknowledge allegiances and influences that are typically ignored or censored. In terms of our positionings in relation to the research we report here, the ambiguities of being inside and outside both orthodox and alternative structures formed part of our research process and dynamic. This multiplicity can create tensions and dilemmas for the researcher, as discussed in Chapter 4, where the commitment to animating women's voices competed with the conventions of writing applications for funding to develop this further. Or it can take the form of a radical partiality and strategic deployment of this, as in Chapter 9. Here the researcher's primary identification was with the work of the organisation rather than with the academic project of evaluating how it functioned. Her position as both participant and as outsider both facilitated reflections on organisational process and in one case enabled the workers to use her 'academic' report to precipitate changes (see also the account of this in Banister *et al.*, 1994).

Moreover, just as feminists challenge the academic–applied and high–low culture oppositions, so we draw upon non-standard resources to supplement and subvert the dominant psychological accounts. In arguing for the need to attend to the multiple and diverse stories of child sexual abuse in Chapter 2, we treat popular accounts as a vital source of alternative perspectives. We take this a step further in Chapter 3, where we deconstruct the serious/trivial opposition to use humour as a conceptual framework by which to examine the misogynist and racist dynamics of psychology.

As the group of women writing this book, we too inhabit a range of institutional locations and political positions. We are clinicians, teachers and researchers. We are lesbian, heterosexual and bisexual. Some of us are mothers. One of us is black. We vary in age and class background. We are all able-bodied. In very concrete ways, therefore, the production of this book reproduces the central questions of commonality and differences between women, presences and exclusions, that form key feminist academic and political debates. As women writing here, 'we' have lived out the discussions of coalition politics (Haraway, 1991; Yuval-Davis, 1993), and the sense in which we are a 'we' is as a provisional and temporary collectivity that is all the more powerful for acknowledging this. This book is the outcome of particular research projects that we are individually engaged with, enriched and developed through group debate and discussion. We formed a group for the purpose of writing this book, and most of us had never met before we embarked on this. We have not always agreed with each other, nor did we expect that we would. The conflict has been exciting and useful. We have had lots of laughs as well as arguments. We have also given each other support to tell previously untold stories.

The presentation of this book as a joint co-authored text challenges the individualistic ethos of academic research which treats writing as the outpouring of a disembodied, singular mind. It stands as a material reminder that ideas are joint productions that eschew individual ownership, even if they are written up by a single author. Of course our primary purpose in writing this was to produce a publication as a vehicle to tell our stories, and as a point of entry and intervention into academic publishing. But the process of meeting in larger and smaller groups, both structured and informally, and of developing a common timetable for the production of drafts, led us to discover both shared and diverse interests and even friendships. Even this Introduction has played a varying role in the construction/production of this book; as constituting it (and us) as a whole entity, and then as a forum in which to discuss our common and different commitments, so that it now speaks retrospectively about what it initially invoked. All this indicates general strategies for the organisation of support and structuring of work that we recommend tutors and students, researchers and practitioners to take further.

As an index of the variability of commonality and differences, the text that follows shifts between a joint 'we' and a singular 'I'. Sometimes this qualifies specific experiences of the original first author of the chapter;

sometimes this identifies variability of opinions within our group. In our discussions of individual chapters we have struggled to maintain a balance between individual experience and group process. The reason why the topics we discuss here were previously hidden and thus call for individual (or joint) articulation is because they have been discounted as 'only personal'. But there are tensions between attending to the specificity of individual experience and risking feeling personally exposed or isolated, tensions which engage current questions about research and writing in both feminism and psychology. Our negotiation of these dilemmas highlights the intervention made by this book.

Thus we do not aim to present this volume as a seamless harmonious whole. Rather, we feel secure in asserting both its common direction and its discontinuities. This represents in direct material form our understanding of our shifting identifications and multiple positions (Burman, 1994a). Even as we write this, we are aware both of the necessity for assuming a common voice, and of the need to qualify this to maintain flexibility and diversity. Rather, the coherence of this book arises from a sustained mutual dialogue, a dialogue between us writing here, and with you in your engagement with what we have written.

Note

1 The Alliance of Women in Psychology is a UK-based network of feminists in and around psychology and allied clinical and welfare services. It traces its origins to Women in Psychology (WIPS) started in 1987 and, like this, functions outside the formal professional and academic organisation, the British Psychological Society (although it has connections with the Psychology of Women Section of this). For details, contact:

Kathy Loudon
15 West Avenue Road
Walthamstow
London E17 9SE

part *one*

Theoretical challenges

In this section of the book we engage with psychological and feminist debates at the theoretical level. Theory informs both research and practice and is the point at which discourses both merge and critically impact with each other. We interrogate institutional narratives, focusing on both psychological and feminist theories. All three chapters see psychology's discourses of women as regulatory. In contrast, we acknowledge feminist discourses as resistive and challenging to normative constructions of femininity. At the same time, we recognise developments and critiques within feminist thinking, especially those which render it plural and critically reflexive. So, while all three chapters aim to displace and disrupt regulating identity, we also challenge our positions within this – as practitioners, academics and feminists. When we write, we adopt fictive identities which we use tactically, sometimes writing as 'I', sometimes as 'we'. Both Chapters 2 and 3 see psychological and feminist theories as narrative fictions. Chapter 3 focuses on psychological discourse as it is implicitly informed by feminist debates on the impact of science on women's lives. Chapters 1 and 2 explore and challenge psychological and feminist theories as implicated in constructions of woman.

chapter *one*

Women, food and fat: Too many cooks in the kitchen?

Colleen Heenan

Today's menu

The subject of eating disorders traditionally comes under the auspices of the medical, psychiatric, psychoanalytic or psychology professions with treatment methods corresponding to theoretical models. It is predominantly women rather than men, who are preoccupied with and seek help for their difficulties about eating and body weight. However, it is rare to find any critical analysis of the social context of aetiology or treatment in the mainstream literature (Hsu, 1989; Dolan and Gitzinger, 1991). Feminist psychoanalytic psychotherapists such as Chernin (1981; 1985), Orbach (1978; 1982; 1985; 1986), Ryan (1983) and Lawrence (1984; 1987) demonstrate that failing to contextualise this subject in terms of gender, culture or history, overlooks the most significant factor; that is, women occupy a paradoxical social position in contemporary western society. They are not just consumers but also objects of consumption.

This feminist psychoanalytic critique has enriched our comprehension of the history and context of prevalent discourses of eating disorders. Nevertheless, radical feminists like Jackson (1985) argue that offering therapy to women with eating disorders involves adopting individual constructs about women's relation to food and weight. This ensures the therapist's regulatory role in reinforcing order amongst 'disorder'. Radical feminist psychotherapist Burstow (1992) suggests there is an 'eating continuum', reminding us that many women are 'troubled' about eating due to patriarchal appropriation and oppression of women's bodies. Recent feminist analyses of the social construction of subjectivity draw on poststructuralist theorists such as Foucault in order to develop further our understanding of the way in which women have come to participate in the surveillance of their bodies (Bordo, 1988; 1993).

This chapter offers a critical analysis of some of the current psychiatric, feminist and feminist psychoanalytic perspectives on eating disorders. I argue that it is essential to deconstruct all of these approaches in order to understand the various discourses of women which each produces and reproduces in theoretical and clinical work. While I am not including an analysis of the medical, psychoanalytic and psychological discourses relating to eating disorders, Chapter 3 uses analogies of humour to examine how psychology constructs images of women. I start with a brief description of the prevalent psychiatric classification of eating disorders in use in Britain and the USA, the DSM-IIIR (cited in Fichter 1990). A short cultural and economic history follows of food and body size in relation to contemporary western society. This offers a broader context for grasping women's experiences of food and weight. Next, I explore how feminist psychoanalytic psychotherapy analyses women's problematic association with food and body weight. This model is critiqued by drawing on other arguments that propose that feminist psychoanalytic psychotherapists adopt the same 'normalising' attitude towards their clients that psychiatry has taken, masked by an apparently feminist perspective.

In the third part of the chapter, I introduce excerpts from a feminist therapy group that I ran for women with eating disorders in order to illustrate the complexities of women's relationship with food, body and weight. The meanings given by the group members and myself to the development and maintenance of their 'eating disorders' highlight that food refusal or over-consumption cannot be seen as simply conformity to social pressures or resistance to them. Comprehending these meanings requires a more coherent account of self, mind and body than is currently employed by either feminist or feminist psychoanalytic perspectives. I suggest this is because we are struggling with whether or not eating disorders are social 'metaphors' for, or individual 'symptoms' of, our times. Post-structuralist analyses (Featherstone, 1991), especially feminist analyses (Bordo, 1988; Butler, 1990a) of 'the project of the body', are useful in moving the debate of 'disorder' versus 'continuum' forward. This has the potential to enhance rather than discredit feminist psychoanalytic psychotherapy. In the 1990s' rush to impose *nouvelle cuisine* on the eating disorder kitchen, I suggest that we have overlooked the appeal of a varied menu.

'Aside' dish

Before moving on I want to locate myself within this kitchen. The kinds of tensions outlined above fuel my interest in this topic. Specialising as a 'feminist eating disorders psychotherapist' for some ten years, I had been attempting to develop a model of therapeutic group work compatible with both my analytic training model and my feminist beliefs. I was also one of those many women who had devoured Susie Orbach's *Fat is a Feminist Issue* in the late 1970s. Her theoretical handle on the complex political and psychological nuances of compulsive overeating spoke to me as a woman who had grown up overweight, at times probably clinically obese. Orbach's book appeared at the time I was not only discovering the power of consciousness-raising and self-help therapy for myself, but also developing my therapeutic career.

The 1980s saw a boom in the publication of material describing and critiquing various models of therapy, especially for anorexic and bulimic women. Like these authors, I wanted to find 'the right recipe' to facilitate substantial and long-lasting change in my client group. Women came to therapy wanting to stop feeling out of control around food, to stop vomiting or taking laxatives, or to learn to feed themselves both literally and metaphorically, in order to meet their emotional needs. While society might have a very disordered attitude to women's bodies and eating, there was no doubt that these clients felt unhappy with themselves. Insights and observations about how British society needed to change its attitude towards women provoked many reactions, but at the end of the day, these women wanted to change *themselves*. They felt they could only attend to the overwhelming distress they experienced within themselves and their families. They wanted to be 'like everyone else'.

There were clear personal resonances for me. At times, I too felt ambivalent about my eating pattern and my weight, but more so about the therapeutic model I was trying to develop. As feminism became increasingly unpopular during the Thatcherite years of the 1980s, sometimes I too wanted to be like all those other male eating disorder therapists who appeared to be constructing tidy treatment models (see, for instance Fairburn and Cooper, 1989). They were tidy because they simply dealt with cognitive and behavioural symptoms. In contrast, my kitchen was becoming increasingly messy. The practice of feminist therapy seemed increasingly complicated due to my growing awareness that being a feminist did not afford me a privileged position outside of the dynamics of gender (Heenan, 1995). The dynamics of working within a women's organisation compounded my dissatisfaction, a subject that Chapter 9 discusses.

My co-authors have asked me to state where I stand in relation to the term 'eating disorder'. I currently take a number of positions and I increasingly feel it is not possible to remain in one place for any length of time. This ambiguity reflects my feelings about my own experiences with food and my body, my subscription to psychoanalytic terminology and practice, and my commitment to poststructuralist deconstruction. As a psychotherapist, when a woman tells me she feels out of control around food, I believe her. Sometimes this is simple in that she has read about or been offered the diagnosis 'anorexia' or 'bulimia'. As you will read in the next section, these include a number of recognisable categorised symptoms. Sometimes this is not so simple, as in the case of women whom I describe as 'compulsive eaters' (Orbach, 1978; 1982). These women also feel 'out of control around food', but unless they have put on enough weight to cause themselves or others concerned to suggest a weight-reducing diet, they have no visibly identifiable bodily 'problem'. This is because eating more than is physically necessary, or eating 'unhealthy' or unnecessary food is 'normal' in the relative affluence of British society today.

The label 'eating disorder' is useful as it offers a framework for comprehending what women often experienced as individual madness or greed. It can be a relief to name a set of characteristics otherwise experienced as shame, moralising and isolation – the woman sees herself as a failure or an outsider, unlike others. Therefore, using the label can mean offering to listen to, or to attend to, distress. But to the extent that these categories offer some women a name or identity, it can also mean exclusion, as I discuss in the next section in relation to compulsive eaters. However, I am well aware that 'labelling' is a very active verb, working to construct both the individual and the social practice, as Chapter 8 highlights in relation to discourses of families.

Many, many women are perplexed and troubled about the amount of food they eat, about their bodies. Who is to say that they are disordered or normal? The feminist wish not to pathologise makes it all too easy to overlook the personal distress – especially perhaps among adolescent women – expressed through their 'troubled eating' (Burstow, 1992). To say that it is the fault of society overlooks the complexity of what is being articulated with and through our bodies.

Feminist psychoanalytic theorists have certainly offered numerous insights into the psychosocial aspects of eating disorders. However, it remains a considerable and constant challenge to enable women to construct satisfying relationships with their bodies. There seems to be an irresistible urge to conform to the 'norm' and to feel bad about deviating from this. My concern is how much I, as a feminist therapist, can respond to women's distress without colluding in this drive towards conformity. As therapists we have privileged access to and insights into our clients' inner worlds. However, I believe that we are still subject to dilemmas about mind, body and self. As a woman, working with women's feelings about their body size and shape and about food, I am stepping into an area that touches on all aspects of my own social and inner life. Readers of this chapter may feel it also touches upon aspects of their lives. Chapters 4 and 5 indicate psychology's false separation between self and subject in the context of research.

However, it is also false to assume a commonality or sameness between author and reader. I am aware I move at times between the use of 'we' and 'they', 'our' and 'their' in writing about 'women'. I also write the chapter as 'I'. In using 'we', I am invoking the common experiences of dominant cultural definitions of femininity. I recognise that not only do these definitions address particular women, they also serve to exclude others. Not all readers will be women, nor will they feel that this chapter speaks to their diverse experiences, their different relationships with self, mind and body, let alone common cultural notions of what these may mean.

And here's what the doctors ordered

While I have discussed my use of the phrase 'eating disorders', it is of course a psychiatric category, included in both the third edition of the Diagnostic and Statistical Manual of the American Psychiatric Association (DSM-IIIR cited in Fichter 1990) and the World Health Organisation's tenth International Classification of Disorders (ICD-10 cited in Fichter 1990). The ICD-10 is becoming more commonly used in Britain. These organisations use the term 'eating disorder' to refer to anorexia nervosa and bulimia nervosa. Anorexia nervosa describes an 'eating disorder' where someone, most often a woman, actively starves herself, losing enough of her body weight (15 per cent) to arouse medical concern. However, the phrase anorexia nervosa is misleading as it means 'loss of appetite'. Anorexics do not lose their appetite; rather they do not eat and, in order to lose weight, they usually exercise frequently. Bulimia nervosa, the eating disorder most currently talked about, means 'an overwhelming desire to eat'. Bulimics 'binge eat' large amounts of food, induce vomiting and/or purge with laxatives, as well as fast and exercise in order to lose weight. Like anorexics, clinical texts characterise bulimics by such phrases as 'fear of fatness', 'relentless pursuit of thinness' and 'overconcern with body size'. Although the majority of bulimics are women, more men now have this syndrome.

'Obesity' is a medical symptom rather than a psychiatric disorder although the ICD-10 makes passing reference to 'obesity associated with other psychological disturbance'. Defined in variable ways, obesity includes an 'excess' of body fat of 20 per cent and 28 per cent for females and males respectively (Bray, 1976), and as 20 per cent above 'normal' body weight. 'Normal' body weights come from the tables published by American life insurance companies using the body weights of their policy holders associated with minimal mortality. Not only do these figures derive from a small self-selected and highly normative population, the body weights have been consistently reduced over the past few decades.

This is in spite of the fact that the weight of the North American and European population has correspondingly increased (Rothblum, 1994). In Britain, the Body Mass Index is now in use instead of these tables.

There are a number of critiques of these psychiatric classifications of eating disorders. Hamburg deconstructs the use of 'symptom' in the context of bulimia, stressing the contradiction between the way the 'Greek roots "sym" and "tom" mean falling-together' (1989: 134), while by contrast, bulimic women really feel they are falling apart. In 'Obesity as a culture-bound syndrome', Ritenbaugh suggests the topic 'cannot be understood apart from its specific cultural or subcultural context' (1982: 351). Swartz (1985b) later extended this argument to include anorexia. However, rather than simply being a passive reflection of the disordered attitude wealthy nations have developed towards food, eating disorders reflect a more widespread social tension where an abundance of readily available foodstuffs competes with a demand for a public image of slimness equated with youthfulness and prosperity (Hesse-Biber, 1991). Consequently, we cannot fully understand the central concern of eating disorders, a struggle to control the consumption of food and the distribution of body weight, unless we recognise that they encapsulate major themes of contemporary capitalist society's 'project of the body'. This 'project of the body' refers to the various ways in which we work on ourselves and our bodies, gaining pleasure in an immediate way, in a consumer heaven on earth. However, these pleasures can only be enjoyed when we possess both the images we are encouraged to consume, and the desire to strive to be better (Featherstone, 1991).

Putting gender on the menu

Feminist critiques of eating disorders focus on women's distinctive role in the history of food and eating. Religious beliefs and cultural traditions have positioned women centrally in relation to the preparation of food, while regulating this practice in order that menstruating women did not 'contaminate' food, demonstrating how notions of purity/impurity link with gender. Chapter 4 describes how feminists have come to re-appraise the medical discourses surrounding menstruation. Perhaps woman's ability to produce breast milk and thus feed infants indicates her most obvious connection with food. However, white women have exploited indigenous women's labour through colonisation and slavery in order to remove themselves from the task of both feeding and raising their children. Toni Morrison's (1987) *Beloved* illustrates this graphically in her use of the analogy of an enslaved black woman having her milk stolen from her at the breast by her white male owners. Employing lower class or caste servants to prepare food and carry out domestic chores remains a status symbol separating women from one class above from those others, below. Thus access to, and provision of, food and care continue to mark out differences between women in terms of class, race and citizenship.

The size and shape of women's bodies also reflect changing historical and economic trends (Chernin, 1981; Orbach, 1986; White, 1991). As Orbach so aptly describes it, '[a]s though they were hemlines that could be shortened or lengthened seasonally, the current aesthetic of women's bodies has been changing almost yearly' (1985: 87). The female body has a lengthy history of reflecting not only the economic climate but also the preferred fashion of various periods. The growth of competing industries in contemporary western society has resulted in the creation of slimming and leisure industries juxtaposed alongside expanding food industries. Once seen as a reflection of wealth, fatness now symbolises downward mobility (Rothblum, 1994). By contrast, slimness is no longer associated with poverty but higher social status. This trend to slimness, even underweight, has continued in Britain since Victorian times. Women are targets for advertisers' messages to eat less and exercise more. At the same time, women are also the key addressees for marketing campaigns to buy and prepare food, and most importantly, to spend more time and money than is necessary for this purpose, in the guise of 'doing the best' for their families. Finally, we need to look 'right' for the part, in whichever clothes the fashion industry currently deems suitable for the roles we take up in contemporary western capitalism's long-running production of the story of the young, white, able-bodied, fit, slim, heterosexual, married woman; the content may change but the play rarely varies. Chapter 7 elaborates on the gendered nature of discourses of care.

When Orbach's *Fat is a Feminist Issue* (1978) appeared on the shelves of British bookstores, the book cover promised women they could 'lose weight permanently'. Inside it was the exciting and challenging hypothesis that women might want to be fat. It was exciting because it offered a psychoanalytic account of what she defined 'compulsive eating', and it was challenging because it offered a feminist critique of why thinness might not be very inviting. Orbach went on to offer similar, though more theoretical accounts of anorexia nervosa, with *Hunger Strike* (1986), as did Lawrence (1984), while other feminist psychoanalytic psychotherapists focused on developing critiques of bulimia nervosa (Dana and Lawrence, 1988) and eating disorders more generally. These have similar catchy titles like *Womansize: The Tyranny of Slenderness, The Hungry Self* (Chernin 1981; 1985) and *Fed Up and Hungry* (Lawrence, 1987).

These authors propose that eating disorders are a physical expression of the contradictions women experience in attempting to meet their emotional needs, symbolised through food and body image. For instance, Orbach and Chernin argue that understanding women's relationships with their bodies and with food requires a twofold perspective. First, it must be feminist, incorporating an awareness of the social conditions for current forms of femininity; second, the perspective must be psychodynamic, comprehending how social processes influence women's mental and emotional processes. This framework explores the way women engage in an internal as well as external negotiation of what the authors argue is a very contradictory social status. Discourses of femininity require women to place their own needs second or to deny them altogether; at the same time, women's social status depends on their ability to nurture at both a familial and an institutional level. Thus, women may come to feel they are 'starved of affection' through emotional overspending and under-nourishment. However, when the dominant heterosexually gendered identity is constructed around this notion of vicarious care-giving, dissatisfaction can feel unwarranted and confusing.

The cult of thinness sold to, and bought by, women replicates this sentiment of self-denial. The socially constructed nature of what we eat and how we eat is imbued with numerous and particular cultural, religious, economic and moral values. Foods are 'naughty but nice', 'tempting', 'healthy' or 'unhealthy'. Words and phrases associated with food and eating have become part of the moral repertoire of the English language, reflected in such metaphors as 'distaste', 'disgust', 'it makes me sick', 'I can't stomach it', 'chewing things over', 'swallowing ideas' or 'digesting thoughts'.

The following statements from an 'eating disorder therapy' group demonstrate the multiplicity of meanings that women project on to food and eating. Lindsay (clients' names have been changed to protect confidentiality) says, 'It's as if the biscuit tin's shouting, "What about me?"' For Pam, 'It's like a statement, isn't it?' Maureen feels, 'It's a defiance, again isn't it?' While Pam next suggests, 'But it's also a comfort though, isn't it?'. She adds, 'It's kind of lots of things. I think that's what food is really. You know, it takes the place of whatever.' Lila says, 'I think it's something you're trying to achieve. I'm just, I'm saying I can do this.' But then she adds, 'I don't think I see it as a treat. I see it as like a punishment.' While these statements arise within a particular therapeutic context, they mirror some of the tensions implicit in a culture which markets food while simultaneously it decries (its) consumption.

Eating disorders demonstrate the ways in which conscious and unconscious feelings about women are split off and projected on to their bodies. Above all, women's bodies are a site for guilt and shame about desire, entitlement, visibility (Seu, 1995). Given that it is much more *normal*, even a communal activity, for women to focus attention on their desirous *physical* appetite rather than on sexual or emotional appetites, it is easy to see how feelings of distress about having an emotional appetite which cannot be fed may be displaced on to the physical. Coward's (1984) thesis, that food is women's pornography, is still appropriate.

Feminist psychoanalytic therapists like Lawrence (1987) argue that the psychological subject of eating disorders arises out of a particular social context; therefore, taking it out of that context, as orthodox approaches do, functions to problematise women. Instead, we need to see that, through being disordered, women are expressing their problems with this disordered society. Anorexia and bulimia are best understood, not as psychiatric disorders or as 'slimming diseases' but as complex ways in which women are saying 'No' to what is expected of them. For instance, the fragile bodies of anorexics grossly over-exaggerate the ways we are urged to be slim. While the anorexic woman is doing as she is told, that is, she is 'getting slim', she has actually appropriated this for her own means. She uses this as a protest rather than simply a compliance. Initially admired for her self-control, she is first envied, then pitied and finally hated. A bulimic woman plays off the system in that she 'has her cake and eats it too'. Binge eating is also a grossly over-exaggerated response to the way we are urged to eat, yet as women we are also urged not to have an appetite. Bulimics make their appetite completely secret, getting rid of the evidence, materially and physically. Weighing more than is deemed appropriate for them means fat women are defying restraint, taking up more space in the world than they are entitled to. They are moral failures, having succumbed to the capitalist message of consumption to 'eat, eat, eat', a sign of the failure of the human mind to control the body or of the body to regulate itself.

But what's cooking here?

Feminist psychoanalytic contributions differ from other feminist critiques in that feminist therapy is part of 'the body project'. Rather than suggesting women focus their energy solely on changing social attitudes, feminist therapists, and I include myself in this, argue that some women may want to explore their feelings about food and weight with a therapist who understands the gendered nature of women's psychological and social identity; that is, a feminist therapist. Orbach (1985; 1986) and Lawrence (1987) outline a model of psychoanalytic feminist therapy for women with eating disorders. This model, based on Orbach's (1982) work with Luise Eichenbaum, uses a (British) object relations model of psychoanalysis to understand the way in which psychological development is gendered. (See Chodorow (1989) for a more elaborate account of feminist object relations theory.) They argue that the formation of the inner unconscious world occurs within a changing social context, an outer world. Psychoanalytic theory suggests that internal representational figures or objects can be split or introjected without conscious awareness. Similarly, these objects can be actively projected out on to external objects such as food or the body. Feminist psychoanalytic therapy for women with eating disorders explores feelings and behaviour around food in order to reveal unconscious contradictions central to women's physical and emotional needs. The therapist does not intervene in clients' patterns of eating or their body size; instead she encourages them to explore their feelings and fantasies about change.

One of the main functions of the feminist psychoanalytic psychotherapist is to articulate these discourses for clients. Working with the concept that the body is an interface between the conscious and unconscious mind within both an inner and an outer world, the therapist interprets the connections between feelings and bodily sensations. By distinguishing the client's 'own' self from her 'represented' self, she re-presents this 'self' to the client, in order to enable her to renegotiate this socially constructed framework. Maureen offers an example of how she is struggling to reframe her perception of herself, constituted by a discourse of acceptable body size:

> when people say to me, 'You do, you do look nice. You've lost weight', it was like food to me and I decided this week that I'm not going to, not, not enjoy it but it's not going to be the be-all and end-all. You know if somebody says to me that I, I look slim which somebody did yesterday and I thought, 'Yes that's very nice', but it, it sort of used to go *to the core of me* [my emphasis].

This text contains a wealth of relevant information not just about the multiplicity of metaphors about food and feeding, but also how they are embedded in gendered experiences of the body. Maureen is complimented about the acceptability of her female body. The phrases 'you do look nice, You've lost weight', focus attention on her body being smaller, more pleasing to the eye. They indicate the public nature of women's bodies, both demanding and eliciting a self-consciousness constructed around body-consciousness. They are 'like food'; that is, they feed her gendered appetite for approval for this body/self. She is unused to separating self from body, used to experiencing compliments as going 'to the core of me', although they relate to her outer appearance. While she distinguishes different selves, an outer layer and an inner core, she also sees the 'core' as more representative of her 'real' self.

While the topic of eating disorders is located within and between mind and body, at the same time it clearly arises out of gendered discourses of normality and abnormality. Prior to defining herself as having an eating disorder, Helen experienced herself in this way: 'I *was quite a health freak,* healthy, slim, no problems at all. I mean a nice size 10. Um, conscious, always conscious about how I looked but I ate sensibly as I remember it but it now it's like there's no control whatsoever' (my emphasis). For Helen, being a 'health freak' was normal for her as a woman, just as it was normal for her to be 'always conscious about how I looked'.

Feminist therapy encourages women to understand their 'real' needs and wishes, to connect, but differentiate between, emotional and physical needs and consequently to articulate and act on them. At times, bodies feel uncontrollable or uncontainable, seemingly having a life of their own. As Helen expressed, 'now it's like there's no control whatsoever'. Physical hunger can also arouse strong emotion. Maureen describes her experience of this clearly, 'sometimes I'm actually frightened of being hungry and I don't know why. If I'm out somewhere and I'm getting hungry, quite hungry and I'm a long way from home, it, I actually feel fear and I have no idea why. I'm frightened of being hungry and I, I don't know what that relates to at all.' As Maureen's therapist, I interpret her fear of hunger as a reflection of her fear of her emotional needs. Reminding her of her needs contradicts the self-denial she associates with being a wife and mother. She enacts this in relation to eating: 'say at a mealtime and there's been sort of, perhaps some leftovers and a fresh lot of food . . . over the years I've found myself, "Oh, that'll do for me." You know, I'll have the leftovers . . . it's good enough for me.' However, she is also expressing her distress in being reminded she has a body that requires feeding. Her appetite arouses too many contradictory feelings as a woman.

Sometimes bodies and minds feel completely merged. Lila describes this when she says:

> I find that I'm stronger when I don't eat at all – when I'm anorexic or whatever and when I'm com-compulsive eating, that's when I totally give up everything and I don't care about anything because there's no other mix? There's no, there's no boundaries – you just eat and eat and eat and eat. There's no stopping you and that's when I become really unsociable and I hate everybody and I hate myself and that's when I shut myself away because I'm so disgusted but there's no boundaries to stop and that's when I become weak, really weak.

Some of Lila's discomfort relates again to shame and fear about appetite. Not eating means she is 'stronger'. Eating compulsively means she is 'weak, really weak'. She is angry – angry with others, angry with herself, angry with containing her appetite – and then exhausted with the struggle. This text again highlights the problematic and symbolic nature of women's appetites which, when unbounded, feel out of control.

But the critics aren't sure they like it

Radical feminists like Cath Jackson (1985) critique *Fat is a Feminist Issue* for betraying a feminist perspective. Jackson argues that Orbach is complicit in encouraging women to lose weight. She states:

> The average diet book sets up standards of success and failure, good and bad. A successful dieter is thin and good. A failed dieter is fat and bad. Susie Orbach makes the same assumptions, with a further refinement. The successful *feminist* is thin; she, lucky thing, has read *FIFI*, has learnt what her fat is saying for her and can now give up her pathetic need for this kind of prop.
>
> (Jackson, 1985: 42, original emphasis)

Writings, mainly from the North American 'Fat Liberation Movement', further reinforce her argument. Anthologies such as *Shadow on a Tightrope* (Schoenfielder and Wieser, 1983) offer personal accounts and theoretical critiques of social attitudes, the slimming, leisure and fashion industries and conventional medicine as well as feminist therapy, in order to highlight the oppression fat women experience in contemporary western society. They emphasise how the stigma of overweight and the external social sanctions against fatness affect women's internal constructions of themselves and how they negotiate their daily lives. They critique authors such as Orbach to argue that when books like *Fat is a Feminist Issue* give the message that 'We want to teach you to help yourself', the implication is that 'we are better than you' (1983: 40). Bovey (1989) further elaborates on the tensions fat women experience in Britain.

However, not all radical feminists disavow psychotherapy. Bonnie Burstow describes herself as a 'radical feminist therapist'. She argues that women's problematic experiences of food derive from the appropriation of women's bodies by contemporary western patriarchal and racist capitalist societies. This appropriation reduces women's bodies to being functional, but functional in meeting others' needs, not their own. Rather than referring to eating disorders, she prefers the term 'troubled eating', because: '. . . there is no disorder here. Trouble with eating can result in medical diseases or "disorders". Trouble over eating none the less is not itself a disorder but a psycho social problem and solution' (1992: 202). Burstow suggests it is more helpful to use the metaphor of an 'eating continuum' on which all women can be placed. Some 'only occasionally worry about food intake as it relates to body image' (1992: 204), while others feel their whole lives revolve around this worry.

However, as Lindsay describes, this continuum is not quite so linear either:

> I don't feel slim. I've been slimmer than this. Some days I'll have what I call a good day which is a slim day and some days I won't . . . I don't know, I suppose I related being slim back to being sort of successful and you look at these models and they're sort of ultra-slim and right successful and I think, 'Oh, I would like to be them' and it's funny but when I was, I was overweight, at least I could put some nice clothes on and get dressed up and I'd feel nice. Since I lost

> weight, I haven't felt nice once the whole time. I can have my best clothes on. I can even be sort of dressed up to the nines and I don't feel nice. I feel worse now really than I did before.

She has bought the marketed myth that slimness equals success, but it appears the goods are faulty. But she is unsure which goods are faulty – is it the product or her?

Critiques saying that Orbach has produced a 'feminist tyranny of slenderness' are, in my view, an over-reaction to her initial attempts to elaborate on the psychological issues around dieting. Her later writing offers a valuable explanation of her understanding of 'the way in which women are schooled to relate to their bodies as their objects/tools/weapons in the marketplace of social relations' (Orbach, 1986: 70, 71). Moreover, while Burstow does include 'overeaters' amongst her 'troubled' eaters she has little to say about their distress. Not only is this approach quite similar to Orbach, but the therapeutic techniques she utilises are from fairly mainstream psychotherapeutic models.

Burstow's radical feminist discourse shapes her particular model of therapy just as psychoanalysis shapes Orbach's approach. Both take a reflexive attitude to the gendered nature of the client–therapy relationship. Nevertheless, Burstow extends this apparently unifying factor by including the impact of social inequalities that operate between women, as well as between men and women. She explores how these power differences enter into her relationship with her clients and actively questions the ways in which she views her clients, the types of assumptions she might make about them and they about her. In addition, she alters how she behaves with her clients in an attempt to equalise their relationship. In contrast, Orbach and other feminist psychoanalytic therapists rarely theorise the impact of social inequalities, apart from gender. They argue that all power differences affect the dynamics of the therapeutic relationship. Rather than eradicating inequalities, they work with both clients' and their own conscious and unconscious feelings about them.

Whatever stance one takes as a therapist or a feminist, it is important to remember that psychotherapy is both socially constructed and historically specific. Our understanding of therapy is bounded by particular discourses that frame not just the therapeutic relationship but the 'truth' of therapeutic insights. Opening the door of the therapy room to competing discourses allows us to locate its dialogue in a wider context. While I have offered a sample of the multiplicity of meanings highlighted by a discursive analysis of client material, the following dialogue between one group member and myself illustrates how I as the therapist, promote particular kinds of discourses. Lila says 'I just want to get rid of of it [the food] as soon as possible, swallow it so I can have more. I don't know.

I just eat everything so fast and I just, 'cause normally there's no, there's no – I don't – there's no thought process, it just happens.' I reply:

> I think the difficulty is, is that there is a process, which is why I'm asking you to try and pay attention to that because it isn't, you know, someone doesn't come along and inhabit your body and go and do this. There, there is a process and there are thoughts and feelings that go on but that, as you're describing, the food blocks out the thoughts and the feelings so that it just becomes, you know, as if the action took place before you know, you even thought about it.

By encouraging Lila to adopt a 'rational' discourse, suggesting that she is in control of her actions, I offer her a number of potentially competing messages. On one level, it is a therapeutic response: 'What's happening to you is not madness but can be understood.' By saying this to her in my position of trust and authority, I also convey, 'I have understood you.' However, by suggesting to Lila that she is 'rational', I may also reinforce her belief that her behaviour is irrational. Not only may this act to underscore the notion that minds can control bodies but it may also serve to blame her for her actions; that is, she *ought* to be able to control her body.

Disrupting disorder

While radical feminists point out that it is all too easy for psychotherapists to replicate the orthodoxy of normality, their accounts still utilise a 'conspiracy' theory to explain eating disorders; that is, there are limitations to their argument that these problems are caused by the imposition of (bad, patriarchal, male) culture over the (good, natural, female) body (Swartz, 1985b). Chapter 2 discusses this conspiracy theory in the context of sexual abuse, as well as illustrating how discourses about 'naturalness' and sexuality are intertwined. Szekeley (1989) challenges the notion that eating disorders are an expression of either resistance or conformity, by asking why some women, but not all, are 'troubled about eating'. Feminist therapists have not been able to explain the different ways this is expressed. For instance, why do some women become bulimic, others compulsive eaters and still others anorexic? While feminist psychoanalytic therapists have developed a detailed gendered analysis of individual women's psychology, Szekeley's observation, that there is still a gap between understanding individuals and explaining social factors, remains valid. Feminist therapeutic theory also limits us to accepting that there is a 'natural' body which can be discovered. Both feminist psychoanalytic and radical feminist therapy are imbued with a philosophy of helping clients 'find the rhythm of their bodies, listen to their bodies'. They also contain an implicit idea that there is a 'true' self – a self that can be found through applying therapeutic technique.

In order to develop the 'feminist social-historical analysis' Szekeley requires, we need to look to feminist post-structuralist theories of the body. For instance, Susan Bordo (1988) comments on the way bodies are 'lived', rather than mere containers, drawing attention to how social practices change experiences of the body. Bordo also disagrees with the suggestion that a woman's use of, or connection with, her body is necessarily resistive as opposed to regulatory, contradicting Orbach's (1986) metaphor of anorexia as 'hunger strike'. She wonders 'Do we really choose the appearances that we reconstruct for ourselves?' (1993: 196). This question is clearly applicable to the issue of eating disorders where women feel particularly caught up in both sides of the experience of both 'being done to' and 'doing'.

Bordo regards pathology as expressive, not as abnormal. She views anorexia as an 'overdetermined *symptom* of some of the multifaceted and heterogeneous distresses of our age' (1988: 89, original emphasis). She emphasises the importance of grasping the multiplicity of the 'cultural currents or streams [which] converge in anorexia . . . axes of continuity' (1988: 90) which intersect in the syndrome. The continuity, synchronicity and historical connectiveness of the axes which intersect in anorexia, allow us to locate and link up the individual, her family and culture, as historically specific subjects. In Bordo's account, anorexia is not a conscious resistance. Moreover, symptoms of anorexia actually preclude extending our comprehension; in fact, they seem to collude with cultural conditions.

In her analysis of anorexia, Bordo utilises Foucault's theory of power as a dynamic, rather than a possession uniquely owned by one party and exercised by them on another (Foucault, 1976). Similarly, Bartky aptly describes the gendered nature of 'the project of the body': 'In contemporary patriarchal culture, a panoptical male connoisseur resides within the consciousness of most women: they stand perpetually before his gaze and under his judgment' (Bartky, 1988: 72). In making explicit the socially constructed nature of the gaze, both authors draw our attention to the way that women's self-images are not reflections but refractions. This is particularly so as it is women's bodies that are mainly used within this 'project' to not only invite, but also mirror, the others' gaze.

'Just' desserts?

Feminist psychoanalytic psychotherapy explores the subtle ways in which our unconscious acts as a gendered panopticon. It also reminds us that there is another world, an internal world, in which we relate to ourselves as parts of ourselves; that is, the psychodynamics of introjection and projection occur internally as well as in relation to bodies or food. Unfortunately, such accounts fail to theorise fully the socially constructed nature of their feminism and of therapy. Thus, they are still open to accusations of having simply donned an 'appearance' while encouraging clients to 'window shop' in the mall of therapy. Feminist psychologist Laura Brown's description of 'the continuing presence of overt and covert fat-oppressive attitudes among feminist therapists' (Brown, 1989: 19), offers disturbing evidence of how feminist therapists subscribe to prevailing images of slimness, on the grounds of health. She makes it clear that their attitudes bely the way they are themselves subject to prevailing assumptions of femininity, and the intense discomfort they experience when challenged about something that is so 'normal', as Helen earlier described.

Not only is their 'feminist' gaze one which is overarching (Spelman, 1988), but so too is the feminist therapists' gaze when they extrapolate from a number of 'troubled' individual women and project on to all women. Orbach's tendency to adopt and use the language (and thus the dichotomy) of 'disorder' and 'order', stems from this therapeutic discourse. Burstow understands that her feminist gaze must encompass the multiple ways in which social inequalities affect women but she still subscribes to the notion that there is a 'self' that can be discovered. This implies that when the therapist manages to scrutinise herself as well as the client, she will find (for example) the real black or disabled woman.

Instead of seeing feminist therapy for women with eating disorders as good or bad, we need to see it as a way of trying to understand how *some* women have internally and externally regulated themselves through their bodies; at the same time, they have publicly resisted mirroring the prescribed gaze. Anorexic women are 'not enough', fat women are 'too much' and bulimic women secretly *have* 'too much'. In many ways, it is bulimic women who exemplify the 'internalised panopticon', while keeping hidden what is meant to be available for public scrutiny: the regulation of their bodies.

'Afters'

Although feminists have fought for women's liberation from her kitchen duties, even in the 1990s much of our attention is focused on this scene of domestic, intellectual and bodily labour. Initially, I wondered if there were too many cooks in the eating disorder(ed) kitchen, as we seem to have been tripping over each other in our haste to have our recipes cooked. Perhaps it is not a question of 'too many cooks spoiling the broth', but rather our difficulty in attending to the diversity of the meals required of us. Feminist therapists find it easier to feed single customers, whereas feminist theorists prefer to cater for large parties, each wanting different dishes. The *nouvelle cuisine* of poststructuralist feminism has a great deal to offer to the theory and practice of feminist therapy. Similarly, psychoanalytic theory is an essential ingredient for poststructuralist thinking (Flax, 1990). In order to develop further an understanding of the subject of eating disorders, the two groups need to swap recipes in order to avoid serving up the same old dishes. In this kitchen, the top chefs are definitely female – the pre-cooked frozen food served up by the psychiatric profession really doesn't merit its widespread consumption.

chapter *two*

Constructing femininity: Models of child sexual abuse and the production of 'woman'

Sam Warner

This chapter moves from a critique of the ways in which child sexual abuse is spoken about and understood, to address how these understandings are part of the discourses which serve to construct sexuality and in particular the category/identity 'woman'. Clearly, stories of sexual abuse serve to construct and maintain binary oppositions of child/adult and man/woman. However, the focus here will be on the production of woman as a crucial, but covert, common term to those oppositions. We begin this chapter by describing our approach. We then identify the assumptions that underpin current ways of theorising child sexual abuse. Feminist as well as mainstream frameworks form the topic for this critical focus. We then analyse the abuser–victim relationship as a particular site of transmission of female identity, and as informing some of the dominant constructions which signify femininity. We will also attempt to identify experiences that are marginal or excluded from contemporary accounts and to reflect on the significance of these absences. Finally, we will offer some analysis of the status of the concept of identity in relation to change: is this a useful starting point or does it hold us in the very categories we seek to disrupt?

Locating the theory

The perspective for this chapter borrows from Foucault's thesis in *The History of Sexuality, Volume 1*, in which he states:

> The central issue . . . is not to determine whether one says yes or no to sex . . . but to account for the fact that it is spoken about, to discover who does the speaking, the positions and viewpoints from which they speak, the institutions which prompt people to speak about it and which store and distribute the things which are said.
> (Foucault, 1976: 11)

While Foucault wrote little specifically about sexual abuse, and in his own analysis of sexuality failed to articulate the different ways that bodies are gendered through discourse, we, like other writers such as Bell (1993) and Butler (1990a; 1993) find much that is useful in his approach. So as feminists we may want to assert that being able to say 'yes or no to sex' does have a critical place within understanding the sexual abuse of children, nevertheless, like Foucault, we do not see this as the starting point of understanding, but rather as part of the mechanism whereby what we 'know' to be sex is transformed into discourse, and which stories sex into being. As such, we share with Foucault the need to shift the focus of investigation to trouble the so-called facts of sex and sexual abuse.

Implicit within the so-called facts of sexual abuse are the values and beliefs which serve to signify what it is to be a 'woman'. Our focus is on the ways sexuality and gender are storied; that is, are produced, maintained and reproduced within discourse. This kind of analysis suggests that identities are socially and temporally located and that there is no real essence of femininity to discover; that identity is fragmented, and as such 'woman' is not a unity. Instead 'she' is fictionalised, or constructed, as unified through the interplay of many discourses; including those around sexual abuse.

Specifically, in this chapter, we explore some of the discursive mechanisms surrounding child sexual abuse which transform bodies into genders and story 'woman' into being. In this text, 'we' functions as the fictional author, to draw attention to the mutability of identity and to emphasise the process of production of this story/identity. We use the terms 'stories' and 'fictions' to emphasise the discursive production of psychological (and feminist) truths. As such, we argue that 'woman', as a category, is produced by language and is, therefore, textually situated. By this we mean that 'woman' as primordial essence is a fiction: rather, the designation of sex is a discursive operation (Butler, 1990a, b; 1993). If 'woman' is fictional, produced and maintained within stories, then there is some justification for locating the interplay of those stories that locate femininity within particular 'bodies' and sex these as 'woman'.

Telling the story: models of child sexual abuse

There are two main areas of understanding child sexual abuse which form our focus here. These are psychological theories and feminist theories. We acknowledge that there are significant variations within both these general fields, but we are more concerned with the central themes which underpin these theories, rather than their specific nuances. So while some recognition of differences will be noted, we want to highlight those assumptions that are uncritically accepted in the application of both these sets of theories.

Psychological models of child sexual abuse – it's a sex thing

Most psychological models of sexual abuse take as axiomatic that first and foremost sex and sexual satisfaction are the precursors to sexual abuse (Araji and Finkelhor, 1986; Frude, 1992). Notions of 'power' are implicated as secondary considerations, in as much as 'power' provides the means to the end. While psychological theorising has developed some sophistication to conceal the essentialist paradigms at the heart of its stories, such assumptions are common and are presented as self-evident truths. A prime example of this position comes from Frude, a practising clinical psychologist:

> There can be little doubt that fathers who approach their daughters sexually are often unsatisfied sexually in other relationships. In particular the marital relationship is usually in difficulties, particularly in the sexual sphere; sometimes the wife is ill or absent, and sometimes the father is a single parent. Incestuous fathers do not seem to have especially high levels of sexual need, but the evidence suggests that the sexual needs are not adequately fulfilled. Whereas other men might cope with this by recourse to masturbation, affairs or prostitutes, the evidence suggests that incestuous fathers often feel that masturbation is degrading or sinful and have similar views about affairs and prostitutes. There seems to be a higher incidence of father–daughter incest in isolated communities and there is some evidence that many sexually abusive men lack the necessary social skills to become involved in stable affairs.
>
> There is a clear consensus within the relevant literature that only a small proportion of abusive fathers are paedophiles. It is not that they prefer sexual contact with pre-pubescent children to that with adults. They seem more often to relate sexually to older daughters; if they 'resort' to their younger children, it seems to be because these are available and biddable. In some ways the activity may be akin to that of the heterosexual who . . . in a prison situation, engages in homosexual activities.
>
> (Frude, 1989: 38)

This quotation draws on a number of psychological approaches and is riddled with normative assumptions presented as truths. The theoretical approaches which are drawn on to understand child sexual abuse include behaviourism, cognitive psychology, family dysfunction and psychoanalysis. While these models do not remain static over time and interpretations vary, some key elements can be described in general terms. However, it is not incidental that the 'big names' in child sexual abuse literature, such as Frude, remain male – who more often than not reproduce the status quo, rather than seek to interrogate it. Here we identify the key assumptions exemplified by the above extract, briefly describe the outlines of the theories this draws upon, and demonstrate their underlying themes about sexual abuse.

Frude immediately contextualises his theory in the 'truth' of common sense: 'there can be no doubt'. Indeed we can have no doubt about the proper role of mothers, which is to act as the sexual receptacle for fathers, and in so doing to protect their daughters from the pervasiveness of male sexual desire. We must accept that sex/desire is always present, is owned by men and directed at women (as wife, prostitute, daughter – other victims are defined by their availability) and that sex/desire is *de facto* heterosexual. These are powerful dicta that shape our lives as 'women' – however crass they appear. The 'power' of these assumptions, in Foucault's terms, is related to their status as 'truth', as part of the given orthodoxy. Such stories are therefore compelling because of their assumed status as 'truth'. These 'truths' of innate (hetero)sexual desire, the pre-supposition of sex and gender, and the implied necessity for the taboo against incest underpin much psychological theorising on the subject. They act as the 'truth context' in which seemingly benign theories can operate.

Cognitive-behavioural theory

From a behavioural perspective (e.g. Simon and Schouten, 1991) all behaviour is understood as a response to reinforcement. From this perspective child sexual abuse can be seen as the outcome of the reinforcement derived from having sex with children, outweighing the negative reinforcement of the taboo *against* having sex with children. While behaviourism, *per se*, does not necessarily presume sex/gender, sexual fulfilment is often accepted as a natural reinforcer, with desire presumed to be heterosexual. This is reflected in the extract from Frude, where he presumes (male) heterosexual desire as a non-negotiable (biological) need to be met, and that satisfaction of this need is justification, or at least understanding, for increasingly removed 'substitutes' for the adult woman/wife.

From a cognitive perspective (e.g. Jehu, 1988), reasoning displaces behaviour as the central motivator for action. Behaviour is seen as the result of individuals following an internally coherent and logical script, which they learn as they make sense of their passage through life. This script may differ from others, depending on particular experiences and understanding. Child sexual abusers are, thus, characterised as suffering from faulty reasoning to account for their abusive actions. So, in the extract from Frude, we are enjoined to believe that child sexual abusers cannot cope with the cognitive dissonance produced by having affairs or going to prostitutes, but can rationalise their 'needs' with their belief systems when having sex with their daughters.

Both of these perspectives appear to reject a simple biologism but, when applied, often still rely on the notion of an innate sexuality – which must be controlled or learned about in a socially accepted way. The lack of theorising around the status of gender results in an acceptance of normative values in relation to which action and understanding is judged. Thus the construction of sex/gender identity is not discussed, but rather assumed. We are born either male or female. The assumption of heterosexuality follows from the assumption of stability of sex/gender identity, as reflected in the above extract.

The systemic-family dysfunctional model

This model (e.g. Bentovim, 1987) takes as its primary focus the immediate situation of the family, as if divorced from other strands of society. Reasons for action are situated, not in individuals, but within the interplay of individuals. From this perspective child sexual abuse can be understood as the result of a family which does not function properly. Focusing on the family unit as a whole can also serve to mask the identity of the abuser. This is demonstrated in Frude's thesis when he suggests that men abuse because their wives are ill, absent or that their relationship is generally in difficulties which means that their sexual needs are not being met. Thus this model, like the cognitive behavioural models, presumes a pre-cultural sexual drive which is gendered and must be controlled.

Psychoanalytic theory

From a psychoanalytic perspective (e.g. Freud, 1905/1977) the taboo against incest is placed at the matrix of the development of (sexual) identity. Heterosexuality is seen as the accomplishment of the denial of the incestuous wish for the opposite sex parent through the resolution of the Oedipus (and in some accounts Electra) complexes. Incest in this formulation is seen as a pre-cultural desire, which is prohibited through the child's acculturation. The result is the naturalisation of male heterosexual desire. Thus it is the *child's* desire for the parent, rather than the *parent's* desire for the child, which is theorised. While the aforementioned psychological theories are seldom used to explore this particular dynamic, we would argue that, in different ways, in practice all rely upon notions of sex/gender distinctions as pre-given and essential.

Additionally, psychoanalysis, unlike the previous psychological theories discussed, is specifically interested in the development of identity, as centred around sex/gender. The development of identity is seen as the process of identification with the same sex parent. It is of little importance that most of us do not live in the family fictionalised in the story of Oedipus: we are all storied within this 'truth', even as we reject it. Identity, then, is a repression of unbridled sexuality, in favour of culturally defined sex/gender distinctions. As, Butler notes according to a psychoanalytic model: 'We take up identifications not only to receive love but also to deflect from it and its dangers; we also take up identifications in order to facilitate or prohibit our own desires' (Butler, 1990a: 332).

Thus psychoanalysis offers an understanding of the gendering process, whereby men become men and women become women. While Frude does not directly access psychoanalysis, as with his account, it relies on a presumption of the primacy of male heterosexual desire.

Underlying themes

Each of the psychological theories outlined above has a different focus of interest and is linked to different, sometimes conflicting practices. However, we suggest that contained within all of them, and articulated in the extract from Frude, are a number of pervasive and interlocking 'truths'. The presumption of sex and gender in turn generates the taboo against incest which, we argue, is intimately associated with the heterosexual imperative. Butler (1990a; 1993) has discussed these in relation to psychoanalytic theory. Here we develop these themes as central to current psychological theorising on sexual abuse.

The pre-supposition of sex and gender

All these psychological stories presume that we know that bodies are gendered and sexed and that these represent some fixed material reality. Bodies are merely the backdrop on which asymmetrical power relations develop whether via reinforcement (behaviourism), mental processing (cognition) or repression (psychoanalysis).

The taboo against incest

The presupposition of sex and gender necessarily gives birth to children who are sexed and gendered. While the child may be seen as sexual, perhaps through the permeation of psychoanalytic theory, this sexuality is treated as initially undifferentiated and therefore, like all sexuality, is considered dangerous. This is because within contemporary discourses sexual desire is all pervasive and acceptable gender roles have yet to be learned. When we talk about incestuous desires or sexual desires in this way, the power relations contained therein are hidden. As Bell (1993: 120) notes, the desire of a child for a parent is different from adult sexual desire, but the discourse of 'incestuous desire' (a term gleaned from psychoanalysis) treats as equivalent the desires of the child with those of a parent. More than this, desire cannot be divorced from the context of its production. In order to direct sexual desire appropriately we first have to define what is inappropriate. Hence the prohibition against incest stories incest into being. Treating the incest taboo as a discursive production does not mean that if we stop talking about incest it will go away. Incest is part of the dominant stories of our time. The incest taboo and the process of incest, therefore, produce gender and sexuality.

Thus the taboo against incest functions as a powerful and uncontested discourse within psychological theories (it is what stops us acting on undifferentiated sexual desires). However, this should be set against the 'will to incest' implied within the same theories, which also accept as given the pervasiveness of sexuality and the appropriateness of male heterosexual desire. The incest prohibition both prohibits incest and calls it forth, and so legitimises both the sexualising of children and the sexual desire for children. Thus the incest taboo does not come after the prior construction of sex, but rather is part of the defining process which constructs sex. This defining process then confers a natural sexuality which serves to conceal the interplay of power relations, which by concealing it, perpetuates it.

The heterosexual imperative

In Butler's account of psychoanalysis, she shows how the incest prohibition is based on an earlier homosexual prohibition. The supposition is that the child will be subconsciously attached to the parent of the opposite sex. This is the point of entry into the Oedipus complex, the 'proper' resolution of which is heterosexual identity. The incest taboo, therefore, enforces both gender identity and heterosexuality. The deployment of sexuality/heterosexuality is instigated through the incest prohibition and the forbidding of the desired object. In naming the incest taboo, therefore, both the prohibition and the desire for the taboo object is created. While this account has particular relevance to psychoanalysis, psychological theories generally take heterosexuality as normative, such that it remains largely untheorised (Kitzinger *et al.*, 1992).

We argue that traditional psychological texts, such as the one quoted above, conflate sexual desire with heterosexuality. The process noted by Foucault and reproduced within psychology of moving the focus from sexual acts to sexual identities (for example, from sodomy to homosexuality), further maintains the organisation of sexuality around the notion of sexual identity: what you do and who you do it with, interpolates you into gender.

Feminist models of child sexual abuse – it's a power thing

Unlike most other areas of concern to mental health professionals, the recent study of and interest in child sexual abuse has arisen outside the academy. Recent concern about sexual abuse has grown out of the liberation movements of the 1960s and 1970s, in which women survivors articulated their abuse. The professionals then took over. The other interesting anomaly associated with this development is that, unlike other areas of medical/psychological concern, the subject/victim of interest has been women rather than the assumed subject of psychology – men. As such, there is a considerable legacy of feminist theorising on the subject. This is also seen in the study of women and eating disorders, explored in Chapter 1.

Early feminist analysis

Early (second wave) feminist analysis understood rape and sexual violence, and within this incest, as tools of oppression of women in the service of patriarchy (Brownmiller, 1975). These aimed to challenge the orthodoxies exemplified in much psychological theorising. Most early feminist writers and activists around child sexual abuse clearly placed themselves within a modernist tradition whereby they sought to expose the 'myths' of sexual abuse (Nelson, 1987). According to this account, rape of some women and girls by some men served all men by keeping all women fearful and subordinate. Incest was understood as an abuse of power, rather than as being primarily about sex. In this analysis of patriarchal society, sexual violence of this sort was merely an extreme form of the oppression that all women and girls experience (Ward, 1984). Thus, the family exists as an important site of transmission of patriarchal values where girls learn their role as passive and available object in the service and ownership of men.

This perspective offered a useful critique of family systems theory where power differences were masked. In this analysis, the tactics of power become the explanation for asymmetrical power relations. In much early feminist writing sex/gender was taken as the truth on which relations of power were constructed. However, this failed to theorise girl and women sexual abusers, as within patriarchy only men are the winners. These difficulties were, to some extent, addressed by extending the analysis of power to include adult power over children: the reason fewer women than men abused was because of their limited access to power within the patriarchy (Nelson, 1987).

Later feminist analysis

This engaged with the contradictions in the argument that incest was about power and not sex (Kitzinger, 1992), acknowledging that rape was a very different experience from physical violence. As such, psychological theories which sought to apply wholesale models of physical violence to sexual abuse (Kempe and Kempe, 1984) were rejected. Later feminist theories built on this to argue that 'the umbrella term "violence against women" failed to criticise sex and the ways in which women have been oppressed through sex' (MacKinnon cited in Bell, 1993: 167). Thus in recent years there has been a move to recognise the place of 'sex' within the overarching framework of power relations within patriarchy. This ties in with a conception that all heterosexual sex is part of the continuum of rape, and that male sexuality is about power: sex and power become coterminous.

Feminism and psychological theories

There has been considerable cross-fertilisation between feminism and psychological concepts over the past decade. A feminist gaze has been incorporated into psychological theorising on sexual abuse, where power and patriarchy are named and discussed (e.g. James and MacKinnon, 1990). Similarly, feminists have sought to apply psychological theorising. In particular, there has been sustained interest in feminist engagement and rapprochement with psychoanalytic theory (e.g. Mitchell, 1974; Brennan, 1989).

Psychoanalytic discourses presuppose gender: man is known through reflection on representations of woman and woman is the lack of masculinity. Butler (1990b) argues that while psychoanalytic stories disrupt the notion of a gender stability they nevertheless institute gender coherence through the stabilising metanarrative of infantile development. The construction of infantile development thus 'instantiates gender specificity and subsequently informs, organises and unifies identity' (Butler, 1990b: 329–30). Feminist analysis not only offers a critical understanding of how sexuality is theorised, but is also part of what constructs it. Feminism, then, does not sit outside culture either and thus is part of this culture's overriding interest in sex.

Underlying themes of feminist accounts

Centrality of patriarchy

Feminist accounts have tended to reify patriarchy as the overarching truism. This has the effect of essentialising both femininity and masculinity. Defining gender hierarchies as stable, even while criticising them, reproduces the problems at issue. Not only does this fail to articulate differences between women, but also differences between some men and some women. To figure such positions as fixed, limits the potential for change.

Early feminist stories which centralised male power failed to account for women's volition. If patriarchy is the central agent, no one is responsible for change. If men are always bad they do not have to take responsibility for individual actions, nor will women because it is never their/our fault. However, the recognition of asymmetrical power relations remains an important story within understandings of sexual abuse.

Rejection of the incest taboo

A particularly powerful and important story which feminist theory has articulated is that abuse is part of (women's) 'normal' sexual experiences and should be understood in relation to existing inequalities of power, the main one being patriarchy. The incest taboo is thus understood in relation to the 'will to incest' contained within normative (male) heterosexuality. Far from conventional narratives of dysfunctional families (voiced by Frude, for example), in this story incestuous and non-incestuous families look the same.

The social construction of the heterosexual imperative

Sexuality/sexual relations are depicted as a key site of learning our place in a patriarchal world. From this analysis (hetero)sexuality is the central site of oppression. Thus it is argued that learning to be heterosexual is coterminous with learning how to be a woman. So women are fictionalised as passive and dependent on men, and narratives of sexual abuse function as key sites for the transmission of this story. Again, this story offers an important challenge to the pre-supposition of sex/gender identities in psychological narratives.

Creating the category – sexual abuse as site of transmission of femininity

At the moment(s) of sexual abuse 'girls' are storied into being and interpolated as female, as victim. At the same time the deployment of sexuality within the victim–abuser relationship positions and confirms the identity of the abuser. Invoking the incest taboo constructs the abuser as beyond control, and as able to abuse within the context of the ever dangerous and sexualised family. So while theories of sexual abuse define all women, they also position those being abused in a particular way.

In order to be 'good' at abusing one must first gain sexual access and then enforce silence and acquiescence. Those fictions which maintain children as victims are deployed at the point of incest to ensure this. 'Girls' come to know who they are through these fictions, now and as adult women. Power is thus not the negation of rights, but operates at the site and production of bodies. Thus the fictions that story woman are told in these early experiences. These include, that she is sexual and sexualising, that she is active seducer and eternal victim, and that she is silent and accepting. The repetition and re-enactment of this relationship stabilises these identities. The girl is interpolated as self-disciplining and self-regulating. Applying Foucault's concept of the panopticon, the girl is trapped in a prison of surveillance, knowing the watch-tower is always there, not knowing if it is 'manned' or not. So, she becomes self-disciplining: always expecting, not knowing when it will happen, only that it will happen. She is held within the disciplinary gaze. As MacCannell and MacCannell (1993: 210) note, '[t]he use of force is unnecessary to the extent that individuals identify with and internalise the gaze of authority'. The words and the methods that the abuser employs to control the child become part of the story that the child is held within: whore, seducer, oozing sex . . . and given *his* centrality in her life these are all the more powerful. Through this repeated experience gender becomes fixed, performed, coherent and has the illusion of arising outside of cultural practices. In contrast to this we would suggest that she is not abused *because* she is a girl/child, but through the abuse is constructed as such.

Who is she? – Constructions of femininity

We have argued that the ways we talk about sexual abuse and the discourses which render sexual abuse possible serve to construct sex/gender identity. So what is the feminine which is storied into being? Within the dominant stories of sexual abuse there are a number of subject positions available to women. Discrete identities as abused or non-abused women are brought forth, and women must recognise themselves as one or the other (and not as some feminist theories suggest, on a continuum). 'Woman' may also be identified as 'mother' – castrating, withholding, colluding – or nurturing. Whether adult woman or girl child, she is gendered and heterosexualised. She is judged in terms of the effects of being sexually abused, and through these 'effects' the category of 'woman' is further reinforced and reproduced. These prevailing discourses of femininity are embodied in laws, institutions and practices of regulation.

Woman is judged both in terms of her responsibility for being abused and in terms of the effects of abuse as she grows up. These fictions, embedded in the way we discourse child sexual abuse, become fixed as internal properties of women. A brief reading of the research literature about effects of sexual abuse gives a clear story of what a good/normal woman should be. A recent review of the literature by Kendall-Tackett *et al.* (1993) lists the possible symptoms which include: withdrawn, neurotic, aggressive, delinquent, promiscuous, immature. (These come from a much longer list – the symptoms are defined within the studies themselves.) Thus sexually abused women who are 'non-pathological' are rendered invisible within much of the research and feminist literature (Finkelhor, 1990). Confusingly, the symptoms associated with sexual abuse are also those associated with women generally. What is 'woman' if not neurotic? How do we differentiate an 'abnormal woman' when women are already defined as abnormal, if the norm is man and woman is signified by the lack of masculinity? There is almost a quantifiable 'woman' such that identity becomes abnormal if it slips out of the bounds of ascription – if you want sex that is too violent or too submissive, you are no longer deemed 'womanly'.

'Woman' is also storied as the eternal child and the girl-child is storied as sexual – provocative and seductive. This is a strongly gendered discourse. Representations of young girls with father figures as sexual partners are acceptable, even celebrated in popular culture. On the other hand, depicting older women or older men with young boys is not acceptable. For example, there was considerable anxiety about the thought of 16-year-old men being able to engage in sexual acts and being 'corrupted' by older men, as expressed in arguments against the lowering of age of consent for gay men. No such anxiety is expressed regarding women of a similar age. So girls are identified as the heterosexual object, and sexualising children correspondingly desexualises older woman as unattractive, as non-sexual.

In this binary system, the world is separated into abuser or victim: the exercise of power can only be at the expense of another; and to be one automatically excludes the other. There is no partial or temporary state: this is your identity. As such, to be positioned within this discourse is to be unable to take/make any decisions. To do so is to risk being the abuser. This connects with early feminist analyses of power that saw it as always dirty and damaging (as explored in Chapter 9). Such conceptions hold women in a state of immobility; for to risk any move is to be positioned as abuser. And to be active is to be masculine.

Women/girls are also interpolated as heterosexual. Through discoursing sexual abuse we all learn what is 'truly' feminine. We need a good man to dominate us and our sexual desires. Our desire is to serve and service 'our man' and if we do not submit we are either 'slags' or 'frigid' or 'dirty lesbians' (Lees, 1986). These fictions signify gendered and hidden power relations within them. We are learning to recognise woman and to measure ourselves against this. It is all these fictions which produce sex and woman as 'docile body' (Foucault, 1977) or woman as pathology. But whatever the injustices of the system, we do know which one we are.

Both feminist and traditional psychological approaches have storied women as victims within the abusing relationship. This has been particularly important within the feminist literature, where it is often argued that the abuser-man's responsibility for the abuse is talked out of the tale by discourses which blame women. As such, it has been important for feminist accounts to story a different identity for abused women which emphasises 'unfeminine' characteristics such as strength, without being then transformed into the abuser. So, within feminist accounts such women have come to be known as 'survivors', although this is not universally such a powerful a fiction as the more traditional ones.

Thus, we have sought to demonstrate that when we talk sexual abuse 'woman' becomes known. We recognise *her* as *woman*, as having a materiality, as a fictive unity. That models of sexual abuse both rely on and produce the fiction of coherence does not imply that we all 'live' this ideal; but rather it institutes the normalising imperative. That is, even when we do not recognise ourselves in the dominant discourses of femininity, we cannot but measure ourselves against them.

Marginal(ised) identities marginal(ised) texts

Both feminist and psychological theories of sexual abuse serve to construct woman as a fictional unity. While the 'woman' constructed by feminisms and psychologies may be antithetical to each other, this very opposition serves further to stabilise identity. In critically opposing the heterosexual imperative, feminists have often made recourse to the 'natural lesbian' (Rich, 1984), which has the function of reifying and stabilising both categories. In order to recognise the discursive production of the category 'woman', a necessary foreclosure must be enacted. The subject emerges against the backdrop of those subject positions not identified, not articulated. These overarching theories story out other subject positions which might also be termed 'woman'.

This is not to say that feminists have not recognised these limitations, but that the underlying tenets of feminist theory, along with psychological theory, fail to articulate different embodiments which might also be positioned as 'woman'. These marginalised identities relating to race, class, age, sexuality, geography do not sit comfortably within the main orthodoxies. While attempts to articulate the intersections of these various texts have started to emerge, such as Melba Wilson's book on black women surviving incest, more often these marginal(ised) identities are found in marginal(ised) 'non-academic' texts, such as novels and autobiographies (Morrison, 1981; Angelou, 1984; Spring, 1987; Danica, 1989). We might also note that while officially marginalised, these are probably read more widely than academic texts. Such accounts offer powerful narratives in which such 'non-women' may recognise themselves, excluded as they are from the main orthodoxies. Maya Angelou's account of literally losing her voice after being raped as an 8-year-old child by a neighbour, is particularly apposite.

Within the collectivity which is 'woman', there are many different subject positions which intersect, transform and reinforce each other. However, subject positions are limited and fixed such that once identified as white/black, man/woman one is differentially able to take up such fictions. Subject positions are not equally available.

There are other fictions which are almost too frightening to be told – or perhaps the fear resides in the subject position hailed by particular stories. If we argue that sexual abuse is a construction, like any other, that defies a coherent and stable materiality, then we open up the possibility of disclaiming its absolute association with harm. In doing this we open a space for paedophiles to occupy. But there is no unity, no one experience to write us all in exactly the same way. To write in these stories of women who are not centrally defined by their lived experience of being sexually abused, for example, only weakens the argument if we cannot understand experience outside of structural absolutisms.

There is another important way that 'women' are storied out of accounts within the academy. Professionals working around sexual abuse spend the majority of their time in the pursuit of 'details'. This is either in terms of the investigation – 'tell us what happened' – or in terms of therapy – 'you have to face it/name it in order to move' on. When this discourse of details is fed back to us in the form of research and reports it is sanitised, positioned 'out there', reduced to numbers, and contained. It is difficult to read ourselves into these accounts, whether we see ourselves as being sexually abused or not. Somehow in the academy the guts and gore and pain and fear which may be a large part of the experience/story is removed. We do not think embodied subjectivities must self-disclose for us, to women's groups or to professionals, but we do think those fictions should be heard, should be accessed as well as the sanitising stories of sexual abuse. This allows us, not to tell the 'truth', but to show how some subjectivities are fashioned. We hear a different story in the media, where sexual abuse becomes a tale of sensation and titillation (Soothill and Walby, 1991). However, within media tales, as psychology, themes of sexually precocious children and culpable women recur.

Finally, within the overarching stories which are feminism and psychology there are subject positions which are difficult to conceive of within those orthodoxies, but that are being opened up and claimed. Pornography, written by and for lesbians, is now readily available in highstreet bookshops (e.g. Califa, 1988). Such writing gives the lie to stability of identity – be that heterosexual or homosexual. *The* lesbian defined in feminist theory (for example, Faderman, 1985) will not enjoy these stories; although some groups socially positioned as lesbian (and bisexual) will. Identity, in practice, is far too slippery. So, fiction is grappling with the (porno)graphic to tell those tales sensationalised in the media and sanitised in the academy, to open up a space that hits out as it draws in. An example of this is Heather Lewis's story *House Rules* (1994) which tells a brutal, bruising story of sex with pain, of lesbian sadomasochism, where physical pain is the narcotic that dulls the emotional edge of sexual abuse.

These marginal(ised) texts and marginal(ised) identities highlight the limits of assuming gender-identity and expose the way power operates to designate subject positions. As Aziz (1992: 303) argues, 'The cost of a "home" in any identity is the exercise of a power to include the chosen and exclude the Other.' So should we move house or move on?

What's in a name? Starting point or limiting condition?

Notwithstanding our deconstruction of privileged feminist accounts, we argue that it is important to privilege (some) marginalised texts, none more so than when challenging normative understandings around sexual abuse. The fact that such abuse continues highlights structures/stories of regulation and prescription. But are we, as feminists, by taking identity as our starting point for a theory and a politic of change, simply reproducing the same categories we struggle against? Alternative narratives are important in challenging the main orthodoxies, but become stuck if their claim to 'rightness' is predicated on claims to the 'truth'. It has been important to tell the story of surviving, not because women are not also 'victims' of sexual abuse, but because this story offers more possibility of change and volition.

As we said at the beginning of this chapter, the issue is not simply whether we say yes or no to sex but to shift the focus to understand what identities are produced and reproduced in the deployment of sexuality, particularly as they coalesce around sexual abuse. This is vital, if we are to disrupt current oppressive forms of identity, to unfix them and thereby offer different possibilities for lived experience.

Identity politics has been important to western feminism. The slogan 'the personal is political' has been the site of resistance and a site of change. This has implied the idea that there is some concrete unity that we can all (re)discover and share. But as Yuval-Davis (1993: 4) argues, should not shared action be about what we want to achieve rather than delimited by 'who' we are? Power is more than the repression of one group by another. Rather power exists in the relationships between people. We cannot then talk about 'women' taking power from 'men'. Such a strategy can have little impact because the bringing forth of gender defines and prescribes and therefore holds. And, as Ramazanoglu and Holland note, '[m]en's grip on women may be fragile, shifting, rooted in vulnerability, easily fractured, but this grip has a temporal and geographical ubiquity and tenacity which constitutes men's power as sturdy and persistent relations of domination and subordination on which women's resistance has made little impact' (1993: 242–3).

We argue that identity politics as a strategy for change can only have limited impact because the focus is ultimately self-defeating: you cannot 'take' power from men if they do not 'have' it, if they too are discursively produced in the same relations of power. This does not mean that we do not recognise that the production of bodies in discourse is not gendered. We agree with Bell, who comments, 'although men cannot be said to possess power, nor to exclusively exercise power, feminist analysis demonstrates the differential and hierarchical positions of men and women in relations which repeatedly accord men the greater access to the exercise of power' (1993: 42).

We have already demonstrated that 'woman', while signifying unity, often excludes more than it includes, and feminism as a politics of change has rejected and been rejected by many who, as 'women', are identified in significantly different ways. So we are left with either extending the category or rupturing it altogether. If we use 'I, as a . . .' as our starting point, the 'I' conceals its own social production; hence the tactical use of 'we' in this chapter. If we stay within the bounds of 'I as woman', even where this contradicts dominant discourses on femininity, we still confirm normative values. To articulate part is to confirm the whole. And, even as the part, this serves to prescribe. For example, as regards sexual coercion, as Avondon Carol argues: 'A lack of desire for an act is all the reason I need for refusing it; there's no imperative to dismiss it as "perversion" before I can reject it as an option . . . By calling some acts "perversions", we over-privilege other acts . . . If only the "perverted" is forbidden, then anything not forbidden becomes compulsory' (1993: 153). But we still need to go further than this to fracture the pre-discursive notion of desire. Like Butler, we believe that we need to challenge the fixedness of sex/gender binary distinctions by disrupting the place of sex as standing outside cultural practices: 'it seems crucial to resist the myth of interior origins, understood either as naturalised or culturally fixed. Only then, gender coherence might be understood as the regulatory fiction it is – rather than the common point of liberation' (Butler 1990b: 339).

We have argued that sexual abuse is so intimately bound in defining sex/gender identities that those identities are limiting, exclusive and undesired. We have suggested that the focus of interrogation should be to locate where and how normative values are produced and reproduced, both within narratives and the subject positions/identities they hail. From this we argue for local and contingent strategies: global theorising predicts global strategies which have failed to effect change. We recognise that each articulation will be different, transformed by other identifications and narrative strategies. As such we reject identity as starting point.

This then is a call to move the focus of theory/politics from identity as starting point to the means through which identity becomes articulated and fixed. We need to identify sites at which disruptions can happen. We do this so we can challenge normative practices which story sexual abuse as contained within the construction and privileging of male over female and heterosexual over homosexual identities. So, how might this be done?

Queering the pitch

If there are no absolute, pre-cultural, pre-discursive identities, we are all caught in and responsible for the stories which render us as bodies in the world. This means we cannot stand back and see abusers as discrete identities, we need to see our place in the story and the potential for change. Queer theory (Golding, 1993; McIntosh, 1993; Harwood *et al.*, 1993) is an attempt actively to disrupt identity as a formative condition for political change. It is a challenge to binary identities, and in particular it fragments sex and gender. It has appropriated a discourse defining shame and pathology to become a discourse of resistance. It is a move away from the static concept of identity to the 'more volatile concept of identification' (McIntosh, 1993: 31). It is, then, a reversal of earlier shifts from discourses of homosexual activity to homosexuality and thus is a disavowing of sex/gender identity as singular or fixed.

While queer theorists have been unwilling to engage with issues around sexual abuse, we see it as having a potential in destabilising dominant discourses of sexual abuse. By disrupting identity, we are challenging the unequal relations of power they are produced in and reflect. In this sense it is important to look at how different understandings of sexual abuse position us as abusers and victims. Sexual abuse is not simply something done by one person to another. Understandings of sexual abuse contain in them the fiction of unitary subjects. Therefore how and why these fictions constrain us in particular and asymmetric relations becomes the site of disruption. There is a need to privilege those stories which disrupt such finite categories and which give way to the possibility of different positions which are fluid rather than ossified into gendered bodies. We need to disrupt those stories which serve to permit sexual abuse. We see queer theory as one tool we might use in pursuit of this.

Our engagement with queer theory is not uncritical. We recognise that this space can also be taken up by paedophiles, but the challenge is to disrupt globilising theories which act as panaceas or justifications for all actions. As we have argued, the aim should be to deploy such tools at specific locations. Queer theory should not halt, but promote further reflection, such that, when we organise around the 'I/we', as we have done in this book, we do challenge, rather than simply accept, the grounds for doing so.

Gendered discourses remain embodied in institutions and laws. As such, queer theory should not be a blanket that conceals different stories relating to class and race as well as sexualities. Rather gender and sexuality should be investigated in the context of the interplay of power in specific cultural and racial locations (Butler, 1993). Queer theory, then, offers a potential for storying ourselves differently. It should not be seen as static, but rather as a fluid and evolving set of fictions which can be tactically deployed. It is a way of troubling the 'I/we' of political struggle, such that identity may be transformed, rather than limit and be limited at onset. We might then produce bodies that are inconceivable within current asymmetric relationships of abuser–victim. Bodies we might like.

chapter *three*

In a bad humour . . . with psychology

Brenda Goldberg

> Jokes, even if the thought contained in them is non-tendentious and thus only serves theoretical intellectual interests, are in fact never non-tendentious. They . . . promote the thought by augmenting it and guarding it against criticism.
>
> (Freud, 1905/1976: 183)

Bad jokes

When we say that something or some situation felt like a 'bad joke', what do we actually mean? What is it about this description that seems to sum up so poignantly the most cruel, sadistic, hurtful and demeaning aspects of a particular experience or encounter? Is it that 'bad jokes' have the capacity to 'twist into' and access our most deep-seated feelings of vulnerability and powerlessness? This is an experience made all the worse by the joke's duality; the way the 'bad joke' often masquerades itself under the benign face of good humour while surreptitiously managing to launch the most penetrating and aggressive of personal attacks. Is it perhaps this aspect, the joke's ability to beguile and entrap us in its seemingly playful context, that bequeaths it its betraying potency? Positioned within such situations, mesmerised and held captive by the jokester's smiling face, and apparent good will, any protester is vulnerable to the charge of being 'touchy' or 'petty'. The 'I was only joking' excuse disarms our rights to criticise; makes one a passive victim, immobilised by, and ever conscious of, the 'can't you take a joke?' accusation. This is an experience particularly familiar to women, where the joke often functions as a vehicle to convey sexual innuendo and misogynistic, sexist material, leaving the jokester protected and inviolate beneath the 'only funning' context and a jocular, banal demeanour.

However, when we make the observation that something felt like a 'bad joke', we are often not referring to conventionally identifiable jokes or joking situations, but to life experiences, social encounters and power relations that seem to mimic the joke's betraying irony; its ability to disguise its underlying destructive and purposeful motives to position us in mortifying, defenceless and objectifying ways.

So what is the quality that distinguishes the 'bad joke' experience from the 'real' joke? Could it be that the 'real' joke announces its arrival through a series of recognisably agreed social clues, codes and signals that prepare and alert us to the fact that what we are about to hear is a fictitious, rather than factual, account? So we can then adopt a playful and expectant mood as we wait to be entertained and amused by the comic's story; anticipate the surprise and pleasure of the punchline? In contrast, the 'bad joke' experience hides its mocking intention beneath an authoritative, truthful and knowledgeable front; and proclaims itself within the respectable, creditable climate of the serious modality; thus robbing us of those vital clues and the right to respond with either amused or scornful laughter.

In this respect the 'bad joke' experience takes on many of the aspects of the practical joke, where the unsuspecting listener, deceived by the apparent sincerity, authority and ingenuity of the practical joker, is in turn mocked and ridiculed for her/his own trusting gullibility and naïvety. Thus the calculating trickster gains sadistic and narcissistic reward for constructing two victims, the manifest object of the joke and his duped listener. He laughs twice over. So the 'bad joke' does not always reveal itself immediately as a 'bad joke'. It is perhaps only later, if ever, that we realise we have been 'had', 'taken in', and betrayed in the most humiliating of ways. That we have been positioned as 'clown' to the jokester's 'straight guy'. And as we walk away from the encounter, and the jokester's smiling face, we take with us an abused and diminished sense of self.

As a female psychology undergraduate it was this duality, this double-edged quality of jokes and humour that attracted me ultimately to do humour research. That, and a significant encounter with Freud's (1905/1976) *Jokes and their Relation to the Unconscious,* which for me at least, seemed to crystallise many of my own responses and vague speculations regarding the 'unconscious' and narcissistic motives underlying many joking and humorous incidents. My interest was further stimulated by the obvious gendered, racial, elitist political content and structure of joking relationships; provoked by the observation that the preserve and mastery of humour was deemed an attribute and prerogative of the white male. At the time it seemed painfully apparent that other marginalised social groups, including women, were just not represented as mainstream humorists. Indeed, they had yet to be acknowledged or credited by western culture as appropriate or talented initiators of humour. When such groups did emerge within the joking narrative, they often served as the objects, the 'butts of the joke'. Or when situated as humorists they resorted to self-derogatory, collusive and self-objectifying humour in their efforts to appease.

So humour reproduces those power and gender, class and race positions rampant in hierarchical and institutional structures, in which the right to command, define, observe and control through narrative is designated the privilege of the white middle-class heterosexual male. These power, class, race and gender positions seemed to me as a female psychology undergraduate eminently replicated in the male-dominated hierarchy, of male tutor/female student relations and the masculine culture of mainstream psychology itself. Studying as a female, and feminist, student, I often felt like the reluctant recipient of a 'bad joke', compelled to listen and collude with a phallocentric discourse that contained me within stereotypical images, while discounting and demeaning as 'unscientific' and 'subjective', my own experiences of being a woman.

I have written this chapter to try to identify some of the 'bad jokes' in psychology that did not announce that they were any kind of joke at all. That hid their own subjective motives and fantastic origins under the respectable cloak of 'science work'. They pronounced their 'truths' within the serious modality, and with the authority and 'neutrality' of scientific language. In this chapter I aim not only to make theoretical and motivational analogies between joking and psychological narratives, but also to allow the humorous and the absurd to perform their own acts of deconstruction, in effect, to turn the tables on the discipline of psychology, by allowing it to experience what it feels like to be the recipient of the joke.

Jokes and their relation to psychology

It might seem somewhat far fetched to equate the pleasurable social activity of jokework to the 'serious' business of psychology. However, such a comparison is not so strange as it would first seem. This is because the content of jokes, and the alliances they forge, express and reflect in ritualistic, metaphorical and symbolic form many of the same meanings, hierarchical power relations and unconscious preoccupations operating institutionally, in psychology, as elsewhere. Douglas (cited in Dwyer, 1991: 3) states that 'A joke is only recognized when it offers a symbolic pattern of a social pattern occurring at the same time.' Thus jokes, like any other narrative form, are never neutral. Popular jokes, like popular theories, are *popular* because they appeal to wider commonly held desires, prejudices and beliefs. The significance of humour as a constituent of both subjective meaning and social relations is amply evidenced by its extensive use in all areas of our everyday life. Humour as a carrier of social meanings, in condensed, concealed and highly symbolic form, serves both creative and reflective functions. Like psychological theory, it is through the dynamic interaction of the teller and listener that the joke, and the object of the joke (or theory), is constructed. Similarly, within this chapter psychology, like jokes, is conceived of as a highly subjective, creative, rhetorical form of storytelling or fictive narrative. That is, despite its claims to scientific neutrality and objective detachment, psychology expresses and reproduces through its theories and practices, its metaphors and language, its chosen areas of research, many of the social, political and economic interests common to the cultural sphere. Therefore mainstream psychology can no longer with any justification claim an apolitical position. Like current 'fashionable' or 'in' jokes, psychological stories are increasingly gaining acceptability within both the public and private domains; they serve not only to reflect but also to construct and pathologise their object in the acts of telling and re-telling.

Like jokes, much of the humour to be extracted from psychology comes from its commitment to identifying difference, and biological theories. Because psychology presumes a notion of a 'person', complete with stable personality and identity, with observable and predictable traits, e.g. genetically predisposed gender, race and class differences, this inevitably leads to a homogenisation of group dispositions and abilities and a tendency towards stereotypical categories. Thus, as with jokes, difference represented through binary oppositions of self and other, like and unlike, functions as an intrinsic part of psychological thinking and theory. This is most evident in the way psychology splits the individual from the social environment, or at best conceives it as interaction of previously separate entities. This conception has its roots in psychology's adoption of a pre-social, pre-discursive and self-sufficient subject, that emerges and develops largely independent of its cultural environment.

So the discourse of individual difference necessarily implies opposition, where each individual is identifiable only through what they lack in relation to an 'Other'. Pathology and exclusion are thus fundamental to both psychological practice and theory. Psychology is governed by the law of normal distribution, whose curve functions as a literally graphic metaphor consigning those on its margins to the realm of pathology. 'Normality' within this framework assumes an invisibility, as the unstated term. It becomes a 'natural', an immutable 'given', protected and immune to analysis through its naturalised status, yet setting the yardstick against which all other categories, or deviants from the curve, are judged. Within the patriarchal culture of psychology, the 'law' and the 'normal' is that as decreed and embodied by the white middle-class heterosexual male. He, like the 'jokester', has the mastery and the power to concoct and circulate stories about psychology's own band of *hysterically, monstrously, madly, insanely funny* people, who do not fit the masculine criteria of what is normal, natural, healthy and bright.

The joke begins

How did the 'bad' psychological joke originate? The bad jokes of psychology, in common with most offensive humour, derive much of their content and appeal from the promotion of gendered, racial and 'Other' group stereotypes. Social, economic and industrial upheavals occurring during the nineteenth century and Lamarckian, Darwinian and social Darwinian theories of evolution, 'natural selection' and genetic inheritance, provided the psychological 'fertile' soil for the hierarchical classification of certain groups along lines of class, race and gender (Chase, 1975; Billig, 1982). These evolutionary tales arose not from any 'real' empirical evidence, but from material, social and political concerns of the day, i.e. the rise of the market economy and the abolition of slavery. Thus these evolutionary narratives functioned as social and ideological metaphors for an increasingly industrialised economy, which required a stratification of its peoples and labour force (Sahlins, 1976; Hubbard, 1982). Theorists projected their own subjective meanings and experiences of western power relations onto the 'natural' world and animal kingdom, and then, interpreted the 'natural', as constructed within those narratives, as a validation of that very same social structure. As Marx pointed out, 'Darwin recognizes among beasts and plants his English society with its division of labour, competition . . . new markets, "invention", and the Malthusian "struggle for existence"' (quoted in Hubbard, 1982: 23). Since nature in her wisdom was seen to favour the 'survival of the fittest', it was no great leap to infer that certain social and racial groups were 'born fittest to survive' (Chase, 1975: 106). Extrapolating from such theories, it was interpreted as only fitting and inevitable that those groups defined as further up the evolutionary ladder were therefore more naturally fit, or chosen, to prosper and rule. Within such terms it became seen not only as desirable, but a duty, to help nature in this selective process. Thus nineteenth-century theories of evolution set the stage for theories of women's genetic inferiority, the eugenics movement and twentieth-century fascism.

An analysis of the origins of psychology is therefore revealing of the implicit sexism and racism of many seemingly benign theories which inform much current psychological knowledge, theory and practice. However, we might hope that with increasing social awareness such 'bad jokes' had gone out of fashion. It therefore comes as something of a surprise to find that such mythical 'old chestnuts' are still doing the rounds.

'Have you heard the one about . . . ?': funny stories from psychology

Of course women know these types of jokes only too well. Biological and evolutionary jokes have long plagued women, and many sexist jokes are variations on the same themes which have positioned women within the 'natural' and the sexual domain; as threats of social and cultural chaos. Jokes from social Darwinism were used extensively during the women's suffrage movement as arguments against women getting the vote (Tickner, 1987; Goldberg, in press). Biological determinism and its associated medical and scientific efforts to contain and control women, to keep them in their assigned place, have been well documented by such writers as Showalter (1987) and Ussher (1991). Probably one of the most bizarre stories of this genre, has been called 'the wandering womb', where the womb was believed to travel in predatory fashion around the body, sapping the mental intellect from vulnerable women. In this case, 'the cure for a wandering womb was to coax it back into place by fumigating the vagina with sweet smelling odours while inhaling noxious odours through the nose!' (Birke and Best, 1980: 90). Unfortunately, these types of 'bad jokes' had rather more serious consequences for women, often leading to medical experimentation and interventions, such as clitoredectomy and hysterectomy (Ussher, 1991).

One of my first encounters with biological and anthropological jokes came within my first year as a psychology student. Even at this credulous and largely uncritical stage in my studies it struck me as a rather strange, comical and somewhat biblical tale. This comic paradigm was known as the *hunter–gatherer* tale, or you could call it 'cave man stories', Adam and Eve revisited, or even the parable of the nuclear family, with its emphasis on gender and the division of labour. What so mystified me at the time, was why we were regressing back to the forgotten beginnings of time in order to understand the social, economic and gender structures of the twentieth century. It was as if two major world wars, the nuclear threat and the women's movement had never taken place. For anybody who does not know the story, within this anthropological tale, the males would hunt and the women would collect nuts and berries, and it is reasoned that all social relations since are merely transformations of this genetically predisposed gendered division of labour.

Commenting on these 'studies of hunter–gatherer societies' and their associated 'psychological studies of cognitive and other social behaviour', Alper (1985: 6) states 'Theories of this type have been based on evolutionary biology, and most recently . . . analogies with animal and especially primate behaviour'. Coward (1984) observes how such 'nature stories' implicitly seek to link the (putatively) aggressive and passive reproductive roles of animals to the complex social relations and economic structure of contemporary society. Animal analogies disregard a post-modern, capitalist, consumer culture based on the appropriation of resources and power relations which, through economic necessity, situate people in positions of dominance and subordination. As Coward dryly comments, 'when squirrels bury acorns they do not have in mind harvesting from the resulting trees in twenty years time and selling acorns at vastly inflated prices to the hedgehogs' (1984: 237). Instead, within such 'nature stories' 'genes' now function as the metaphor of capitalist exchange between men and women. In such tales, 'genes' as commodities are 'bartered' and 'traded', to ensure a 'profit' and 'return' to the 'traders', in the form of healthy offspring and improved genetic 'stock'. Thus, these 'nature stories' implicitly promote the inevitability of instinctual human heterosexual behaviour, whereby, 'all mating, parenting and territorial behaviour is seen as a sort of economic calculation for the future. Both animals and humans share this common concern – to perpetuate their genes' (Coward, 1984: 237).

That these sorts of jokes are still alarmingly popular, and sell-worthy, was brought home to me by a recent television programme, *The Human Animal* (made by that observer of human and animal behaviour, Desmond Morris) where once again modern man as breadwinner was shown to be merely replicating his aggressive hunter instincts as he brought home the metaphorical 'bacon' or 'kill', in the form of the monthly wage packet. Again, within this story the male was cast as hero, while blatantly ignoring the fact that, no, women were not out picking nuts or berries (unless at the supermarket), or keeping the home fires burning, or producing genetic progeny, but were out catching their own, rather more meagre 'kills' and wage packets, as they now (as always) made up a major part of the workforce. It would seem that when social or economic factors dictate, instincts or innate tendencies go out of the window. For many women the 'survival of the fittest', means the ability to take and tolerate low-paid part-time tedious work so that their dependants, sitting round the communal hearth, might have a chance of survival.

Hunting and gathering 'sex differences'

Another comic genre that I encountered very early on in my psychology degree might be encompassed under the general heading of 'the sexual joke'. Now this joke had a very wide and popular appeal, and managed to manifest and insinuate itself, in its various forms, in almost any part of the discipline you could care to imagine. It seemed that no topic or area of research was too important or trivial to evade this comic narrative. Such jokes usually made their appearance under the theme of 'sex differences'. Between 1974 and 1994 there were 23,698 papers citing sex differences

(*Psyclit* an electronic database of psychological literature). I learnt very early on, within my first term, to anticipate references to sex differences with both suspicion and dread. Like the worst of offensive sexual jokes, I always knew that I was about to be insulted. And although the joke would be stated with scientific authority, and couched in scientific terms, the attack would be of a highly sexualised, gendered and personal variety. At first, I understood the joke as something to do with 'my brain being on the wrong side of my head', or how we as women were so 'stimulus driven', grounded in the social context, that it affected our ability to think in sufficiently rational or abstract terms. The particular paradigm or debates did not matter; I knew that, as a woman, I would always end up on the losing, 'less than', 'inferior', pathological side. I now recognise such psychological jokes as having such scientific 'punchlines', as *brain lateralisation* (or specialisation), *visual–spatial ability, verbal ability* and *field dependence/independence.*

It's the way you tell um

Like most jokes, 'it's the way you tell um'. The art is to present the joke's content in such a way as to ensure that men always come out 'on top'; 'It seems that if sex differences . . . do not exist, then they have to be invented' (Kinsbourne, 1980, cited in Bleier, 1988: 154). Bad jokes such as the 'hunter–gatherer' have increasingly been superseded by psychological research which seeks to link 'sex differences' to genetic differences in brain and cognitive functioning (Kimball, 1981; Alper, 1985). This change of strategy has occurred in order to give such psychological, biological theories scientific credibility and respectability and also, as a response to feminist politics, problematising gender and sexual identity since the 1960s (Alper, 1985; Bleier, 1988). Such research has increasingly centred around the paradigm of 'brain lateralisation' or brain 'specialisation' as it is perhaps more revealingly called (Alper, 1985).

Brain lateralisation research is premised on the assumption that men' and women's brains and cognitive abilities have had to develop in disparate ways, 'to fit men and women for their different social roles in hunting and gathering societies' (Sayers, 1980: 51). It is reasoned that in his role as hunter, man had to develop his visual–spatial skills, while women in their more nurturent, related roles had to develop their more communicative and verbal (gossipy?) talents. Thus certain psychologists argue, that while men's brains have *got bigger, progressed, developed, evolved,* become *more* asymmetrical, and thus *more specialised* in visual–spatial ability and right-hemisphere functioning, women's brains have hardly evolved beyond their original, prehistoric state: 'there are a large number of women whose brains are closer in size to those of gorillas than to the most developed male brains. This inferiority is so obvious, that no one can contest it for a moment; only its degree is worth discussion' (Gould citing Le Bon, in Bleier, 1988: 49).

Despite persistent and consistent evidence that sex differences have just not been proven to exist, and that the differences between individuals is far greater than between the sexes (Alper, 1985), this obsessive hunt for sex differences has developed into a 'comic saga' of ceaseless experiments characterised only by their circular reasoning and farcical, convoluted and improbable interpretations of data. The underlying, tendentious motive for such research is that it seeks to link men's 'supposed' superior visual–spatial abilities to their greater capacity for rational, abstract reasoning.

Bleier (1986: 61) cites one such case, by Gershwind, documented in the journal *Science* (1983), which confidently and authoritatively announced, 'Math Genius may have Hormonal Basis', and 'testosterone effects on the fetal brain can produce superior right hemisphere talents, such as artistic, musical, or mathematical talent'. However, what the article did not state, was that, having found no collaborative human studies to substantiate the claim, the scientists had to make recourse to experiments on spatial ability in *rats*, in a desperate attempt to try and confirm their hypotheses. As Bleier quips, 'I am aware of no studies showing that female rats get lost or fall off cliffs' (1986: 60); and equally we might bear in mind that one does not often encounter many rats showing artistic or musical abilities either.

Even if one accepts the terms of these debates (which I do not), there is no logical reason why women's more dispersed, symmetrical evolution, their left-hemisphere bias and their 'superior' language abilities could not be given an equally positive interpretation, especially since the left side of the brain has been cited as the hemisphere of logical thought and sequential reasoning (Alper, 1985). As Bleier points out (1986: 56), 'The only reason for believing that using both hemispheres symmetrically in cognitive processing is inferior is, presumably, that women do it and men do not.'

However, no matter how absurd, such 'bad jokes' have real social and political implications for women. Such jokes as the 'rat story' enter the 'psychological joke book'; get passed into educational and popular circles, as support for biological theories purporting men's superior conceptual and creative abilities. Even though women's greater mediating and verbal talents might be seen as an asset in managerial posts, such theories have been more often used to relegate women to repetitive menial tasks (Kimball, 1981: 322). Or they have been used to dismiss women back to the home and their domestic, reproductive duties (Kimball, 1981: 319).

Brain lateralisation has also been put forward as an explanation of women's supposed 'lack of sense of humour', where it is argued by psychologists that, 'the right hemisphere (the "male" side) [produces] awareness of incongruous relationships, whereas the left (the "female" side) can barely comprehend incongruities, or jokes . . . which means that in public places women look round to see who else is laughing and men immediately discern the absolute signification of incongruity and thus the hardcore of humour' (Gagnier, 1988: 136–7). Are you watching someone else as you read this?

However, like the tendentious joke, psychology's compulsive need to establish 'sex differences' might serve more covert, sexual, aggressive and regulatory functions. Foucault describes how discourses on sex arising in nineteenth-century western Europe, established sex as an integral part of identity, firmly and biologically inscribed on the body. Paradoxically, rather than sex being repressed, the very discourse of repression compelled us to want to tell all, to confess our sex, our desires, in an effort to know and understand the nature of our essential being. Thus, around this period there arose a 'scientia sexualis' (Foucault, 1976: 68), a plethora of medical and scientific discourses, dedicated to the 'analysis, stocktaking, classification and specification' of sex, through which the authorities could 'police, monitor and regulate population and reproduction' (Foucault, 1976: 24).

Therefore, psychology's obsession with 'sex differences', these pseudo scientific discourses, allows for women's bodies and minds, activities and desires, to be legitimately studied, 'penetrated', 'controlled', 'looked at' and discussed in covert sexual terms without the observer having to admit to sexual interest directly. Commenting on the genesis of sexual humour Freud concludes, 'the desire to see what is sexual exposed is the original motive'; the observer, 'now the listener, becomes the person to whom the smut is addressed . . . laughing as though he were the spectator of an act of sexual aggression' (1905/1976: 141–3).

Like conventional sexual jokes, these 'sexual' discourses not only satisfy voyeuristic fantasies and purposes, but also serve, like male banter, to strengthen male bonds and interests in the objectification of their 'Other'; while effectively disqualifying women, through their 'natures', from entering the cultural and political arenas. Elena Lieven (1981: 203) explores the investments behind the appeal of nature: 'If it's natural, we can't change it'. Therefore, increasing and equalising social and educational opportunities or making interventions becomes not only redundant but also a waste of economic resources. Social deprivations caused by class, race and gender can be conveniently and guiltlessly filed away under the heading and rationale of genetic biological determination. Like jokes, biological and evolutionary explanations are versatile; through reformulation or creative 'jokework', they can be manipulated to convey whatever you want them to.

That these types of discourses have real, political repercussions became apparent in recent debates about 'sex differences' (again) in educational achievement, sparked off by the reported trend of girls taking the academic lead, not only in traditional female subject areas, but in mathematics and the sciences as well. Since women's so called lack of visual–spatial skills has been theorised as the prime reason for their lack of mathematical success, this might be thought seriously to challenge and disprove such biological theories. But apparently not. Now males' lack of communication skills and their 'macho' hunting instincts, which previously had guaranteed their success in such subjects, are paradoxically what hold them back, discriminating against them and their academic achievement. Obviously lack of educational success in any social group needs to be addressed, but the terms of the debate were themselves revealing.

First, the widespread consternation it caused suggests a challenge to dearly held commitments, 'Have girls had it too good for too long, while society has complacently accepted that "boys will be boys?"' (Melkie, 1994). Second, we can note the alacrity with which the issue was taken up, as evidenced by the immediate planning of measures to provide the educational opportunities to amend the situation and redress the supposed gender imbalance, 'Professor Michael Barber . . . called yesterday for a radical rethink of attitudes to equal opportunities' (Melkie, 1994). Thus in this instance, it would seem that 'biology' is not 'destiny', and that biology can be changed by meeting increased social and educational needs. Here biological theories have rebounded, imploded in on themselves, by becoming such an integral part of everyday common-sense thinking. Despite girls' greater academic success until adolescence (Unger, 1979), it has been assumed that the male biological 'surge' would come unhindered to the rescue, simply by virtue of males' superior right-brain 'specialisation' and the inevitability of the evolutionary course. So girls have doggedly invested in hard work and taken advantage of their allegedly greater educational opportunities, conscious of their 'inferior' genetic status. But males, confident in their biological superiority, have simply waited to be rescued by their genes, 'girls are more positive about school, and are better motivated . . . Yet more boys than girls think they are able pupils and fewer think they are below average' (Melkie, 1994). Thus in this instance, biological theories have turned back on the tellers and males have become the recipients of their own evolutionary joke.

A colonial joke

A particularly nasty 'colonial joke' is currently enthusiastically being circulated by J. P. Rushton, professor of psychology at the University of Western Ontario. He has picked out of the evolutionary hat the outdated (and discredited) science of 'craniometry', and the dubious evidence of 'A French colonial army surgeon [from] (1898)' (Rushton, 1988: 1013). Rushton seeks to link the genetic and reproductive lives of 'dandelions, fish, flies, milkweed bugs, and field mice' to the complex social, economic, sexual relations of different human racial groups (1990: 196). In this project, the professor enlists three varieties of what he offensively terms 'oids', 'Mongoloids', 'Caucasoids' and 'Negroids', in which comparative measurements of brain, penis and vaginal size between the three racial groups are related with dizzying and murky 'logic' to all manner of cognitive, moral, social and sexual behaviour (Zukerman and Brody, 1988: 1026). Reproduction, parenting styles and fertility rates are incoherently and nonsensically correlated with intelligence, genitalia, brain size, drug and sexual abuse, criminality, sexually transmitted diseases, personality traits and (even) '*dancing styles*' (Zukerman and Brody, 1988: 1026, my emphasis). Yet again, the 'mean distribution curve' is enlisted to situate the white man as the 'normal' respectable average both in brain size and penis size, '*between*' the more precocious, physical development and rampant sexuality of the black man, and the 'less', 'more delayed', 'more introverted and more anxious' 'imperturbability' (does he mean inscrutable?) pathology of his oriental 'Other' (Rushton, 1988: 1012–14). As with jokes, Professor Rushton's choice of terms and metaphors are often more revealing and suggestive than the manifest content.

Certain images suggest themselves when reading the professor's papers. He infers brain size via the crude means of measuring head size, a dated practice of the nineteenth century, cited by Zukerman and Brody (1988: 1026) as 'used to "prove" 19th century theories of racial superiority'. The mind boggles at how the professor set about determining the relative size of genitalia. Did he follow Middlemist and Knowles's example, by resorting to peering underneath lavatory doors using, 'a periscopic prism imbedded in a stack of books lying on the floor of the toilet stall' to gather visual evidence of his 'subject's' arousal (1976: 544)? Or did the various groups of 'oids' passively submit to the scopophilic, scientific gaze, as the professor, with ruler poised, collected his scientific data? But no, apparently, there is a whole array of psychological and scientific literature dedicated to the relative size of genitalia (Rushton, 1988: 1015). So Rushton's 'bad joke' has more insidious and widespread implications. It suggests that perversion, science and sadism are close bedfellows in psychology.

Like the content of most racist jokes, many of the myths, fantasy images and stereotypes of the black male that still pervade western culture, and the professor's text, derive from the eras of colonialism and slavery. Europeans played an active role in the construction of current meanings of black masculinity. During the 'civilisation' of Africa, white colonialists took with them their own definition of white masculinity, as 'rational' and 'cultural', and perceived in the black man's apparent uncivilised state only the antithesis of that 'white masculinity'. The black male, by a process of projection and 'splitting', became the 'Other' of the white man, a representation of what the white male needed to repress and disavow in himself – the sexual, the physical, the natural and the 'feminine' – in order to maintain his own semblance of masculine identity and civilised status: 'The white man's unadmitted – and apparently, to him, unspeakable – private fears and longings are projected onto the Negro' (Baldwin cited in Segal, 1990: 176). Thus the black male, through unconscious fantasy, became an object signifying both fascination and danger, representing those 'uncontrollable', repressed sexual desires and forces which the white man feared had the power to destroy, not only his own construction of manliness, but the very fabric of white western culture itself.

> If the black, the savage, the nigger is the absolute Other of civility then it must follow that he is endowed with the most monstrous and terrifying sexual proclivity. If you are a white woman, you are in constant danger of being raped. And if you are a man then you can be fucked such that every vestige of morals, and civilization will be drained from you.
>
> (Mercer and Julien, 1988: 108)

Thus, the stereotypical images of black masculinity, the phallic, the sensual, the animal, the child, the 'feminine' arise from the white man's paternalistic appropriation of the South, where 'The black man yet again represents the body; the white man, the mind . . . in most respects the very same polarity usually drawn between the "feminine" and the "masculine" in white discourse and consciousness' (Segal, 1990: 180).

Rushton also offers (and lingers over) some highly titillating and graphic descriptions of black women. But the professor's main interest centres on the phallic and castrating threat posed by the black male. When black women do enter this evolutionary script they feature more as reproductive 'vessels', rather than significant actors in this tale of the 'ascent of *man*'. The issue of the 'invisibility' of black women is a 'silence' taken up in Chapter 5.

Professor Rushton justifies his recirculation of racist and sexist myths in the name of presenting truth with his comment, 'Social scientists have spent enormous effort investigating how "stereotypes" are perpetuated but in recent times they have spent very little time investigating the veridicality of aggregated perceptions' (1988: 1039). So we urgently need to ask, is this science really 'disinterested'? Or are there more insidious, tendentious motives being promoted and concealed within the narrative? It is perhaps salient to note that the professor's interest in fertility rates and sexual practices always returns to themes of 'invasion', racial purity and population control. Citing Fisher (1958), Professor Rushton 'suggests', '*the great civilizations* [my emphasis] decayed because the ruling groups failed to reproduce themselves, having lower fertilities than the ruled groups' (1988: 1039). Moreover, Professor Rushton's dedication to scientific research rather than his social and moral responsibility to his fellow human being, is succinctly summed up by his statement, 'fearfulness about injustice resulting from the overgeneralization of differences in group means to particular individuals should not keep us from vigorous research' (1988: 1021).[1]

The question is, if there is no evidence for such racist and sexist psychological theories, how have they become such an established and acceptable part of both psychological literature and thinking? Is it because, like well-worn jokes, they become such a familiar part of comic folk lore or scientific mythology that mere constant re-telling establishes validity? Eventually, as with jokes, we no longer question their dubious origins or motives. Their status as old favourites, popular psychological stories, becomes evidence enough of their apparent truth.

However, once in circulation, such dubious 'evidence' justifies a host of equally suspect research, all in mutual corroboration, but whose very foundational basis is fantastically flawed. Like castles of sand, psychological myth builds on psychological myth, until we have erected a whole 'scientific' edifice of myths, maintained by circular self-reference, and their comforting status as psychological 'classics'. As Nietzsche states, 'truths are illusions of which one has forgotten that they are illusions, worn out metaphors' (cited in Hekman, 1990: 27).

That Professor Rushton's theories were published in such a prestigious publication as the British Psychological Society's *The Psychologist* attests to their acceptable, creditable, academic status within the psychological community. The trouble is, that like any successful joke, these stories do not depend for their circulation on the truthfulness of their content, but on their ability to exploit the unconscious infantile, sexual, racial fears, desires and anxieties of their audience. Therefore, for the joke or theory to be successful, the teller and audience need to be psychically compatible to release the same repressions in both. As Freud (1905/1976: 203/183) observes, this creates 'for the enemy a host of opponents where at first there was only one'.

The danger of these 'bad jokes' is not that they are being circulated by your 'common' bigot. Such 'bad jokes' carry conviction because they tend to be told by 'experts' and humorists skilled at their craft, who have built up a reputation as proficient and authoritative story-tellers. 'Scientific theories about race and gender differences have always been put forward not by cranks but by recognized and distinguished scientists of their day' (Bleier, 1986: 57). Like the myth-tellers of old, these 'experts' spellbind their audiences through the mystifying tropes of their rhetoric, such that the listener has to actively penetrate the duplicity and ambiguity of the narrative or 'jokework', to fill in the gaps, to solve what is left unsaid, to comprehend what is being indirectly conveyed through the narrative. To 'get the punchline'.

Arousing tales or how 'sadism demands a story'

My interest in humour has of necessity involved an extensive search of the current humour research and literature. It is therefore appropriate to end this chapter by giving an account of one such experiment, which although chosen for its humorous content, also exemplifies many of the reasons why I have chosen to reject traditional cognitive and social psychological explanations of humour. The following example is by no means atypical of humour research in general, and demonstrates psychology's ability to so decontextualise and atomise its topic of research that it loses all relevance to any personal experience or social situation. It also demonstrates an almost seemingly unbelievable naïvety, which succeeds in reducing the most complex and pleasurable of human experiences and social behaviour, that of humour, down to the absurdity of a Monty Python sketch.

It is perhaps necessary to set the scene for this comic episode by giving a summary of the aims of the experiment. The research by a Mark Winkel (1993), was concerned with the 'Autonomic differentiation of temporal components of sexist humour' (sex differences again). Just in case the title is not entirely self-explanatory, the purpose of the experiment was to try to distinguish the cognitive and the emotional components of humour. Simply put, he set out to measure the period between understanding, and reacting to, the joke. To this end, a whole arsenal of sophisticated, psychological, technological equipment was used in order to monitor and register the subjects' psychological and physiological responses (arousal) to sexual and sexist humour.

Within the sterile confines of the laboratory, the passive victims were bound and trapped in a chair. Electrodes (administering 10 microamps of electricity) and monitoring equipment were strapped to chest, neck and hands. Video cameras were strategically placed, so as to catch on tape every change in pupil size and facial expression. The 'subjects' were also expected to press a hand held button, 'while they fixated on an "X" located on a white wall four feet away' (1993: 34). Thus rendered helpless and immobile, the participants were then subjected to the further humiliation of having some disembodied, amplified, voice verbally 'flash' sexist jokes at them, at the rate of 3.5 jokes per minute. Thus, the experiment starts to read like some bizarre form of research into the effects of human bondage or sadomasochism, rather than research into the 'arousing' effects of sexist humour. As Mulvey so aptly observes, 'sadism demands a story' (1975: 14).

So what did this state of the art experiment hope to accomplish? In the words of the researcher, the 'purpose of the experiment was to obtain [the subjects'] *natural responses*' (p. 33) and to improve on previous experiments by presenting stimulus material, '*in a more social context*' (p. 31, my emphasis). Conscious of the need to simulate real life experience, Winkel allowed subjects five minutes to 'acclimatise', and instructed them to, 'ignore the electronic devices as much as possible' (p. 33). It does not seem to have occurred to the experimenter that enlarged, dilated pupils, a pounding heart and sweating are also the signs of anxiety and fear. Thus psychology's bad jokes not only incite racial and sexual violence but in this case come close to direct torture. However, the punchline to this story must come from the researcher's determination to eradicate all possible 'confounding variables' in his pursuit of humour's essence: 'Subjects were screened for cardiac anomalies and particularly large and curved eye lashes. None were dismissed for cardiac abnormalities; three, however were dismissed for large eye lashes' (p. 32).

Conclusion

The examples of 'bad jokes' given in this chapter have of necessity been limited, reflecting my own areas of interest and concern. However, there are still an abundance of strange and comical tales circulating in psychology, about, for instance, the 'handicapped', the 'bad' and the 'mad', and it is hoped that this chapter will inspire readers to become adept at spotting their own 'bad' psychological jokes.

I suggest that one needs to develop a sense of humour to do psychology; as encouraging a critical and sceptical perspective, a necessary survival strategy and source of resistance against psychology's fundamental racism, gender bias and latent misogyny. It is also possible that humour might offer some protection against the dangers of collusion, by offering another perspective by which one can start to appreciate some of the sedimented, political preoccupations underlying the 'bad jokes'.

However, I have been acutely aware during the writing of this chapter, that by simply recycling these stories and using the author's language and terminology I run the risk of recommitting the offence. This is a very real dilemma, not only for this chapter but for deconstructionist attempts generally. However, the alternatives to doing this work are similar to those when presented with an offensive joke. Do you walk away and pretend you have not heard it? Do you laugh hollowly but collusively, so as to avoid confrontation, and the allegation that 'you can't take a joke'? Or do you make a rumpus, metaphorically slap the person's face and tell the person responsible that you find the story offensive? The trouble is, that, like many popular 'bad jokes', these psychological stories are still in circulation and gaining in popularity. To keep quiet will not alter that fact. At least by taking a critical stance, and by creating a space to 'laugh it off', there is the possibility of introducing a different perspective and an alternative interpretation of psychology's covert and subjective investments which some narrators, readers, users and students of psychology might take on board.

Note

1 I have made no attempt to offer conflicting 'empirical' evidence against the professor's arguments because I consider his conclusions and analyses as just too absurd to warrant any counter argument. If readers feel the need for such evidence I would suggest that they read Zukerman and Brody (1988) who thoroughly discredit his account. Further, I have omitted much of the content of the professor's conclusions, terminology and remarks, because of their scopophilic quality. This serves to transform much of the 'humour' to be derived from the narrative, from the 'merely' comically sexual, to the pornographic and obscene.

part *two*

Reflecting on research

This section of the book takes up some of the methodological issues posed by reflexive approaches to consider how these enter into feminist psychological research. The three chapters in this section address in different ways the impact of institutional structures on the privileged meanings that command articulation in research to analyse what is rendered absent or silent. They trace through a progression from feminist engagement with dominant definitions of research topic and process in attempting to secure funds in Chapter 4, to, in Chapter 5, exploring the meaningful experiences of non-cooperation and exclusion in research that corresponds to a more pervasive (including feminist) failure to theorise adequately the relations between 'race' and gender. Chapter 6 focuses on a specific area of silence over personal safety brought about by the convergence of discourses of empowerment in research with residues of positivism which erase researcher subjectivity.

All three chapters speak using the personal 'I' of the original researcher. The project of owning and naming the experiences described in these chapters has been significant for their authors, and their accounts here testify to a writing and discussion process that enabled new perspectives to emerge. The production of these singular voices as 'I' has been wrought through a collective process, and 'we' present them here as individual in part to assert their personal significance and specificity as much as their wider relevance. While questions of research process take centre stage in this Part, the role of emotions and personal involvement which forms a key theme in this section is taken up in later chapters, as is the question of the strategic deployment versus the call to take issue with specific research topics. The question of the adequacy and appropriateness of invoking a collective 'we' to identify feminist experience and activity is discussed here in this Part in terms of the multiple forms of power relations operating within research processes, and is developed more generally in the final chapter and Endnote.

chapter *four*

Heavy periods: The process of collusion and compromise in research

Jane Marshall

> From a starting point wherein I wanted to learn about, and ideally add to, our understanding of women's experience of menstruation, I had evolved a series of experiments in which menstruation had become a variable on a par with stressors such as sleep loss, heat, noise etc. It had become rationalized, compartmentalized as a stressor, and thus devalued. I knew in myself that women's experience of menstruation could not be meaningfully conceptualized in this limited way.
>
> (Ussher, 1990: 50)

The focus of this chapter is an exploration of an account of women who seek help for heavy periods, which was produced to support an application for research funding. This is contrasted with other accounts produced in the course of the research. I consider how I split off my interest in women's accounts of problem periods from my desire to design 'respectable' research, placing what women had to say as secondary to 'objective' measures of outcome. This chapter describes how I acted on internalised assumptions to subvert my feminism and conform to a particular discourse.

The research involved interviewing women who had been referred to a hospital outpatient gynaecology department with the complaint of excessive menstrual blood loss, the medical term for which is menorrhagia. I wanted to identify what the effect of providing women with the opportunity to talk about their concerns would be on outcome in terms of women's satisfaction, uptake of surgery and perceived severity of symptoms. Undoubtedly I was interested in the women's accounts, but did not see a record of these accounts being the primary focus on which to base any conclusions. However, in piloting a semi-structured interview, I became caught up in listening to what women had to say, interviewed more women than I needed to to make a convincing study, and started to feel uneasy about the way in which I had formulated the research in the funding application.

Once I began to reflect on this I became aware that I had produced differing accounts of the proposed research. I will use these to illustrate the collusion and compromise engendered by the research process. An extract from the research proposal forms the first 'account' to be considered here. It had been written for potential funders, the ethical committee and the institution hosting the research. When I started to take a critical look at this original research submission I realised that I had also produced a second account with a different emphasis for the staff at the gynaecology clinic, and a third oral account with yet another emphasis, for the women I was to interview. The last account to be considered here is actually a collection of quotations selected from the 24 transcripts of my interviews with women. It is my interpretation of these women's comments which served to challenge some of my assumptions about women who present with heavy periods. I conclude this chapter by considering ways in which we can avoid collusion and maintain our integrity as feminists and as research psychologists.

Background to the research

My interest in menorrhagia research was prompted by an awareness of the prevalence of women's discontent with periods and the frequency with which women undergo hysterectomy. A Mori survey in 1990 reported that almost a third of women of reproductive age complain of excessive menstrual blood loss. Although only a minority of those women take the complaint to the GP, the number is rising (Barlow and McPherson, 1988). There is a positive correlation between going to the doctor with this complaint and the receipt of surgical investigation and/or treatment (Coulter *et al.*, 1994). One-third of all gynaecology outpatients are referred for this reason and a woman is more likely to be referred to a gynaecologist if she herself has a preference for surgical treatment. Sixty per cent of hysterectomies are performed for menorrhagia (Barlow and McPherson, 1988) and treatment with surgery is becoming increasingly common. Around one-third of wombs removed from women under 45 have nothing obviously wrong with them (Lumsden, 1990). While some causes of excessive bleeding can be identified, excessive loss without obvious cause is labelled 'dysfunctional uterine bleeding' or 'menorrhagia of benign origin'. New technologies have been developed which allow for less invasive ways of checking for malignancy and for removing the lining of the womb without removing the whole organ. However, there is a danger that these technologies replace hysterectomy without addressing the existing concerns about how menorrhagia is assessed and without hearing women's concerns and treatment expectations, given that it is a problem which often presents no threat to physical health.

Differing accounts of the research

My attempts to appeal to different audiences reproduce variable discourses about women and about my role as a researcher. At the outset I was aware that I had a mixed agenda for doing the research. In part it related to an altruistic desire to see an improvement in women's experiences of health care, and in part it related to professional issues and the wish to expand the role of clinical psychology in relation to health services for women. I viewed research in a hospital gynaecology department as a potential vehicle for achieving these aims. I selected an area which affects a significant number of women and for which referral to a gynaecologist often leads to surgery. In contrast to the menstrual cycle, menstrual bleeding *per se* has generated relatively little psychological research.

I believed that one way of fostering a more psychological approach to healthcare for women was to formulate research which would be of interest to those with the power in the health service to propose changes and argue for funding to bring about new approaches to the delivery of healthcare. Peckham (1991) argues that one of the main objectives of research in the health service should be to ensure that healthcare interventions within the NHS reflect scientific knowledge. However, there is a difficulty with the definition of the construct 'scientific knowledge'.

Lyne de Ver (1994: 13) considers the role of clinical psychologists as researchers in the NHS and argues that they are required to have a 'good awareness of other people's priorities and a willingness to find a way to influence or work meaningfully with these'. Attempting to understand other people's priorities can lead to a process of arranging an argument for the research you want to do and selecting research literature to justify the argument. In addition, the current split in the UK National Health Service between purchasers of health services (including research projects) who want value for money, and providers who want to get on with the job with as little interference as possible, means that the researcher can be placed in a position of being seen as a potential agent of change by the former and a potential threat by the other.

Thus I was in a position of attempting to find out, or to imagine, what other people's agendas were and tailoring my own priorities to fit them. In addition, a desire to avoid personal rejection, which, exacerbated by my gendered position as a woman entering a male-dominated hierarchy, probably influenced my wish to produce an 'acceptable' scientific discourse. It was only in thinking about this chapter that I became more aware of the process I had been engaging in. The conflicting feelings I experienced when formulating the research would have been much easier to deal with, had I understood the nature of this process at the time.

The first account

My focus was mainly defined by the current backdrop to the funding of research in the NHS which is, in theory at least, to achieve the best possible value in terms of cost effectiveness. In my written rationale I therefore used the language of 'costs' – first, financial; second, in terms of mortality and morbidity; and, lastly, the costs to the woman of a stay in hospital and recovery following treatment and the possible effects on her children. Nothing there about the costs to the woman of not being heard!

The receiving audience for the first account was the regional health authority research and development committee. I wrote the two paragraphs below as part of the summary required by the committee.

> There is considerable evidence from research that a sizeable proportion of women receive treatment for gynaecological symptoms for which there is no firm evidence of significant abnormality or disease. It has been shown that between 38 and 57 per cent of women who attend hospital believing their periods to be abnormally heavy are in fact experiencing loss within the normal range. Objective assessment is rarely used and thus treatment is often given in the absence of objective criteria.
>
> It is suggested that women may lack knowledge about the normal range of menstrual flow, may be anxious about change in flow and, most importantly, may use concern about their periods as a focus for other anxieties or depression. These women and those whose flow is indeed outside the normal range may have anxieties about serious disease and anxieties about hospital procedures.

This was the concluding paragraph of the same submission:

> Given the high level of psychopathology amongst gynaecology patients there is a delicate balance to be achieved between taking the patient and her complaints seriously and running the risk of reinforcing a 'career' of medical investigations. There is evidence that some

> patients, having exhausted the options offered by the GP, confound the specialists in one discipline and move on to one or more others. Since what usually motivates the patient is a high level of anxiety rather than malingering, there is a case to be made for intervening before such 'careers' are far advanced and phobic states well constructed and less amenable to intervention.

I start out by expressing implicit concern about women receiving medical treatment when there is no objective evidence of a medical problem. In order to secure the agreement of the host institution I believed I had to disguise my criticism of existing medical services. I therefore move on to focus on women believing their periods to be heavy when they are not, and reflect on the reasons for this. While there may be some value in considering a complaint of menorrhagia in the absence of an objectively heavy loss as evidence of psychological distress (Greenberg, 1983), the effect of menstrual taboos on the dissemination of knowledge needs to be considered. How is a woman to know what is a normal or excessive blood flow if it is something that is rarely discussed? The role of those in powerful positions (doctors, male partners) also exerts an influence in various ways. This was highlighted by a woman who came to a Well Woman Centre without her husband's knowledge since she said that he refused to allow her to go to the doctor for treatment of heavy periods.

It could be interpreted from my first account that I portray women as mistaken, lacking knowledge, anxious and somatising. It is not so much the reporting of the research findings which is problematic, but rather the way in which my argument is structured and developed. From my initial contact with the hospital I sensed that a psychologist who is interested in what gynaecologists are doing represents a threat. Thus it is acceptable for 'patients' to have psychological problems but not for medics to have psychological problems around their treatment of women. On the other hand, listening to women served to reinforce the idea that it is important not to take a simplistic view. A multidimensional theoretical model which incorporates feminist and systemic ideas (Goldner *et al.*, 1990) recognises the complex interaction of variables which influences thinking and behaviour – in this case those of the woman, doctors, peers and family, and sociocultural forces which are a part of this. The temptation is to simplify and scapegoat the medical profession as a counter to the implicit devaluing of women. However, analysis at different levels is possible so that one analysis does not exclude others.

At one level I took some pride in the concluding paragraph of my submission, probably because I thought that I had succeeded in tapping into what I perceived to be the audience's belief systems. I focused on women's psychopathology, not doctors' psychopathology. In this account women become 'patients'. I do not specify whose agency ensures that 'a delicate balance be achieved', but I pose women as exhausting the offers of the GP and subsequently confounding many more medics. Thus I have completed my argument that it is women who need sorting out. I then propose that they be assessed, counselled and offered psychological therapy. This lends credence to the use of my clinical psychology skills. However, earlier in my submission I was using a different language about giving women space to talk about why they had come to see a gynaecologist, what anxieties and questions they had and what they expected and what they wanted to happen, and proposing that they have the opportunity to come back and talk further if they wanted to. Again this shift exemplifies the tendency to adjust the language in order to gain 'respectability' for research.

Questioning my first account also led me to read more about feminist research, reflexivity and discourse. Thus the discourses available to me changed and led me away from a research model which requires subjects, controls, hypotheses, variables and quantitative data. It led me to ask such questions as: How much do we know about women's experience of menstruation and particularly about periods that are perceived to be unacceptably heavy? What is it about the interaction between a woman and her doctor that leads so many women to be referred to gynaecologists? What is it about the interaction between women and gynaecologists that leads to so many women having surgery? Additionally, how many women fail to go to a doctor and are putting up with symptoms which constitute a risk to their health?

The first question above suggests a focus on women, and the second and third a focus on the medical profession. Certainly, it is tempting to take a critical view of the way menorrhagia is managed by the medical profession. However, my research proposal, written with an awareness of the medical profession as the receiving audience, backs away from a critical view of the medical management of this problem and, instead, ends up by pathologising women.

The second account

I wanted to gain the confidence and support of the staff of the hospital gynaecology clinic. It was not possible to meet with the staff so I prepared a written account of my research and invited feedback. I will briefly consider how this account highlights a shift from the first account.

> It is clear from many research studies that there are considerable psychological aspects to the problem which women present with at gynaecology clinics. I have selected the area of Menorrhagia as the focus of my research since a significant proportion of women who

> believe their periods to be abnormally heavy have been found to have a menstrual blood loss within normal limits. Since many of these women go on to have surgery it seems important to gain a greater understanding of what women are distressed about, what ideas they have about what is normal, and what treatment they are expecting.

The extract here presents a different emphasis from the first account above. While I still portray women as having mistaken beliefs about their menstrual loss I go on to emphasise the importance of understanding women's perceptions, expectations and distress. It now seems to me that the shift in this account is because my audience this time were all women (nurses and a receptionist). Since I was not conscious of this shift at the time when I wrote it, it suggests that, whatever our expressed commitments as feminists, the process of compromise and self-censorship is deeply ingrained.

The third account

This account was one which I prepared and then refined in order to explain the study to the women I wished to interview. This account was not given in written form but delivered verbally to the women in the study.

> I am a psychologist who specialises in women's health. Part of my work is in the two Well Woman Centres locally, where women come with all sorts of problems and sometimes are referred here. That work has given me an interest in the reasons women come to a gynaecology clinic and how they feel about it. If you agree to it, I can get *some* information from what the doctor's letter says, what Mr X's opinion is and what treatment he recommends and the results of any examination or tests if you have any.
>
> However what it says in the doctor's letter and in the medical notes is never the whole story and usually doesn't refer to the worries and questions women have. What I'm really interested in is what *you* have to say about what the problems are, how you feel about being here, what you're expecting and what you're hoping for and any worries or questions you might have. As well as giving *me* a fuller picture, it may be that important information comes out which could lead to improvements in the service women get. I would hope also that you may find it *helpful* to talk about things in more detail before you see the consultant.

In this account to each woman I interviewed I was attempting to establish my credentials, not by expounding on my knowledge of research findings and methodology, but by talking about my past experience of seeing women in Well Woman Centres. In doing this I place myself in a more central position – not as a dispassionate observer, but as someone whose interest has been prompted by my meetings with women. However, it is evident that I chose to maintain a stance as a woman *working* with women, i.e. a professional position rather than presenting myself as a woman interested in women because of my personal experience. At the time, my concern was to establish some credibility both with the women and with the gynaecology staff since I wanted to conduct research which might exert some professional influence on the way in which gynaecology departments respond to women. I feel reasonably comfortable with the position I adopted since it is likely that the women attending were expecting to be seen by professionally trained individuals. To be interviewed by someone presenting their personal experience would not only have flouted role expectations but more reciprocal disclosure may have been experienced as intrusive. Equality in such situations is elusive and it is necessary to acknowledge the institutional power relations (such as those between psychologist and patient) which necessarily enter into the interviewing process (Ribbens, 1989).

It was, in fact, only in writing this chapter that I reflected on where my interest in women's health research comes from. My first thoughts were about my past involvement in campaigns for a woman's choice on abortion and how this political involvement led me into having an instrumental role in the setting up of a Well Woman Centre within the NHS. From there I have broadened the development of my work as a clinical psychologist by focusing on the psychological aspects of women's physical, as well as mental, health. Further reflection, however, took me back to adolescence when the (boarding school) doctor dismissed chronic thrush as normal. This male doctor was also renowned for getting girls to remove all their clothes except their knickers and making them touch their toes, regardless of the complaint. I am not aware that this was ever challenged. It now seems to me that my adolescent rage (I would not have called it that at the time) is what brought me into working in the field of women's health. What I have in common with other women, therefore, is having experienced the power accorded doctors, having a health complaint dismissed and being viewed as a sexual object.

At the time of deciding to research the area of menorrhagia I had felt that it was a positive thing that I had not experienced menstrual problems, and that the area I was exploring would not be biased by my experience. It is interesting that when Sophie Laws wrote *Issues of Blood: The Politics of Menstruation* (Laws, 1990) she did not make her own experience visible but decided to comment on this later (Laws, 1992: 118) in an article saying that 'drawing attention to one's menstrual pain in public is disapproved of in this culture'.

Although I do not place my personal experience in the foreground it has a place in a more covert way in the manner in which I ask questions and make comments. I respond differently to different women depending on my perception of their preferred style of communication and level of comfort with the interview situation. Some women seem more interested than others in wanting to look for areas of common experience. It seems to me that offering a woman space to talk about her unique experience while at the same time acknowledging our common experience is a complex process. Nevertheless, it would be interesting to know whether relating my adolescent experience would have led to different accounts from women.

This third account of my experience and stated interest in women's health is an attempt to establish some credentials for my interest in listening to women. I then communicate my interest in what the woman herself has to say as opposed to anything that doctors may write about her. The emphasis is different from my first account which professes an interest in exploring 'psychopathology'. It is not that my intentions were different when I wrote the different accounts but that 'psychopathology' is the psychologist's equivalent of the medical terminology which converts 'really heavy periods with no obvious physical cause' into 'dysfunctional uterine bleeding'.

I let each woman know that I am interested in her, ask why she has come and explore her questions, hopes, fears and expectations. It also seemed important, first, to acknowledge that by talking to me women were helping me with my research and second, that I hoped their information would contribute to improvements in services for women. I express my hope that the discussion would be helpful to them as a preparation for seeing the consultant. I also offered to send the results of the study to women who wanted to receive them.

Other factors which are relevant are, first, what my accent, dress and white skin colour communicate (charles, 1992), and second, how the way in which I structured the interview and the sorts of questions I asked affected women's responses (Roberts, 1992), as well as the impact of audio-taping the interviews.

In this third account, therefore, I have declared myself as a woman interested in women and women's experience. I could have given an even more subjective account by placing my own experience before the woman. Nevertheless, the account is less 'objective' and therefore less distanced than the first account. It places women's experience as important, valid and central.

Accounts from women

In addition to the factors which influenced the exchanges between the women and myself, there will be a further distortion of their views brought about by the process of selection and interpretation in presenting these particular accounts. Nevertheless these accounts provide a richness and challenge which 'objective' research using questionnaires would not be able to do. The accounts are based almost exclusively on white women's experiences, which in large part mirrors the fact that the local population is predominantly white.

Many women launched into their accounts without waiting for me to finish explaining the study and formally securing their consent, while a few were anxious and may have perceived the request as an imposition. While consent is a complex issue in itself, this willingness to talk suggests a lack of other opportunities for women to speak about menstrual problems. It certainly felt at times that my invitation to talk was implicitly a reversal of the taboo about talking about periods (Laws, 1992).

Women's presentation of their problems

I was struck by the graphic nature of some women's descriptions.

> I woke up in the middle of the night one night. It was just as if someone had been murdered.

> You get a bit frightened really because you think it's not going to stop. It's like stop and that's gushing, well not gushing, but trickling and you think it's not going to, a bit frightening.

> Most of them are pretty normal, but I do get the odd one that's really horrendous, and I seem to swell up like a poisoned pup.

They suggest a complex set of reactions possibly made up of fear, disbelief and even disgust. Consistent with research findings elsewhere, there was a wide range with regard to how severe symptoms were perceived to be, such that some women appeared to minimise apparently severe menstrual problems and others expressed considerable concern at apparently less severe symptoms. However, a pointer to the variation in the perceived severity of symptoms lies in the range of symptoms that women presented. Often there was a mismatch between the stated reason for referral in the GP letter and the concerns expressed by the woman. Some women expressed doubts about whether the consultant would be interested in anything other than accounts of blood loss. This is important since symptoms such as cyclical breast tenderness will not be alleviated by some forms of surgical treatment, with the likelihood that the woman will feel dissatisfied with the treatment given (Slade *et al.*, 1991). If she feels she does not have permission to give a full picture, her concerns may not be heard or may be dismissed as insignificant.

> They say cancer isn't hereditary, but nearly all my family have died from cancer . . . My mum died of cancer, my grandma died of cancer, all my granma's sisters died of cancer of the womb.

Weijts *et al.* (1991) found that women generally present their anxieties to gynaecologists in covert ways with, for example, implicit allusions to the possibility of malignancy or with pressure for more drastic medical intervention. They found that doctors responded either by exploration, immediate reassurance or by negation of the expressions of anxiety. Women's accounts suggest that it is important to find out about a whole range of symptoms which may or may not be related to the menstrual cycle, and to hear and address women's concerns, particularly the fear surrounding cancer.

Women's 'psychopathology'

The medico-psychological model subsumes women's fear of cancer under the category of 'psychopathology'. However, using normalising language, it was clear from women's accounts that there was often considerable past or present distress. My dispute here is not with identifying the 'psychology' of health concern, but with the label 'pathology'. My perception of texts in this field is that there is often an implicit view that women are pathologically prone to exhibit psychological problems. I take the view, rather, that distress is often understandable and to be expected, given the reality of women's experience.

> My daughter died 2 years ago.

> My husband left me, I had to change house, er, then my son was in a coma for six months and I was nursing him. Things keep cropping up with him and I haven't had time to think of myself and all of a sudden I thought there is never going to be a right time for me.

For some women, their usual everyday pressures were made more difficult by the menstrual symptoms or the taboo surrounding the discussion of them.

> It's even when I go to work people even know when I'm having a period because I look so ill . . . It makes me very bad tempered, it makes me really bad tempered and I'm inclined to snap at everyone . . . Actually my husband even went to the doctors and said he was about to have a nervous breakdown if he [the doctor] didn't sort me out with it.

> I'm all right at home, but men are pratts you know and I do lose my rag you know [laughs], but the boss is aware I think because obviously he's married and he just steers clear [laughs].

A woman's current pressures and/or past distress could make certain symptoms less easily tolerated. It may also be difficult for a woman to protest about, or even acknowledge, everyday aspects of her life (e.g.

being dominated, undermined, objectified), so that a change in her menstrual pattern could become a focus for that distress. Greenberg (1983) suggests a variety of theories about the mechanism that might be operating, including a suggestion that depression may trigger a physiological reaction which upsets the hormone balance, and hence produces excessive menstrual blood loss. Certainly, several women interviewed were confident that stress was a contributory factor.

It is likely that there was also hidden distress which women did not tell me about because I did not provide the opportunity. Draijer (1989) quotes a study by Ribberink and Slurink (1988) which found that more than 40 per cent of gynaecology patients questioned about sexual abuse mentioned one or more 'severe' experience. This sample showed a higher prevalence and greater severity compared with a general population sample. A history of abuse could have a bearing not only on how women normally feel about the functioning of their bodies, but also on their reactions to being physically examined by doctors (Domar, 1986; Areskog-Wijma, 1987). Some women expressed a generalised fear of hospitals. Reactions to the prospect of an internal examination varied widely, as did views about the gender of the doctor.

> How do I feel, I don't feel anything really because I think I'm used to it. We've had that many D&Cs and um, I'm not a person that gets embarrassed easily and I don't think there's any need to get embarrassed anyway, because if you've had a baby I think you lose all your shyness anyway. It wouldn't worry me if I was lying on a bed there and there was all students round me, it wouldn't bother me at all.

> I think I'd prefer a woman doctor, I mean I've got a male doctor . . . I don't know, not that I'm embarrassed, I just feel they understand the other side of a woman more. Not so much in medical, the problems of a woman more than what a man does, but they've all sat the same exams and they've all got the same experience. I suppose that was a bit stupid really talking like that.

The above extracts suggest something of the complex process we have to go through to tolerate intimate medical examinations. While the gynaecologist has a medical framework for the encounter, for women genitals and their function have both positive and negative associations (Wijma and Areskog-Wijma, 1987). In order to engage with the process we have to surrender privacy and deny our sexuality (Lachowsky, 1989) at the same time as we encounter a heterosexist and restricted view of sexuality.

> If I was married perhaps I would have said to him, you know, will my sex life change, but umm, that's gone anyway, that's flown out of the window.

> Sometimes they ask 'are you sexually active?' and things like that and I don't know what to say to that because they automatically mean the other you know.

Women expressed other fears which could be interpreted as relating to issues of autonomy and control, such as the desire to be awake or asleep during investigation and treatment.

Women bring the great richness of their lives to the medical consultation but are expected to leave this richness at the consulting room door. Nevertheless, perceptions, beliefs and fears will be influenced by present and past experience and will in turn influence the medical consultation and therefore treatment. Acknowledging women's experience may well lead to different outcomes.

The referrer

Women's comments echoed Coulter *et al.*'s (1991) findings about the variability of GPs' responses.

> Incidentally I saw a doctor at the end of last year and she said she couldn't do anything for me because the problem was normal for me which was ridiculous to my mind . . . because there comes a stage where you think, you know, this is supposed to be such a natural thing, how can it cause me so much distress and so much pain?

Some accounts talked of the care and respect with which they were treated, with information and explanation being given and treatments tried before a hospital referral was made. Other women were surprised either by the haste with which they were referred or by their complaint being apparently taken more seriously than they had taken it themselves. This led me to speculate about doctors' reactions to menstrual blood and whether some doctors prefer to leave the examination of (bleeding) women to the specialist. Coulter *et al.* (1994) found that women were almost twice as likely to be referred to a gynaecologist if their GP was male.

A significant number of women reported that their GP had led them to expect the surgical procedure of dilatation and curettage (D&C) which is of doubtful value in diagnosing malignancy and only temporarily helpful as a treatment. This is a cause for concern, since the procedure involves a general anaesthetic which carries its own risks. However, once the expectation has been set up by the GP that an operation under anaesthetic will establish whether there is any malignancy and effect a cure, then the woman may feel cheated if she is not offered this and she may exert pressure for surgical treatment.

It is evident that there is a need for GPs to be aware of how their knowledge, assumptions and attitudes regarding menstruation influence their referring pattern and the expectations they give women and hence influence outcome. Since the outcome may be the removal of a healthy womb and possibly a woman's continuing distress, this is not a matter to be taken lightly.

Women's expectations regarding outcome

Women's accounts of what they were wanting to happen with regard to their presenting symptoms highlight the complexity of women's experience and the relation to our bodies.

> I could do without my periods all together now. I feel as though, I'm 44 nearly and I've had enough really, but I could be going another 10 years. Umm, but as long as they regulate it that would be acceptable and I don't particularly want to take tablets to do it, I don't really like taking tablets.

> I'd be really frightened if he said anything about an operation or anything like that, I'd probably collapse on the floor before hand.

> I don't necessarily want anything to happen if the medical profession could see fit that whatever's going on to cause me to have the period I'm having is in their opinion normal well that's fine. I'll just get on with it.

> I don't know. I've left my mind open, I don't think about it, just see what happens.

Coulter *et al.* (1994) express surprise that only 40 per cent of women expressed a preference for treatment when asked in a questionnaire. However, it is evident from women's comments that there is a complex interaction between attitudes, beliefs, knowledge, emotional responses and historical experience regarding symptoms, treatment process, menstruation and the womb.

Ambivalence was common.

> I mean now that my son is older my husband and I can go out a bit more and I don't want all this nonsense, it could go on for another three or four years . . . If they were normal, like once a month you could probably put up with it . . . Well I'd rather not have the operation let's put it that way. Urm, I think but if I've got to have it I've got to have it. But if I could do without it, if I could be certain that the tablets would control it, there's no problem, I could live with that.

An additional factor was women's roles as carer and the effect that treatment would have.

> Surely I might as well have a hysterectomy because I've got a family history of cancer of the womb and it plays on your mind . . . Umm

> I'm hoping that he'll say leave it and see how we'll go on, not because of myself, but because of my [disabled] son.

A couple of women referred to their infertility:

> I suppose really I'm also thinking that at my age I don't need them and umm, I've never had children, I've really wanted children and umm, I thought well at my age I don't see why we should have them.

It seems to me that this woman was saying that she is disappointed with her reproductive organs which, having failed her, nevertheless provide a regular and disruptive reminder that the opportunity to have a child is now past. Other women express similar feelings that menstruation no longer holds a positive function and therefore removal of the womb appears a reasonable option. This raises wider questions of women's choice over reproduction and fertility. However, the important issue is whether women are in a position to make an informed choice over treatment for their periods. This means having information about whether symptoms are outside the normal range, whether they present a risk to physical health, what the treatment options are and what the benefits and possible side effects are. Hufnagel (1990), for example, argues that hysterectomy can negatively affect women's orgasmic response. Women cannot make an informed choice if their own questions about sexual response are not given a voice.

In conclusion

> I think they should look at the whole person rather than just isolated, one little bit, because that might, in my opinion tell them a lot more about what is actually going on than they know about. It could be lots of other associated things.

The aim of this chapter has been to describe the way in which *hearing* the women I interviewed allowed me to hear myself and challenge academe's demands for 'objectivity' (Hallam and Marshall, 1993). Some of the things I heard, or interpreted, women to be saying were that their concerns are rarely talked about in such detail, that doctors would only be interested in the labelled problem, that the reality and complexity of their lives should be left at the consulting room door, that sexuality should be invisible, and that medical examinations and hospital procedures can be experienced as traumatic. These accounts challenge the implicit assumptions and the conclusions of much research into menorrhagia, which largely ignores the complexity of women's concerns and the powerful role of doctors. Women's position(s), life experiences and emotional reactions are frequently subsumed under a label of 'psychopathology'. Having applied the label, research studies then seek to find ways to identify which women fit the label so that they can be prescribed a more psychological treatment approach than those not so defined. My own study, which seeks to assess the value of offering *all* women the opportunity to be heard, challenges these pathologising research discourses. However, I find myself anticipating that the very ordinariness of 'offering all women the chance to be heard' will be devalued and dismissed by those with the power to approve and fund research.

Listening to the women at the gynaecology clinic made me more aware of the powerful nature of the process I have engaged with. I began to realise that, in my pursuit of academic respectability, I had ignored the *emotional* investment I have in doing research and in striving to give women a voice. As long as I ignore my own voice, my own experience, I run the risk of being assimilated into the main (male) stream 'objective' view, or of patronising women by assuming that I am addressing their needs rather than my own. I run the risk of becoming yet another professional attempting to 'speak for' women. Unless I take as central my own connections, identifications and investments, I start to see myself through 'the eyes of the other' (von Foerster, 1991) and my vision is obscured. I begin to act as though 'feminist' is a dirty word, something risible so that speaking a discourse of feminism will result in my ideas being dismissed. If I fail to look to my own experience then I am less likely to be aware of the devaluing of women in many scientific discourses: 'Extreme, alarming and persistent forms of pubertal haemorrhage are mostly seen in spoilt, often only, children with overanxious parents' (Tindall, 1987: 529). This is clearly pejorative, but frequently the devaluing is implicit, difficult to see and difficult to challenge. The internalised power of 'the other' can lead us to forget and even feel uncomfortable with other celebratory discourses:

> There is something numinous, mysterious and awe-provoking in the ability of women to bleed regularly without dying – much as the moon diminishes and finally dies away, but returns from death. This blood is an indication of the miracle of life – because the woman does not die, and because it means she can bear children.
>
> (Hall, 1991: 170)

In attempting to bridge the communication gap between the speakers of such accounts as these, we run the risk that feminist discourses are submerged in deference to the dominant male discourses.

Thus, to be able to speak with my own voice, I need to hear the voices of other feminists in order to challenge the dominant 'other' whose voice is strengthened if I work in isolation. Meeting with others and reading a broader range of texts can answer 'the continued need to challenge patriarchal knowledge and practices, which variously obstruct, oppress, expropriate and oppose our feminist aims and achievements' (Kennedy *et al.*, 1993: xv). Nevertheless, allowing oneself to discover a shared discourse can be a difficult process in itself, since it is easy as a novice researcher to assume that any problems encountered in discussing research with supervisors and others is attributable to inexperience or incompetence. The other chapters in this section also highlight the pitfalls of conducting research in privacy and isolation.

As a white middle-class feminist I am not going to hear *all* women. Some women may not want to talk to me, and those that do may re-present what they think I want to hear for me to re-interpret and re-present for publication. Research does not produce universal truths, but we must make the connections between our lives, our politics and our academic experience to develop feminist research which challenges dominant discourses and gives voice to our own and other women's experience.

chapter *five*

Black parent governors: A hidden agenda

Robina Ullah

This chapter is a reflexive analysis of my experiences as an undergraduate conducting a piece of research in 1992–3. I will suggest that the difficulties I experienced illuminate the issues that I set out to investigate. My analysis is structured around an absence, a silence, which as Foucault argued, can be interpreted as informative of the constellation of power/knowledge relations that maintain it. In Foucault's terms, 'silence itself – the things one declines to say, or is forbidden to name, the discretion that is required between different speakers – is less the absolute limit of discourse, the other side from which it is separated by a strict boundary, than an element that functions alongside things said, with them and in relation to them within over-all strategies' (Foucault, 1976: 27). My initial research topic was to investigate the experiences of black parent governors within inner city primary schools, and it arose from the then current promotion and discussion of parental choice and parental involvement. I began my research full of enthusiasm and certain that I would have dozens of 'subjects' to interview and no shortage of material for analysis. This chapter reflects on why this did not happen, and the role of racism in this process. The type of racism I will be discussing was institutionalised and not necessarily direct or intentional. Rather, bureaucratic delays facilitated non-compliance with my study. I will also look at the ways in which I was positioned in the study which were not always advantageous in 'getting results'. I will first give a brief outline of the topic of research, and then I will describe some incidents that occurred during the process of conducting the research. These experiences literally form a 'case study' for exploration of the relations between race and gender as they arise in research processes which illustrate the urgency of exposing and challenging institutionalised racism and sexism.

Policy and practice

The original topic of my research was to investigate the experiences of black parent governors. My initial interest arose from consideration of new legislation and media hype concerning parental power and choice, as well as about the more long-standing debates over the educational needs of black children in Britain.[1] Moreover, an additional reason for looking at this issue was that in 1992 the first four-year term of statutory parent governor office in British schools had ended. This was therefore a good moment to explore how successfully the theory of parent governors' participation had been put into practice. There were also reports in the press of the practical difficulties facing parent governors. These were, first, that governors felt dissatisfaction concerning the amount of time and commitment that the role of parent governor involved. Second, the reports not only voiced the difficulties parent governors experienced in getting time off work to attend meetings, but also discussed the stress of dealing with the management and running of the school without having sufficient background support and training.

There has also been little formal research carried out, and my research may illuminate why. At this point, I will outline my position in the formation of the idea for research, for, as Wilkinson (1988: 494) suggests, '[f]or the individual his or her research is often an expression of personal interests and values'. In this instance, my personal interests revolved around the fact that I am a parent, I am black and I am a woman. I wanted to find out how black parents are represented on school governing boards. One of the few pieces of research on the topic of parent governors found that school governing boards were not representative of the population as a whole or of the schools that they govern. Deem *et al.* (1992) found that of the 250 governors in their study only 33 per cent were women and only 8 per cent were black, and out of these only a tiny fraction were Local Education Authority (LEA) or co-opted governors. In their sample 40 per cent of the parent governors were women and of these most were white. Similarly a NFER study (Streatfield and Jefferies 1989, cited in Deem *et al.* 1992) of 500 schools in 10 different LEAs in 1988 found that 41 per cent of the governors in the school were women, but less than 3 per cent were black. They found that black governors are noticeably absent even in the schools where a high percentage of the pupils were from different ethnic backgrounds. This context of much public and press discussion and little research played an influential part in my final choice of topic. A further factor that influenced my choice was that current government policy claims to uphold parental power, in particular through such documents as the Parents' Charter.

The rallying cry of 'parental choice' of late 1980s Britain was given some institutional expression in the 1980 and 1988 Education Acts (see also Chapter 7, this volume). However, LEAs did not view this as a particular priority as they saw local management of schools (LMS) more in terms of hiving off the funding for schools, buildings and staff, rather than extending parents' rights. While the current legislation is claimed to place parental influence and choice as central, as Johnson (1990: 104) points out, 'there is some evidence to suggest that, parent power may be illusory'. In particular, choice and empowerment are not necessarily equivalent. In 1988 the Consumers Association found that only 25 per cent of parents had attended a parent teacher association (PTA) meeting in the past 12 months and only 9 per cent had attended a school governors annual meeting (Johnson, 1990: 103).

A further key element in this political climate is how an uncritical celebration of parental choice can lead to a collusion with racism, as was highlighted by a recent case in Dewsbury where parents of 26 children refused to send them to a school where the majority of the other children were Asian. At the time the law was such that LEAs could place limits on the number of pupils in each of its schools and the Secretary of State claimed that he had no power to intervene. The LEA later reversed its decision after a judicial review in the High Court. The 1988 Education Act allows open enrolment so that schools are forced to accept children up to the limit of their capacity. Although the Dewsbury parents denied being motivated by racial prejudice, what cannot be denied is that new regulations could lead to racially segregated schools. In November 1987, Baroness Hooper, the Under Secretary of State for Education stated : 'If we are offering freedom of choice to parents we must allow that choice to operate. If it ends up with a segregated system then so be it' (quoted in Johnson, 1990: 103).

Given the current discourse of parental choice and power, I wanted to document how parent governors are recruited, trained and supported. In Manchester, a 'multicultural' city with a substantial proportion of the population composed of minority communities, there are a number of leaflets published in community languages such as Punjabi and Chinese. These introduce the concept of parent governor and then go on to give contact details of where to get further information. A survey carried out by the Labour Party reported that two-thirds of the authorities questioned were experiencing difficulties in recruiting parent governors, a quarter of them saying that the problem was serious. While the Labour Party supports the idea of parent governors and has identified a number of shortcomings in the present arrangements, it claims that all parents have not been informed adequately of their rights under the Act and has criticised the lack of training available (Johnson, 1990: 104).

In my research I discovered that places on LEA training programmes were often oversubscribed so that there was no guarantee of parent governors receiving adequate background knowledge before making decisions on matters relating to the running of the school. Johnson (1990) also points out that there is a risk of middle-class bias in school governing bodies, with the evidence pointing to the active involvement of relatively few parents. Given that governing bodies have increasingly greater financial responsibilities, business contacts or acumen may become a major criterion for election. In the case of parents from middle-class backgrounds, they may have the resources available that will enable them to act as school governors and exercise their parental choice. Hence the problem facing working-class parents as well as those from ethnic minorities is that if they become school governors they may find that they lack skills and influence. They may therefore become token representatives in contexts where schools lack resources of real, as well as cultural, capital (see also Sarup, 1991).

In terms of my original research topic, the notion of parents taking an active role in their children's education through parental involvement in the classroom, or through the roles they played in the management of the school through their presence on the school governing board, was underscored by the current political discourse of choice. But these choices cannot be exercised unless there are adequate resources to fund the training of parents for their role on the school governing boards and provide them with training and materials in a language that they are able to understand. These are prerequisites for them to be able to make a genuine contribution towards the running of the school.

In mid-1993, some indications emerged of problems in this process. I include this information as the historical and political backdrop to my own research in this area. In June the *Daily Mail* published reports from the Audit Commission about questionable practices by school headteachers managing school budgets. These claimed that headteachers were awarding lucrative contracts for equipment to their wives, husbands, children, friends and moonlighting teachers. They also often failed to keep proper records of how the money was being spent. In addition, the Commons Report 'Adding up the Sums' (June 1993) looked into how schools have coped since the government reform allowed them to control their own budget from April 1988. This found that in nine out of ten cases the headteachers had complete freedom in how they spent their money and were rarely challenged by governors. This report highlighted that the school governing board was playing the role of a 'rubber stamp' on decisions that the head had already made. These reports tie in with my own and other research suggesting that most governors do not receive adequate training and information about issues relevant to the running of the school, and tend to accede with whatever the head proposed.

Mahoney (1988) documents the following comment made by a senior LEA official while discussing proposals for training, 'You're not going to teach them their rights are you?' This symptomatic comment flies in the face of earlier recommendations of the Taylor Report (1977) that all governors should be given the opportunity to inform themselves on matters of educational theory and practice.

Black parents' involvement and choice

Closely related to questions of parental involvement is the fact that many children in inner city British schools come from families whose first language is not English. Very often the parents of these children may have little or no command of English. In this case, they may be unable to understand the literature that is published about parent governors. In response to this criticism LEAs point out that it would cost them a lot of money to translate relevant documents and, through shortage of funds, are unable to do so. But if no interpretation facilities are available, then this renders such training sessions as are provided useless for promoting the involvement and representation of this group of parents. With these shortcomings, then, the much vaunted Parents' Charter is not fulfilling its function in providing parents with choice and freedom in their child's schooling, owing to the lack of provision for the needs of parents from ethnic minorities.

During my research I attempted to obtain figures in relation to the numbers of parents from ethnic minorities serving as parent governors. Despite practices of 'ethnic monitoring' across the LEA, I was informed that it was not possible to get this type of information as not all individuals were willing to divulge details of their ethnic origin. Here the discourse of choice and self-designated identities has worked to obscure the documentation of lack of representation. There has, however, been an increase in the collection of 'race' data in post-war Britain and the use of these statistics to inform immigration laws and other policies. A debate correspondingly surrounds the usefulness of 'race' statistics as a weapon to fight racial discrimination within the political system centrally and locally. The questions in social policy surrounding the relevance of collecting ethnic data via the national census criticisms are summarised by Leech (1989, cited in Ahmed and Sheldon, 1991). Apart from the problem of accurate definition in reporting of ethnicity, black groups have campaigned to have the ethnic question(s) removed because of the abuse of such information in immigration and policing policies. In this context, and alongside the development of multicultural policies, 'race' as an analytical category has lost favour and the notion of ethnicity has now been popularised. Nevertheless, problems remain with the racial/ethnic descriptions currently in circulation which are reproduced in policies and records (Carter and Williams, 1987). These define race and ethnicity by colour, and treat as equivalent those identities arising from notions of nationality (e.g. Pakistani, Indian) and geographical regions (African, Caribbean).

Hence the political will of both the central and local government to fight racial discrimination by the collection of such data has been questioned (Sivanandan, 1990). But more recently some benefits have been put forward for the collection and disaggregation of race-based information (see Anthias and Yuval-Davis, 1992). Some sources of central government funding, such as Section XI, require local authorities to have accurate figures so that they can apply for resources with which to tailor their services to meet the needs of the local people. It is also argued that ethnic data can help in situating services in appropriate localities and provide evidence of discrimination at different levels within an organisation, on the basis of which it is argued it can then be tackled. It is also claimed that such information can be used to provide 'baseline data' for policy formation (but see Dorn and Hibbert, 1987).

These benefits indicate possible uses for accurate documentation available concerning the racial and ethnic backgrounds of parent governors. While race and ethnicity are problematic categories, I retain the term 'race' here as a social construct with links to racism, old and new. The use of ethnic data has implications for dealing with the ways that racism affects communities and individuals in terms of, for example, definitions of their needs, and evaluating provision and adequacy of services. It is also necessary to be aware of assumptions that 'all members share the same experience and interests' (Yuval-Davis, 1993: 6). Such assumptions are often structured into policies made in relation to black people, where they are grouped together as if homogeneous. When looking at the representation of black people on policy-making committees it is also important to recognise how, as Yuval-Davis (1993: 6) says, 'anyone who can claim to be a member of the grouping can claim to represent it to outside agencies and benefit from it, no matter how different s/he is in terms of class, power, gender, etc. from the majority of the people claimed to be represented'. Such literature as is available on consultation practices between local authorities and minority communities (e.g. Gibson, 1987) suggests that these marginalise precisely those groups – including women and young people – traditionally under-represented within those communities (as elsewhere). Thus the statutory obligation for consultation and representation between school and 'community' can become an occasion to reinforce existing chauvinisms rather than extend democratic rights.

This review of the political issues at stake and the scant literature on black parent governor participation all emphasises the need for proper consultation and democratic election processes. So ethnic data may be useful to a researcher theoretically, and may be used to make a useful assessment of service needs on the basis of information on the ethnic mix of its population. This is how I arrived at the conclusion that LEAs should adopt an approach where they can determine the ethnic mix in their schools to monitor the representation of black parent governors on governing bodies. Otherwise, it is futile to have legislation that calls for parental power and choice when the parents are being denied their rights through lack of representation.

The process

What now follows is an account of what took place in my attempts to pursue this research, and why in the end I was left pondering the significance of various incidents and responses I encountered. In a sense, my research process highlights the institutional processes and investments mobilised by questions of the representation and participation of black people within supposedly democratic structures. Owing to the need to protect the identities of the schools and individuals involved, I can only give generalised descriptions. This, however, does not detract from my argument as I am concerned not with particular schools and individuals, but with the institutional processes such specific instances illuminate. I present the following four examples as intimating what lies behind the slogan of parental choice, and the silences on actual participation.

Approaching black parent governors

In the process of trying to collate data for my research I first approached the Governors Training Unit of the LEA where I found that the workers were enthusiastic about my project. In particular I assessed that this was an area of concern for them to the extent that a post had been appointed specifically to promote the participation of black parent governors. I set out my research proposal of exploring the experiences of black parents on governing boards through a short interview, and I was provided with names and contact numbers of black parent governors. However, the black parent governors I contacted met my request with a variety of responses. Some parents did not want to be interviewed, but said that they would fill in a questionnaire if that was of any use. One said that he was too busy and could not help. Some said that they would have a think about it and get in touch if they decided to participate. None did so. The others explicitly refused to take part.

As a student researcher, I felt aware that I was relying on the goodwill and commitment of the individuals I approached. Lacking the power of a professional position that would command greater respect for the topic of my research, I was met with a silence. Interestingly, a year later, in the different position of a bilingual support worker in a school, I encountered neither a shortage of information, nor such obstacles in gaining access to parents or schools. All this says much about the social structuring and effectivity of my position as a black woman parent. Looking back now, it seems quite clear that these parent governors were not willing to participate in the research. From their silence the conclusion that I now come to is that they did not want to admit the limited extent of their roles within the governing body. As it was, some of the governors indicated that they were not on the key sub-committees where decisions are made before they go on to be presented to the school governing body as a whole and finalised. Some of the governors I talked to made observations and comments about their position, but this was only once they were assured that their comments would be 'off the record', that there would be no recriminations, and that their identities would not be revealed. They echoed the concern, documented from other studies that, 'lip service is given to equal opportunities with no strategies for serious implementation' (Zmroczek and Duchen, 1989: 609).

Approaching the schools

As I was unable to 'get access to subjects' in the conventional psychological sense, I tried another approach. This time I telephoned a number of inner city primary schools listed in the telephone directory to ask if I could interview their black parent governors. While again this produced no offers of participation, this approach was most revealing in terms of other people's perceptions of me. A few of the schools explained their refusal to participate in terms of not having their full quota of parent governors. They excused themselves from involvement in my study by saying that they were in the middle of elections because the four-year term of office had ended. However 'reasonable', this explanation seemed to indicate rather than solve the problem: not only could I not distinguish how many parent governors were black, but once again questions about black people's representation were getting submerged within general limitations and procedures of institutional bureaucracies. Some schools said that they would pass on my request to the governing board who would then decide whether they wanted to take part in my project. While clearly this is a proper procedure, both they and I knew that this process would take more months than were now available to me for this project. In the event, none did respond. Others refused outright, saying that they were already assisting students in a number of projects and could not take on any more.

Moreover, while making these enquiries and asking for information on the phone I experienced apparently helpful responses until I disclosed my name. Immediately the person on the other end of the phone became eager to end, or to hurry along, the conversation and very often halting comments were made such as, 'you don't sound . . .'. Such surprise and equivocation over my socio-cultural identity was, I feel, a racist reaction. As my study was asking questions about (what I now understand is) a sensitive area, perhaps I should have anticipated the defensive reactions and responses of these various schools. However, that my position of parent, female and black person combined to warrant the non-advancement of my project in these ways exhibits precisely those processes that prompted my study in the first place. In this case racism was operating on a subconscious level, since doubtless the respondents felt that they were giving adequately valid reasons for not participating. But if we treat this as the stopping point, this then sets them free from any sense that they should have participated. In addition, the underlying reluctance to reveal who was on the governing board also avoided putting them in a position where they would have had to come up with adequate reasons for not having sufficient representatives from the black communities. This part of my study also reflects processes and practices underlying the general failure to set up arenas for consultation from members of community groups.

While engaged in this process, I lost contact with my informant in the training unit who had taken voluntary redundancy after a period of extended sick leave. This left me with a lack of support from the LEA governors training unit despite their initial commitment. I became even more isolated and puzzled about why this topic was so difficult to research.

Observing a general governing board meeting

Eventually, when time had nearly run out, I was given the opportunity to attend a governors' meeting at a school and to observe the proceedings. The governing body was made up of thirteen governors, seven men and six women. There were two female parent governors and one male parent governor who was also the chair. The rest were members of staff and representatives of the LEA and the council. This meeting took place in the staffroom and there were no formal seating arrangements. The meeting lasted approximately two-and-a-half hours. There were 14 items on the agenda and they covered a range of topics including the completion of Standard Assessment Tests (SATS) and the results of the Inspector's Report on reading.

The meeting seemed very preoccupied with handing out the Inspector's Report, and looking at the teachers' re-scheduling list. Three of the governors, the two women parent governors and one teacher governor, remained silent throughout the meeting. The LEA governors left an hour after the meeting started. It was the chair who kept the meeting in flow and determined which items should be discussed in the sub-committees rather than included on the agenda. The two headteacher governors were the ones who made the most contributions throughout the meeting.

This meeting highlighted the parents' lack of involvement with any major decision-making as, for example, any matters concerning finance were left to be discussed in the sub-committee where they were not participants. They stayed silent even when there was obviously (or so it seemed to me) a need for a parental point of view, as in the statementing of particular pupils. My observations of this meeting showed that even though the governing body may be made up of a number of people, in the end those on the sub-committees make most of the decisions, and these are also the ones who are most informed. In the meeting that I attended the decisions had already been made in the sub-committee and were just being finalised in the general meeting. None of the governors objected to any of the suggestions put forward.

Moreover, despite the fact that the pupils were around 40 per cent black, this was not reflected on the governing board in terms of representation. While I cannot claim that this meeting was representative of all school governing bodies, given the history of my limited access these dynamics seem likely to be more than unique. David (1989) points out that including parents as governors opens up lots of opportunities for particular non-representative parents to claim a voice they do not speak for. This was highlighted in the governors' meeting that I observed when the dominant parent governor appeared to be directing the decision-making process, although not in the interests of all parents. Parent governors can exploit their position to their own personal advantage. The picture emerging from that meeting emphasises the need for proper consultation and democratic election processes, which leads me to my final incident.

Observing an election of parent governor

This incident reveals the extent to which apparently independent processes of community (in this case parent) representation can be influenced by professionals. Events leading up to the election of a parent governor in one school I observed involved a meeting to which all the parents of registered pupils were invited to meet the three candidates standing for election. The meeting was informal and there were no representatives from the governing board to explain the role of parent governor. The meeting was well attended and lasted for an hour, and the parents were given the opportunity to introduce themselves and say how they felt that they could represent parents on the school governing board. One of the candidates during this meeting was not able to answer any questions posed about the role of parent governor. However, this parent went on to be elected. What emerged some seven months later when this parent governor then resigned, was that parents of the pupils had been lobbied in a number of ways to give their vote to this particular parent. The individual who had done the lobbying was an influential member of staff, the home–school liaison teacher. This meant that she had influence especially with the parents who were bilingual and who turned to her for explanations on a variety of school matters such as translating letters for them. The motive for such election engineering was to exclude another parent who was considered to be 'unsuitable' by the teacher because she was vocal and regarded as not conforming to traditional community values.

This incident indicates not only undemocratic processes, but also how claims to respect cultural diversity can reinforce static and reactionary definitions of gender, 'culture' and community practice (Hatcher, 1987; Saghal and Yuval-Davis, 1992). It also highlights basic inadequacy at even the most token level of practice, since the parent governor also later disclosed how she did not receive adequate support, and therefore could not actively take part in the meetings. By resigning a short period after she had been elected, she was admitting that the role of parent governor carries more responsibility than parents are led to believe. She found herself in a situation where she was voting with the majority of the white governors rather than being able to express the needs of the black community she was supposed to represent.

A similiar incident in Birmingham at Springfield Primary school in 1989 highlighted the lack of communication in the functioning of the governing board. This involved the appointment of a home–school liaison teacher, the job specification for which had not taken into account the parents' wishes to employ a bilingual teacher. The governors, apart from the chair, had not even been aware of the post until it had been filled. The problem here lies with the Education Department in failing to ensure that the governors had been properly informed and had the training and ongoing support to take parental concerns on board and to put racial equality measures into practice. More generally, the precondition for parents to have their voice properly heard is that they are adequately represented on governing bodies.

Conclusion

Looking back, I can see how a number of factors were influential in the responses I received while trying secure participants for my research. Ann Phoenix (1994: 50) discusses the forms of influence and impact of gender, 'race' and social class in negotiating with respondents. As I have already pointed out, research by Deem *et al.* (1992), shows how school governing bodies are largely composed of white middle-class males. I can now see how all these factors came into play while I was trying to find research 'subjects'.

Edwards (1990), in her study of mothers returning to education, found that the black women she approached were much more suspicious and reluctant to take part than white women. She attributes this not only to the fact that she herself is white, but also to questions over informed consent – since the educational institutions in which the women were studying passed on their names to the researcher without first asking for their consent. Similarly, since I was given names of black parent governors without their consent, this perhaps partly accounts for why I found them unwilling to participate. I should also point out that most of the names that I was given were men's, and therefore I can see now how my gender and race may have influenced non-cooperation. But this again restates the problem: why were there so few black women parent governors? In addition, my project thus illustrates how simple methodological 'fixes' such as 'colour matching' can ignore other structural power relations entering into research, such as class, cultural codes, gender and age.

Phoenix also talks about negative reaction to researchers and her experience of 'white interviewees being visibly shocked, when she turned up for appointments' (Phoenix, 1994: 55). She relates this to her colour as this was the only additional feature that became 'visible' on meeting face to face. She suggests that it is not unusual for black researchers and academics to encounter such reactions of surprise. This is what I experienced while asking for help on the phone, only it was my (Asian) name that made me 'visible', so that personal meetings did not even take place.

Throughout this project I found myself trying to undertake research in situations where I felt oppressed and dominated. I relate this to the fact that I was a black woman researcher. It is not possible to be certain which of these factors was the most influential. I can only comment on how these positions combine. As a student, there was also an added disincentive to secure the schools' participation because it was assumed that my results would not be published or reach a wide audience: my research could therefore be treated as unimportant and there was nothing for anyone to worry about as nothing would be revealed of my experiences. Thus the marginalisation of my experiences as a black woman were compounded with the powerlessness of the position of student researcher.

For my part, I also feel that too often I took a passive role in not pursuing requests once I had received a refusal to participate or non-response. At the time I felt worried that I would be seen as aggressive and 'looking for trouble' where perhaps no problem existed. What I was trying to research was black people's experiences on school governing boards and, as Phoenix (1994) points out, questions relating to 'race' are controversial and thought-provoking. This was demonstrated in her study where her interviewees wanted feedback on her views of how they had responded when they had been asked questions in relation to race: what they wanted to know was whether they had come across as being racist. In addition, the topic I had chosen for research can also be described as 'sensitive' in Lee and Renzetti's (1993: 5) definition, that is, a topic that is seen either as threatening to those being studied, or as inviting unwelcome effects. So, the parents who spoke in confidence to me did not want their opinions revealed for fear of repercussions. My research therefore highlights the complexity of power relations, not only in terms of how these structure what is available to be documented, but also how silences indicate sites of oppression and exclusion. The process of silencing my efforts to give voice to black parent governors can therefore be seen as indicative of more general strategies used to suppress their perspectives.

Much psychological research suggests that 'matching' of researcher and researched is desirable in order to minimise the impact of power inequalities in social research. One reason why I faced problems was that I had to approach interviewees through white contacts. But even where social/cultural identities matched, as with my contacts with black parent governors, other power relations can come into play. Thus the history of my research reproduces the history of its topic. Just as I emerged frustrated and dissatisfied from this research, black parent governors expressed their dissatisfaction about their role on school governing bodies. They felt that they were there as token representatives and that no one was really interested in what they had to say. There is criticism here of how governing bodies function in that the presence of co-opted (non-parent) governors and LEA representatives can be intimidating and can effectively de-skill parent governors. This issue of power was highlighted in a 1987 report by the Exeter Society for Curriculum Studies which stated: 'New parent governors express resentment at the political nominees on governing bodies. They also experience acute feelings of anxiety about their own shortcomings doubting their ability to both understand the education system and to represent faithfully the views and interests of parents' (quoted in Golby and Brigley, 1989).

These local and current questions of power need to be contextualised within the histories and geographies that, in some sense, have overdetermined them. So it is not surprising that black parent governors are reluctant to engage with or discuss the politics of school governance, since they suffer the legacies of the social structuring of cultural inferiority wrought by the British imperial tradition. Suspicion combines with pressure to conform and not complain in ways that make it difficult for black parents to dissent in decision-making processes among white-dominated governing bodies. My account of the influencing of a supposedly democratic election for the post of parent governor illustrates how experiences of racism intersect with reactionary definitions of gender within minority communities.

Even though policy statements commit themselves to the promotion of equality for all people, all too often this is not achieved. Troyna points out that 'while the existence of racial inequalities alerts us to the existence of institutional racism, the relationships between the various mechanisms said to exemplify this concept operation aid the causation of racial inequalities is rarely specified or demonstrated empirically' (Troyna, 1988: 162). I have described how delegation of power within the governing bodies is another site for the covert exercise of dynamics of exclusion through the structure and membership of sub-committees, in particular the finance sub-committee, who have access to information (such as school budgets) before the rest of the school governors. In the study by Deem *et al.* (1992), only four schools had any black governors on these finance sub-committees.

In my research I found that black parent governors did not want to be interviewed and thus, through being unable to address my research question, my experience paradoxically both mirrors and answers features of that question: that is, that black people – and especially black women – do not have access to the institutional forms of representation that would enable them to make their voices heard. However, there are a number of additional points that I want to clarify. Maynard (1994: 15) points out that black writers have emphasised the importance of recognising that experience does not necessarily equal 'truth'. Rather, this provides the basis from which to address both similarities and contradictions in women's lives, and to develop theories about how these might be understood collectively. Brah discusses how the notion of experience is important, 'as a practice of making sense symbolically and narratively; as struggle over material conditions and over meaning' (Brah, 1992: 141). My research challenges traditional feminist work in that black women are in many instances excluded from feminist writings and, as Zmroczek and Duchen (1989: 607) report 'there are very few Black women in research positions in institutions'. Perhaps this could be one reason why my research was met with what I can only describe as 'disinterest'. However, black feminist writers, such as Patricia Hill Collins and bell hooks, are now calling for feminists to recognise the black women's differences as a resource by which we can expose the 'underside' of oppressors and oppressed. As Collins puts it: 'the theoretical and analytical development of this knowledge is that to be a black feminist is to inhabit an ontologically distinct set of experiences' (Collins, 1986, cited in Stanley and Wise, 1990: 30). Further, she argues that this knowledge should be used as the basis of a black feminist standpoint. Thus my frustrated and frustrating research experience reflects aspects of the oppression of black parents (perhaps especially black women) in paralleling how and why they were not active as parent governors.

Bhavnani (1988: 42) talks about power relationships between the researcher and researched, and goes on to say that 'messiness' in the research is what is important as this can provide a starting point for the analysis of power relationships between the researcher and researched. In my study, the power to access and motivate participants to take part was very much under the control of the schools and other officials, as they were my first port of call. This absence of conventional research material has left me with a catalogue of incidents and responses which constitute the 'messiness' on which my analysis here is based. Bhavnani (1988: 43), also reports that 'social psychological research has ignored the power inequalities resulting from hierarchical loadings assigned to socially ascribed characteristics'. While research can be seen as giving a voice to those being researched and potentially empowering them, it can also be part of a disempowerment 'because it reproduces social stereotypes of those who are the subjects of the research' (Bhavnani, 1988: 45). In my research, I did not set out to reinforce any stereotypes of black people. Nor do I see this account as fostering stereotypes. Rather, my analysis documents the stereotyping of black parents, particularly women, who are subject to racism both in their role as parents and as school governors.

Even though I did not have any interviewees for my research and in the end had to rely on analysis of the *absence* of 'data', I want to emphasise that this should not be seen as 'bad' research, as a project with 'no data'. Rather, taking my own experiences of research seriously has illuminated my topic of research. The difficulties I encountered demonstrate those strategies of exclusion and marginalisation of crucial relevance to the democratic participation of black parents as governors in schools.

This project therefore illustrates the analytical/methodological strategy of making the silences speak; of theorising the power structures that enforce or create such absences. While psychology has tended to investigate what is observable, my account here demonstrates the insufficiency of this positivist approach. Instead we have to question why it is that some events can be documented while others remain undisclosed. This corresponds to a theoretical silence within feminist accounts, of failing to articulate forms of gender as structured by race and racism (see Afshar and Maynard, 1994). This recognition has led to a recent re-evaluation of the complexity of forms of feminism constructed within, as well as against, histories of racism (Ware, 1992; Frankenberg, 1993), which form the starting point from which to theorise differences between women *as power relations*, rather than equally valid variations. In this project, my positions as black, woman, parent, researcher, were inextricably linked and all became interwoven within the narrative of frustration and equivocation that I have presented here. I draw on my experience here as a political resource to be mobilised, rather than an account to be accorded the status of authentic truth. These reflections on research thus challenge both psychology and feminism to analyse the intersections between gender and other relations of inequality as they are played out in institutions, including those of research practices, for our mutual and further subordination.

Note

1 The term black is used here to denote all people subject to racism on the basis of skin colour.

chapter *six*

Keeping mum: The paradoxes of gendered power relations in interviewing

Karen Taylor

> I have come to believe over and over again that what is most important to me must be spoken, made verbal and shared even at the risk of having it bruised or misunderstood.
>
> (Lorde, 1984: 40)

This chapter tells *my* story of research experience. I want to illustrate the vast difference between what is written about the research process and what happened to me, and I suspect, to many other women researchers. I was a funded research assistant on a project evaluating employment policies within a large firm. The policies aimed to integrate the needs of working professionals with family commitments, with the needs of a professional workplace. The project involved interviewing women professionals, their line managers and the women's partners. It was the experience of interviewing the men in this study which leads me to speak out about the role of research methodologies and their effect on personal safety. Little has been written about women interviewing men, this chapter draws on my own experience of interviewing to address this silence.

The positivist legacy

Although the methodological implications of carrying out research in a positivist paradigm have been well documented, and, to a great extent, rejected, by feminists (Oakley, 1981) and others, they still leave a legacy that is difficult to resist. Many social science textbooks still include chapters that encourage the researcher to go to the interview situation with the impression that it is possible to become a neutral person for the duration of the interview. They imply that personal emotion and subjectivity can be put in a neat box before turning on the tape recorder. This dehumanising process is supposed to allow the researcher to generate unbiased, objective data that can be analysed by totally disregarding the presence of the interviewer.

> The interviewer's job is fundamentally that of a reporter, not an evangelist, a curiosity seeker, or a debater. Interviewers should take all opinions in their stride and never show surprise or disapproval of a respondent's answer. They should assume an interested manner towards the respondent's opinions and never divulge their own. If the interviewer should be asked for personal views, they should laugh off the request with the remark that the job at the moment is to get opinions, not have them.
>
> (Selltiz *et al.*, 1965: 576)

This approach to 'data collection' is one that forces the interviewer to present a blank screen to 'an informant' in order to be an 'objective' sponge that soaks up all the data without any personal investment. More recent publications do little to dispel this notion of the interviewer's role. Breakwell talks about the need to control 'interviewer effects' by using the same interviewer for all the interviews. She argues that this will avoid generating 'biased data', since 'This serves to hold constant the stimulus provided by the interviewer' (1995: 239). This approach forces the researcher to lose any sense of identity of their own and to become part of the project. However, the research interview is not a clean cut data collection process, nor is it necessarily a friendly, egalitarian, conflict-free encounter. It is a social relationship that cannot transcend inequalities structured around gender, race, age, sexuality and disability. It cannot leave the realities of the outside world outside the interview room. Nor can we pretend that the places where we conduct the interviews do not also enter into their meaning and process.

Feminist challenges to positivism

Academic culture remains powerfully influenced by positivism. Our daily discourses are littered with positivist values, especially those of objectivity and validity. If a piece of research does not contain numbers and 'facts', it is considered 'soft' and 'unscientific'. At a paper given at a research seminar for psychology students, I was asked how large my sample was. When I replied that I had at that point interviewed 18 people, I was then bombarded with challenges questioning whether I could comment on emerging themes as the study was not 'big enough' to be valid or representative of working parents. As a researcher doing a qualitative study, there is a pressure to carry out in-depth interviews and analysis, and yet still feel the need to have 'enough' cases.

Feminists have challenged the notion of the research experience being 'hygienic' and scientific, and have been highly critical of disempowering effects of positivist research (Oakley, 1981). Feminist critiques have looked at the production of research, the methodology, and the relationship between the researcher and the researched (Harding, 1986; Stanley, 1990; Stanley and Wise, 1993). Feminists have challenged the role of 'objectivity' in the research process, and stressed the importance of the subjective experience.

Instead we feel that social science researchers are taught to mistrust experience, to regard it as inferior to theory, and to believe that the use of research techniques 'can provide data unclouded by values, beliefs and involvements' (Stanley and Wise, 1993: 153).

In discussions of feminist research, reflexivity has become central to the research report. Reflecting about the experience of researching allows the 'messiness' of the process to have an equal part in the writing up. Many traditional academic social science projects are written up in such a way as to reinforce scientific paradigms of idealised research practice. Such pieces of work exclude the failures, the difficulties, the learning as you go along and, above all, 'what happened'. Instead what usually occurs is an account of 'what should have happened'. 'The difference is that feminist researchers tend to be much more open about this process and can therefore be seen by some as a threat to research orthodoxy' (Scott, 1985: 74). The danger of failing to reflect these research experiences in reports is that important theoretical and political issues get privatised and individualised as personal inadequacies or mistakes. I am writing about these experiences out of the conviction that they are not peculiarly mine, but offer insight into the structural dynamics of research relations.

Interviewing men

Within recent feminist research there has been a move away from researching specific aspects of women's lives towards a focus on gender relations. This has meant that feminists have not restricted themselves to only researching women's lives but to include the lives of men (McKee and O'Brien, 1983; Layland, 1990). While there is currently a burgeoning literature on masculinity and gender studies, feminists have for some time argued the case for in-depth research on men as central to feminist analysis and interventions. 'If feminist researchers continue to focus on women there is a danger that in continuing to place so much emphasis on researching the relatively powerless that we partly reinforce and rephrase what we already know' (Scott, 1985: 81).

The public/private debate

Traditionally men seem only to be conceptualised in the public sphere, rarely are men located in the private sphere of their homes. While women are consigned to the research areas of motherhood and division of labour, men are seldom asked questions regarding the domestic running of their lives. This means that spatially men are located in the boardrooms and shop floors of the workplace, while women provide us with detailed accounts of the daily running of the household and family.

Within the study of work and family, the role of fatherhood has increasingly become a legitimate research topic. Many researchers feel that change cannot be effected by concentrating solely on the role of motherhood. It is argued that the role of fatherhood needs to be altered if the workplace is ever going to become a place where women can compete equally alongside their male counterparts. Hence in order to understand more fully the work and family interface, and to place men in the private sphere of the family, the research project for which I was working included, as a vital part of its design, interviews with the partners of the working mothers of the study.

The study

In this section I will briefly outline the rationale and context for the interviews, before moving on to present some specific incidents that arose.

The firm

The firm that formed the focus of the study was a traditionally conservative organisation. It was an international firm with many offices throughout Britain. Unlike the sort of organisations discussed in Chapter 9, the firm was male-dominated with large wage differentials between the (almost exclusively female) secretarial support and the technical partners at the top (all male except for the senior personnel partner). During my entire contact with the firm over a period of two years I never met or saw any staff of a different ethnic origin to my own (white), so I can only wonder how a black woman interviewer might have felt and fared in this position (see Chapter 5, this volume). Although most of the offices I visited had disabled access, I did not encounter anyone with a disability. As the firm had no equal opportunity policy and certainly no monitoring policy that I could gain access to, I was unable to find any information regarding whether my experience was accurate of the organisation as a whole.

The study for which I was researcher was concerned with evaluating a number of personnel employment policies that had been introduced by the firm to encourage staff retention. A number of trained women professionals were leaving the firm to have children and not returning to work because they were only being offered full-time employment. Many women have cited this as a reason for not returning to paid work as they cannot combine a full-time post with family commitments (McRae, 1991). The scheme offered a reduced-hours policy which allowed staff to take up to ten hours off a week without losing any other staff benefits, a career break option of up to five years and a part-time working policy. It was not a big surprise to find that, although the scheme had been available to all employees, only one man had opted for reduced-hours working. He did not want to be interviewed.

Contacting the participants

I contacted the women who had taken maternity leave in the last three years through the personnel officer of the firm. She gave me a list of women's names and departments and I wrote a letter inviting each woman to be interviewed about their experience of being a working mother. I explained about the nature of the study and their role within it and that I would give them a copy of the transcript of the interview and safeguard their complete anonymity. At this point I also asked whether I could interview their partners and their line managers. In retrospect, I feel this approach discouraged women from the study who may have felt that their 'families' did not fall into the category of the 'universal nuclear family'. It also meant that lesbian mothers might not have volunteered for fear of being 'outed'. I gave these letters to the personnel officer who sent them to the women's home addresses along with a letter from the company stating their support for the study.

I had given my phone number at work as the contact number for the study, and after a while women who had received the aforementioned letters started to ring me and ask me more about the study and the promise of anonymity. Some women decided that they did not want to be involved with the research. However, the majority of women agreed to be interviewed and also agreed that I could interview their partners and their line managers. I was to carry out the interviews with the women at their place of work (the firm had agreed as part of its support for the project to allow employees to take an hour off work fully paid to do the interview), and they were to be the first members of the research triad to be interviewed. All of the women apart from one were married and initially I contacted their male partners through them. Subsequently I contacted the men directly by phone either at their workplace or at home. As none of the men worked for the same company as their female partners, very few of them would agree to be interviewed at their place of work as they could not legitimately take time off. We therefore negotiated a time that I could come to their house and carry out an interview. Talking to the men in their own homes would, I assumed, locate them very firmly in the private sphere, and I felt that this would enable me to see for myself how they 'really' coped in the domestic setting. This was perhaps the first key error I made in treating abstract theoretical commitment (to changing the gendering of the domestic sphere) as translatable directly into research practice.

The fathers

I had a great deal of difficulty devising the questions to ask the fathers. There was very little material I could find at the time written about interviewing men, especially fathers, and about the conflicts between the workplace and family commitments. I also felt there was a lack of focus to the interview. The boundaries of what was 'appropriate' were unclear. I was unsure whether should I be asking the men about the firms' policies or only about the direct effects upon family life, and whether I should ask about how they felt about their partners' decisions to return to work. In effect I was unsure where to position the male partner's accounts in relation to the female's. I wanted to empower the working mothers by placing them at the centre of the study and did not include my power relationship with the other interviewees in the equation. I assumed that, as an interviewer, I had power and I could pass this to an interviewee.

I did not, at this time, think about how the men would perceive being interviewed, and how they would react to my positioning of them in the research. Looking back, I had definite areas that I wanted to discuss with the women in the study and their line managers. However, the role of the fathers within the project was much less clear and more problematic.

During all this time I did not come across one article or chapter that alerted a female researcher to the particular difficulties of interviewing men. While feminist reflexive accounts were exposing the 'messiness' (Bhavnani, 1988: 43) of the research process and the experience of taking part in research projects as a researcher, there was not one whisper of the power relationships between a man and a woman in the research interview. I now want to explore the costs of and investments in this silence.

The interviews

It was with an intention of being a 'good' interviewer who did not seize the power during the interaction, and who tried to make the interview an empowering experience for the interviewee, that I put together my research questions and set out to interview the 'participants'. It was the lethal combination of a naïve empowerment model and a desire to be an 'objective' interviewer, that allowed me to become a mere extension of the study. Not only did I deny my subjectivity and emotion as valid responses but I put my own safety at risk in what emerged as being a dangerous situation.

The following account draws on the transcript of the interviews themselves, the field notes I made following the interviews, and a difficult process of sitting down and remembering the actual encounter and the feelings I remember having. Obviously time has lapsed since the event and I am sure there are aspects that have been omitted, whether due to an inability to recall everything that happened, or a desire to sanitise the experience. I have struggled in writing this reflexive account, weighing up the anxiety of exposing my vulnerability in a public forum for an audience to judge, alongside the desire to alert other researchers to the dangers of interviewing men in their homes. My purpose in writing this is not to provide a 'complete' picture or a confession to elicit sympathy, but to suggest practical recommendations to improve the safety of researchers.

The first scenario

I arrived at the house of a female professional I had interviewed earlier in the day in order to interview her male partner about his reaction to the employment policies and how he felt they affected the family. The house was in a suburban area and was quite a long walk from the train station. By the time I actually arrived at the front door it was about eight o'clock in the evening. A man came to the front door and I explained that I was the researcher from his partner's company who would be interviewing him for the purposes of trying to find out how families were coping with the combination of careers and dependants. He invited me upstairs to the lounge and asked whether I wanted a cup of coffee. It was at this point that I remembered that his partner was not going to return that evening as she had told me earlier that day that she had a meeting and would be staying overnight. The house was spotless and the young child had already been put to bed. We chatted for a while about the research in general and then we sat down in the lounge to start the interview. I felt he was a little reluctant actually to get going, so I got out the tape recorder and asked him to say something so that I could test to see whether it was working.

I started the interview by asking very general questions about the age of his child and how he managed on a daily basis and how he felt they coped as a family. The responses to these questions is the subject of my MPhil and are not relevant here (but see Taylor, 1995). However, when I came to the area of his workplace and whether he felt his workplace was 'family-friendly' he started to talk about the problems he was having at work. At first I supposed I was simply playing the role of 'listener', which was what I felt I ought to do. As he continued I felt his comments were not really relevant to the study and I tried to get him back on line with further questions. He turned these back round to the problems he was having at work. I then felt as if I was becoming less of an interviewer and more of a counsellor, for which I am not trained. It was at this juncture that I began to feel that this was not a simple interview as the previous ones had been. I looked at my watch and saw that it was now ten past nine. The thought that went through my head was that he was going to continue in this vein for hours 'if I let him', and that what he was talking about was not pertinent to the study. I managed to ask my last question which was open-ended, but I was already trying to think of ways to bring the interview to a close. Yet again he brought the topic round to his work and continued talking. By this stage all that was going through my mind was to round the interview up and get home. Eventually I interrupted him and turned off the tape as a way of ending the interview. He carried on talking and, whether, out of politeness or because I still had my interviewing 'mask' on, I nodded and smiled at his barrage of talk about his own work problems. I began to pack my research equipment into my briefcase and sneaked another look at my watch. The time was now twenty to ten and I was starting to worry about the long walk back to the station, the train journey back to the city and the underground journey back to where I was staying. At this point I stood up and put my coat on, picked up my briefcase and began moving towards the stairs. He immediately jumped up and walked round the coffee table and into the open plan kitchen. This directly closed my access to the stairs and my way out.

For the first time that evening the nagging discomfort erupted into huge alarm bells in my head. I was alone in the house of a complete stranger and his partner would not be returning. Nobody had the address or phone number of where I was, and nobody except for the friend at whose house I was staying, was expecting me back that evening. I felt simultaneously panicky and annoyed. Why had I not told anyone? How long would it take before somebody actually started to worry? If he did anything would I be able to overpower him? Once again I tried to hide the emotions from my face but I felt that he was aware of the thoughts rushing through my mind. I stepped forward to get past him and he stepped back still blocking my exit. I can't remember anything that he was saying. I was just nodding. I kept stepping forward and he kept talking and moving backwards. I told him that I was going to miss my train and connections if I didn't leave straight away.

He then started asking me where I was staying and I again tried to get past him. He then started walking down the stairs and I followed. He got to the bottom of the stairs and stood there, but made no attempt to open the door. I realised that the keys were in the door and remembered that I had gone up the stairs first on the way in and therefore I didn't know if the door was locked. He carried on talking and I blatantly looked at my watch and said that I really had to leave. He unlocked the door and opened it but stood in the way. I could see outside and went towards the door, he made no effort to get out of my way and I had to slide between him and the door frame to get out. Once outside I ran from the house up the road and all the way to the train station. When I got there, there was hardly anybody around, I went to my platform and found that I had another 15 minutes to wait before the next train. After about five minutes, two young men came and stood on the platform. They asked me for a cigarette and when I said I had none they started trying to talk to me. I ignored them and just looked at my watch. The train duly arrived and was empty, I waited for the two men to get on and then got in another carriage. They walked through into my carriage and started walking up and down. I sat in my seat and stared out of the window. We reached another stop and I saw another woman and her children had got into the next carriage so I picked up my stuff and went and sat next to them. The two men followed me into the next carriage, but left soon afterwards.

Since this night I have spent a great deal of time thinking about what happened and more so about what didn't happen. At first I felt that I had over-dramatised the situation, nothing had actually happened, I hadn't come to any harm. I obviously had an overactive imagination. He was simply a man that was unaware of personal space and it was my inability to cope with physical closeness that had caused me to panic and overestimate the danger of the interaction. I told nobody about this apart from my friend who had witnessed the state I was in when I arrived at her flat.

The second scenario

The second experience I will narrate concerns an interview with a senior manager from the firm that was taking part in the study. This took place about three months after the above interview. I arrived at the offices of the company with my tape recorder and was told to wait in a large boardroom. I set up my tape recorder and waited. Nearly quarter of an hour later a man appeared. I started to introduce myself and he nodded and waved his hand at a chair at the other end of the table to where all my equipment was. I immediately felt a dislike towards this man but moved everything down to the other end of the table. I tested the tape to ensure it was working and I started the interview. His views on women in general and women 'returners' made the hairs on the back of my neck stand on end. I felt a huge physical revulsion towards him. I sat stony faced while he told me that people who were not the main breadwinners were less committed to their work, and that his politics were 'on the right side of Attila the Hun'. I went systematically through all the themes of the interview and turned the tape off after about 25 minutes. He seemed shocked that the interview was so short, so I shrugged and said that he had answered all of the questions. I packed up my briefcase, shook his hand and walked out of the building.

On the train on the way home I began to write up my field notes. I began to feel a little guilty that I had finished the interview so abruptly and had not followed on from any of his comments. But I had enjoyed turning off the tape. I had taken control. While still functioning as a competent professional I had let my emotions run riot. I had not cared whether the interview was 'good' data. I had listened to my emotions and it was as a *woman* I had turned off the tape, not as a *researcher*.

Power relations

The power dynamics present in any interview situation are complex and often subtle. The positivist tradition reduces the interaction to a simplistic two-tier hierarchy of researcher/researched. This approach places the interviewer in the most powerful position, that of information gatherer, with the 'subject' in the least powerful position, of answering questions for the purpose of academic knowledge, thus reinforcing gendered notions of disclosure or confession as disempowering. Some feminist researchers have also seen the dynamics in a similar light, encouraging a presumed allpowerful researcher who, instead of questioning subjects, empowers them by allowing and encouraging participation in the project. However, both these perspectives deny more complex power relationships within the interaction. McKee and O'Brien highlight the 'weakness of the model which characterises the interviewer/interviewee relationship as being an active/passive or a hierarchical dominant/subordinate relationship' (McKee and O'Brien, 1983: 149).

Gendered power dynamics

Almost all of the men I interviewed for the research controlled the boundaries of the interaction. It was difficult actually to pin down many of the line managers to commit themselves to a time as they were too busy to be interviewed. Often they would arrive late or cancel at the last moment. The time limits would often be set by them and one particular male manager spent five minutes telling me how he could only give me an hour of his time as he was so busy. I finished the interview precisely one hour later and he kept me another half hour telling me how far he travelled into work every day and also how far other people in the department travelled every day. My experience echoes those of other women researchers.

> What I learnt was that senior men would react to me as a young woman in a relatively marginal position no matter what I did, and that this reaction was just as much data as anything else that happened in the interview.
>
> (Scott, 1985: 76)

Despite following a similar structure, the men's interviews were shorter than those of the women, and they generally offered little insight into their views on their own personal relationships and the role of men within families. As with Scott's study of male lecturers and post-graduate students, the power did not rest in the hands of the interviewer to be simply handed over to the interviewee:

> although we had set up a qualitative interview we were not in control of what actually happened and many of them seemed to be responding to a hidden structured questionnaire.
>
> (Scott, 1985: 76)

The power dynamic present in the interviewing of men by women reflects that of the wider structure of society. As a dominant group the men resist traditional research power dynamics of the researcher/researched. This highlights the dangers of assuming simplistic and naïve conception of power relationships in the interviewing process. Participants in the research were not passive and subordinate and have many resources to both resist and intervene in the interview and the research (Banister *et al.*, 1994). When these factors are placed within the context of women interviewing men, the result can take on the form of sexual harassment (McKee and O'Brien, 1983; Reynolds, 1993).

Power in the private sphere

This complex dynamic of power relations becomes more problematic when combined with the feminist desire to challenge the traditional gendering of the public–private division by locating male participants in the private sphere, the home. In the second scenario I was able to exercise my right to take back the control of the researcher from the gender power conflicts by virtue of the location, the public sphere of the workplace. This contrasts with my first experience in that I perceived myself to be in a much safer position and was therefore able to assert the little power I felt I had as a researcher to terminate the interview. Therefore the power dynamics between interviewer/interviewee and between woman/man alter according to the location of the encounter. The public sphere offers a much greater protection to researchers carrying out interviews with male interviewees who might see the interview as a way of exercising their power, or who exercise their male power by resisting interviewer dominance.

Subjectivity and silence

At the very end of their valuable and rare chapter on interviewing men, McKee and O'Brien (1983) write about an incident in their study of lone fathers in which a male interviewee had offered to give the interviewer a lift to the station. Without apology or explanation he had driven past the station, angrily discussing the way his ex-wife was raising their son. They describe how the female interviewer had been worried and insisted that he let her out of the car at the third station. However the authors make fairly light of the occurrence in their summing up: 'Although he did not initiate any physical contact, his unpredictable behaviour in the car left the interviewer very relieved to have "escaped" and at that point glad that the study was not longitudinal in nature!' (McKee and O'Brien, 1983: 150).

Personal safety

It is this suppression of the issue of personal safety within the research write-up that is most disheartening. If this incident had happened outside of the research context the female researcher's reaction might well have been one of terror and anger. When I first read this passage I was enraged by the trivialisation of such a dangerous occurrence, where the devaluing of the researcher's experience is so apparent. What is worse is that the combined effect of treating these situations as avoidable, and of overestimating the power of the researcher, as positivist research does, is that the blame falls on the researcher. McKee and O'Brien comment:

> In these interviews, the researcher employed a variety of strategies to offset any risk of sexual confrontation: taking conscious decisions about make-up and clothes; and maintaining a 'professional' manner when ambiguities arose. The *props* on these occasions were *things* rather than people: the tape-recorder, the clip-board and interview schedule – although the presence of children and others was also a mediating factor.
>
> (McKee and O'Brien, 1983: original emphasis)

According to this theoretical approach, the reason why I had been intimidated was due to the fact that I had not been 'professional' enough. Assuming that harassment can be avoided by the type of clothes or make-up a woman wears is both sexist and naïve. The assumption apportions the blame upon women researchers: women who dress professionally do not get harassed, thus if you are harassed it is your fault. Unfortunately despite all my 'props' and professional attire I was still harassed. I had been in a house alone with a man who was not prepared to be a powerless interviewee. This individualising of wider social structures only assists in the internalisation of responsibility for such experiences and consequent silences about the potential for exploitation.

> These theories serve to displace structural problems into disagreements between individuals, or, to put it another way, to make general social problems appear as the product of individual guilt or failure. Such theories have no difficulty in surviving, unless we confront them with experiences which conflict with them.
>
> (Haug, 1992: 25)

Feminist silences

While many feminist researchers have emphasised the importance of analysing the experience of carrying out research, there are still taboos regarding what is spoken about in reflexive accounts. Personal safety is an area lurking in the background, the unnameable danger in the shadowy streets, which as feminist accounts of violence have demonstrated (cf. Maynard, 1993) contrary to popular myth, is more likely to be encountered at home rather than outside. My first scenario illustrates how being located in the private sphere, the male interviewee's home, was more dangerous than the public sphere, the train station. There is a difference in the way that a woman can deal with harassment which is dependent upon location. While I was in the home of the male interviewee I had few resources other than my 'clipboard' to deal with the harassment; I was powerless in his environment. Once in the train station I was able to get on a train, move carriage and sit with another woman – the environment was not controlled by the two men.

Breaking the silence of the research experience is difficult. Research can be especially isolating if your experience of carrying it out is not reflected in other reports. However, the failure to address this is not simply an oversight; it is a resounding, deafening silence about the whole experience of being a woman researcher. This self-inflicted cage of silence does not protect the researcher, nor does it promote the growth of ways to understand research processes. The only thing it protects are the power imbalances between men and women that are already in place, as Haug points out: 'Silence is another way of coming to terms with the unacceptable' (1992: 22).

Theory and experience

Notwithstanding the feminist emphasis on subjectivity, as a research resource functioning within the genre of academic social science research, there is a real danger in suppressing these experiences. The goal of objectivity is so heavily thrust upon us as researchers that we become our own censors. The classical mandate for objective research combines with the traditional trivialisation and marginalisation of women's experiences of violence so that when I felt that I had been both manipulated and harassed by an interviewee, I felt shame and guilt. It was *my fault* and therefore I had not told anyone. I internalised the entire encounter as being of my doing and I said *nothing*. A few months later when I read my field notes I was amazed by the strength of my feelings. Re-visiting the notes alarmed me. It couldn't have been that bad, I told myself, I must have over-reacted. I censored my subjective feelings, I erased their validity and protected the men I had interviewed. Why? I had mentally erased the experience from my memory and had further distanced myself by assuming that the words had been written during a heightened emotional state and were, therefore, less valid.

> The language of theory exerts a conceptual imperialism over experience. In effect, there is a power relationship between theory and experience, and one consequence is that women are not only alienated from theory but also experience itself.
>
> (Stanley and Wise, 1993: 162)

The domain of research is not so precious that it can be elevated to a state where the people involved are no longer human. The research interview, while artificial, is as human an encounter as any other. So much research discounts this reality, and fails to theorise the research encounter as a social relationship, as an interaction between two people, in this case, a man and a woman.

Practical steps

The issue of personal safety needs to be addressed not only within the interviewer/interviewee interaction, but also within academic departments. Other organisations have addressed the problem of personal safety for researchers by outlining safe practices and policy guidelines. Manchester University's Department of Social Policy and Social Work has compiled a personal safety policy for researchers which includes both definitions of safety and practical procedures (AUT). Research should be seen in 'job' terms like anything else, other jobs that involve working outside the 'public sphere' have addressed the issue of safety. However, safety for women is often neglected, despite the work of organisations such as the Lamplugh Trust, and women continue to carry out their work in potentially unsafe environments. There are issues of structural power within organisations and who has the right to work in a safe environment. The situation within academia is that most social science research assistants are female and are on the bottom rung of the academic ladder with little power to challenge existing procedures. Safety is not acknowledged by many institutions as an integral part of the commitment to and costing of research.

An issue that arose in group discussion of this chapter was the commonalities and yet specificities of the positions of women academic researchers. Many women professionals routinely interview men in their homes, and as such this chapter connects with a range of experiences that are not particular to academic research. On the other hand, there may be reasons to suggest that academic researchers may be among those who are most vulnerable: unlike other professions, such as health or social service workers, researchers do not have the power of the state behind them. The researcher is reliant upon the goodwill of the interviewee in order to 'collect data'. This constructs a qualitatively different set of positions for the researcher and the researched.

Department responsibilities

Below I outline ways of improving personal safety for researchers that departments should cost into their research funding. They should:

- Adopt a policy of commitment to safety. The policy should outline: first, safe procedure; second, definitions of safety that allow this to be defined according to individual interpretation; third, a commitment to the inappropriateness of 'blame'.
- Purchase mobile phones for use by staff and researchers working off-site, especially at night.
- Purchase personal safety alarms.
- Provide a telephone answer machine for staff and researchers to use in out of work hours.
- Appoint a member of staff responsible for safety issues.

Researcher responsibilities

From my experience of research interviewing and taking part in this jointly authored book I recommend that researchers set up discussion groups for peer counselling and supervision. Talking about the experience of being a researcher is an invaluable way of breaking the silence and the isolation inherent in this work. Finding out that you are not alone is empowering, it is an important step forward in believing and valuing your experience.

Another valuable lesson I have learned is to tell someone where you are going. Departments should set up either a person who is responsible for the safety of researchers or, an answering machine, as Manchester

University has done, that researchers can access out of work hours. In this way supervisors (or members of staff responsible for safety) could alert relevant authorities if a researcher had not contacted the department by the arranged time. Researchers should have the right not to interview if they feel that a situation may be dangerous or unsafe and the right to take somebody else along to the interviews.

Keeping mum?

The power dynamics in interviewing need a more complex feminist analysis. Power is not just experienced within one framework or dynamic but is constantly shifting and being resisted by both parties in the interaction. There is a need to unpack the layering of power within the interaction and appreciate that the power is not binary (Kristeva, 1981). It could be argued that previous moves by some feminists towards empowering interviewees have been sexist in their treatment of the interviewer. They maintain women's traditional role of putting others first, being 'nice', behaving as a 'good girl'.

The theorising of the interview as a social relationship that encompasses all the power dynamics that are present in every interaction is the starting point of any intervention or research process. Pretending that the research interview is not 'contaminated' by outside power structures only serves to reinforce positivist claims of how interviews should be carried out. It is impossible to become a non-person for the duration of an interview; we cannot remove wider power structures from the encounter.

Silences need to be broken; research reports should not pander to the whims of positivists by 'cleaning-up' the reflexive account. Research is messy and complex, it reflects the world in which it is constructed and all its power relations. The reflexive account is the opportunity not only to say what really happened (whatever it 'really' was), it is also a chance to theorise the experience and look closely at the effects of power relations in the interviews. Remaining silent about power conflicts only serves to reinforce power imbalances. The research process can be isolating and lonely, we need to write about the whole experience, not a 'hygienic' account that devalues personal experience and denies the opportunity to discuss issues, such as personal safety, in an open debate.

I have described the pressures towards 'keeping mum' in this chapter in three ways. First, in relation to the damaging imposition of silence upon the female researcher, I have highlighted the theoretical and institutional structures that encourage women to 'keep mum', that are used to justify not speaking about the research process and have kept women in fear of naming their experiences. Second, I have questioned the assumptions underlying the liberal naïve empowerment model, where 'keeping mum' centre stage in the project – in the sense of structuring the project around working mothers – in this case led to a failure to think through the complexities of research rationale and process. Finally, by 'keeping mums' in the public sphere and fathers in the private sphere, the issue of safety was cast within traditional oppositions, rendering outside the realm of public discourse questions of harassment and violence. Just as, more generally, these questions are associated with 'the outside', the streets, this silence renders women's experiences individual, private, shaming. Personal safety must be acknowledged as an integral part of the research process. Researchers, like everyone else, must have the right to work in safe environments where personal safety will not be ignored as a result of 'keeping mum'.

part *three*

Institutions, interventions and difference

The final section of this book turns its attention to psychological and feminist research and practice in three settings: educational case conferences; debates related to 'family policy'; and women's voluntary organisations. As Liz Stanley notes in *Feminist Praxis* (1990), feminism is both theory and action. It is appropriate, then, that this last section focuses on three practical settings for feminist and psychological analyses, recognising the way in which these analyses influence, and are influenced by, current social and political contexts.

It is in the arena of practice that differences, tensions and conflicts *between* women become impossible to ignore. The call in these chapters is to move beyond a one-dimensional definition of 'woman' (usually arising from a dominant white, eurocentric, middle-class, heterosexual and non-disabled perspective), so that women can form coalitions around research, practice and political action in which difference is the starting point, rather than an essentialist similarity.

These chapters also turn their attention to the dominant sexist, heterosexist and racist definitions of 'what women are like' which exist in political policy, organisational practice and psychological theory. In the first chapter in this section, Deborah Marks uses the context of educational case conferences to discuss the discourse of 'caring' which is firmly embedded in notions of femininity. As Deborah suggests, this discourse leads to conflict for women 'professionals' between caring for and regulating children, a conflict further confused by current discourses about motherhood and childhood.

Panics over 'monstrous children' described by Deborah are closely connected to panics about 'monstrous mothers' discussed by Pam

Alldred in the second chapter of this section. Pam looks at the way lone mothers have been described in recent media debates prompted by changes in 'family policy'. She demonstrates how psychology informs popular representations of single mothers and lesbian mothers and how this discourse confirms dominant definitions of 'ideal womanhood', often implicitly endorsing oppressive patriarchal and racist concepts. Pam considers the responses feminists can make to this discourse and concludes by saying that feminists must develop pluralist coalitions and strategies to respond to family policy debates.

Pluralism is a theme of the last chapter in this section which ends the book on a note of challenge to feminism and feminists to move forward in recognising, managing and celebrating difference between women. Catherine Bewley draws on research and experience in feminist organisations (voluntary organisations run by and for women from a feminist perspective) to critique concepts of power developed in both organisational and feminist theories. Catherine's call is primarily to feminists to engage effectively with issues of power between women so that more focused and diverse coalitions can develop in organisational settings.

The three authors take different approaches to their personal location in the chapters. Catherine's location of herself in her chapter acknowledges her personal and political involvement in feminist organisations, whereas Deborah presents her material as if she were not present at the meetings she describes to reflect her sense of being an outsider at the meetings. In contrast to both these approaches, Pam uses the rhetorical 'we' to emphasise her call to feminists to respond to family policy debates.

Difference is a theme of this section and these three chapters express differences in the focus of their critiques; in their research and writing approaches; and in the political locations of their authors. Nevertheless, what the authors have in common is a commitment to engaging with their differences and a challenge, not only to psychology, but also to feminism.

chapter *seven*

Gendered 'care' and the structuring of group relations: Child–professional–parent–researcher

Deborah Marks

> The 'professionals' and their 'clients', live within the carefully crafted, mechanical embrace of 'care'.
>
> (Davis, 1993: 199)

Introduction

This chapter examines discussions taking place in education case conferences on the topic of educational provision for pupils identified as having specific special educational needs. I review the strategic employment and functions of discourses on 'caring' within the case conference to argue that discourses on and related to providing 'care' play a key role in the interpellation of participants into a variety of gendered subject positions. The chapter draws upon discourse analysis (Parker, 1992) and psychoanalysis (Ernst, 1989) in order to highlight some of the gendered power relations between the groups of service providers and between the providers and recipients within the case conferences.

These positions can be organised into a series of oppositions: the professional, carer and regulator; the child who is innocent and culpable; the mother who is pathological and irrelevant; and the father who is absent. These roles do not operate alone, but are produced in relation to each other. I argue that these gendered discourses map out, constitute and over-determine hierarchical relationships, differential access to power and rights to speak within the meetings. As such, they illuminate how the public domain of work exists in relation to and thus reproduces the division with the private sphere, through the gendered distribution of power/knowledge (cf. Pringle, 1989).

This chapter is the product of a study of language in education case conferences. The focus of the study was on the way in which pupils were discursively positioned in group discussions, as having some form of special educational need. By examining the language within case conferences, the research aimed to identify some of the rhetorical practices which served to reproduce patterns of inequality within special education. This analysis raised questions not only about the constitution of the pupil but also the social relations between participants within the case conference (Marks, 1993).

The chapter begins by describing what case conferences aim to do and exploring some of the tensions which typically emerge between participants in the meetings. Second, I explore some of the issues around providing 'care' and how this activity has become gendered. I speculate on possible psychological or inter-relational (or, to use psychodynamic terminology, 'psychic') and political motivations for the production and reproduction of 'caring'. The relationships between the professional, mother and child are elaborated. Third, I examine the implications of caring within three specific case conferences, in terms of the positions open to the absent 'subject' (the children, whom I will call Vivien, Charlotte and William), the mothers and the professionals in relation to one another in the meeting.

Case conferences

By bringing together the group of people who are directly involved with the child or young person's education and welfare, the case conference is concerned with offering participants an interdisciplinary decision-making forum. Recent years have seen an increase in parental involvement and calls for greater collaboration between professionals. There now seems to be a general acceptance of the need to 'work together' (Hanko, 1991). However, a number of studies have found difficulties in exchanges between professionals and carer, identifying feelings of powerlessness (on the part of parents; see Tomlinson, 1981) and anxiety (on the part of professionals; see Cornwell, 1989; Marks, in press a). Parents' groups have complained that decisions often appear to have been made in advance, by a select groups of professionals. There has been a move in British education towards involving parents in decision making. This includes a number of programmes involving parent–teacher collaboration. Many parents of pupils with no identified 'special needs', or with 'severe learning difficulties' are implicitly entrusted with involvement in decision making. 'Parent power' is always mediated by a variety of social factors, such as 'racialised' status and class categories (see also Chapter 5, this volume). However, the (albeit chequered) increase in parent power has been much more limited in relation to dealing with parents of children identified as having 'moderate learning difficulties' and 'behavioural problems'. Bennathon (1989) writes,

> Parents [of children with no 'organic' physical or mental handicap] do not join support groups. They feel themselves commonly to be part of the problem, a view they are often allowed to keep by the professional workers.
>
> (1989: 84)

Professionals have been accused of engaging in stigmatising and stereotyped assessments of parents (Tomlinson, 1981). Thus, despite a rhetoric emphasising consultation and parental involvement, parents frequently remain marginal and powerless.

The social construction of relations of care

How do caring roles impact on decision making within education case conferences? Caring is seen in this chapter as a socially constituted and relational activity, which locates problems within specific individuals, whose vulnerability is identified and reproduced. Discourses in case conferences do not simply 'refer' to a fixed person 'outside' the meeting. I argue that discourses constitute and refashion the 'subject' at specific moments, for particular rhetorical effect (see Henriques *et al.*, 1984). Caring is a gendered activity which both binds and separates women as professionals or mothers (see Dalley, 1988).

It is helpful to outline some of the constituent ideological components of caring, before going on to discuss how discourses around care are manifested within educational decision making. Caring discourses can be found within a specific field of organised activity. However, it is not enough merely to focus on the site of their production, since locally produced discourses operate as part of a matrix of inter-relating discursive practices. These practices operate beyond their immediate spatial and temporal location (Parker, 1992). It is helpful, therefore, to identify a series of commonly used categories, embedded within a range of cultural and institutional practices, before elaborating how they were employed in the case conferences.

First, I review some social functions and psychic positions which discourses on care make available. Second, the consequences of gendered provision are elaborated for the parent/guardian of the case conference child or young person. Third, it is argued that caring discourses constitute the 'attributes' of the child.

The provider of care

According to Acker, gender is implicated in the creation and conceptualisation of work. A job appears to be an 'empty slot, a reification that must continually be reconstructed' (1991: 168). The concept of 'a job' is thus presented as being abstract, bodiless and gender neutral. However, categories of workers are divided, among other ways, along gender lines, in terms of the division of labour, space, power and activity. Elsewhere in this book, we discuss how power relations are reproduced in feminist organisations. Here, we take up these questions in relation to the use of educational and psychological expertise and gendered investments in particular (supposedly gender neutral) discursive practices.

Feminists from a variety of perspectives have argued that the imperative to respond to the needs of others has fallen disproportionately on women (Dalley, 1988). Women make up a large part of the caring professions (Chodorow, 1978). Given the long-standing cultural association between women and discourses of care, it is helpful to make some speculations regarding psychic and political investments which women might have in caring.

Psychic motivation for care and gender identity

Work in disability studies, such as that of Swain *et al.* (1993), have drawn attention to the needs of professionals to position recipients of care in specific ways. While striving to 'empower' recipients of professional services, the professionals simultaneously disguise their own dependency. Professionals depend on their clients for their jobs. In other words, they need clients to be in need.

Psychoanalytically oriented (object relations) feminists such as Orbach (1990) and Ernst (1989) have argued that women's social position as carers has powerful significance for the construction of female identity. This is because anxieties around 'neediness' are particularly intense for women. Orbach writes,

> Many girls grow up hearing the explicit message that they should not expect anyone to be there for them emotionally . . . [By contrast] Men's apparent independence, then, rests not on their lack of need for others, but on the fact that their dependency needs are in some

> way legitimised and at least partially addressed by their wives, without their existence being acknowledged.
>
> (1990: 4–5)

Because girls have learned to repress their own neediness and convert it into 'relationally directed activity; to emotional ministering and the midwifery of others' (Orbach, 1990: 4), many turn, when they grow up, to the caring professions. Attending to the needs of others may therefore represent a vicarious form of care, which the carer has been unable to obtain for herself. It thus becomes a crucial weapon in an armoury of defences against acknowledging and attending to her own needs. The woman no longer sees herself as potentially vulnerable, but rather, as Ernst puts it, 'all powerful in her capacity to nurture and heal others. The others are, in phantasy, totally dependent on her . . . She lives out her phantasy that she can control difficult, painful and intractable feelings and circumstances' (Ernst, 1989: 109). In this way, a sense of self is constructed through attending to the needs of others.

Anxiety about issues of care and its relationship to identity are thus structured by gendered relationships. Caring may be seen as one element in the way in which femininity may read as a constellation of signs (see Cowie, 1978). Caring may function in providing external evidence of 'womanliness'. This 'socially constructed fiction' thus comes to be subjectively experienced and lived 'as fact' (Walkerdine, 1990).

The evidence that women are disproportionately involved in caring labour is certainly borne out in the case conferences (see Marks, 1993). Despite the gender-neutral rhetoric of parental involvement, it is women, as mothers, who tend to be the primary caretaker and are therefore most likely to attend the case conference meeting to discuss their 'charge'. Mothers are therefore most likely to be subject to the benign, but surveillant, professional gaze. Women also tend to occupy a disproportionate percentage of the more directly caring roles within education. Women are less likely to be headteachers, especially in secondary schools, but more likely to occupy welfare and pastoral roles.

Collaboration in case conferences

Having explored possible psychic investments in caring, it is important to relate those roles to the material constraints under which women operate in case conferences. As has been mentioned, case conferences are concerned with collaboration between professionals drawn from a range of differing institutional bases and sharing divergent histories. The history of special education has documented numerous ways in which professional rivalries and conflicts have been played out (Ford *et al.*, 1982; Rose,

1985). From the beginning of the provision of compulsory education in Britain, the medical and psychological professions struggled for dominion over the power to define special education needs. The legacy of this is that case conferences are riven by hierarchical tensions between different professional groups.

As in Chapter 4, where we examined women's experience of heavy menstruation, women often fail to be heard in matters which they have direct experience of. Despite the democratic rhetoric of giving everyone a 'voice', different categories of participants in the meetings are positioned along a continuum of degrees of 'expertise'. Rights to speak tend to be correlated with lower levels of contacts with the child and the greater access to 'abstract' knowledge. For example, educational psychologists have greater rights to prescribe 'solutions' to problems, than teachers. Collaboration may appear to emerge naturally out of mutual concerns to solve a problem. However, this image belies a more complex process. Professional differences are an intrinsic part of multiprofessional collaboration. Conflict is rooted in different institutions which case conference participants are members of. However, caring has become an imperative within special education, particularly since the 1981 Education Act and its focus on 'needs' and the near orthodoxy of child-centred approaches to education in the 1970s. This works to produce particular effects. It renders expression of professional differences inappropriate. It foregrounds a particular, needy, often sentimentalised, image of the child. As one teacher stated in an interview, using 'you' in the sense of 'one', to generalise her experience, 'you're not here to talk about differences, are you?' Collaboration in case conferences assumes an image of the 'disinterested professional' who joins with others to 'help'.

The analysis of the case conference shows that, in the face of the (apparently unwritten) strictures against the expression of conflict, caring seems to operate to mystify differences, and rally opposing factions into 'agreement'. In paradoxical ways, while unifying the professionals against the recipients of care, it also seems to offer those who are lower in the hierarchy and most involved in direct care, the opportunity to speak. While they might not have access to rarefied 'expertise', they usually have greatest contact with the child, placing them in a powerful position from which to adopt emotional discourses of caring and determination of need. This brings us to the position of recipients of professional services; first the child and second, the parent.

The recipient of care

Having looked at some of the psychic and socio-political functions of caring discourses, it is important to explore the corollary of care; that is, being cared for. In contemporary western culture, a high value is placed on 'independence'. Being dependent on others has negative connotations. (Yet the social organisation which creates such 'dependency' is rarely questioned.) Some of the dangers of being a recipient of care need to be outlined.

If the wish of the carer is frustrated, then she may come to resent the 'ungrateful' recipient or those perceived as being responsible for the problem. While the person in need is often positioned as innocent, the person who resists being positioned as grateful recipient may suddenly become identified as pathological.

The case conferences exhibited such oscillations in the position of 'special' pupils. For example, the accounts of pupils shifted between expressions of affection and hostility towards the child with 'problems' or 'needs', depending on the specific requisite rhetorical task. People in the meeting were called together to debate the needs of a particular child, rather than, say, the social organisation of the school (Marks *et al.*, 1995). The case conference is thus explicitly individualising. Accounts of childhood or the 'child' do not necessarily contain within them images of specific children. The focus is on the extent to which the child or young person conforms to this abstract general 'norm'.

This chapter is written against a current moral crisis about childhood. I follow James and Prout (1990) in seeing the category of childhood as being socially constructed. Childhood has come to represent, for adults, a nostalgic 'lost' era of innocence and safety. When children violate categories of innocence they disrupt adult investments and desires to 'return' to a (mythical) past. One way of resolving the dilemma of how to categorise children who fall foul of these idealised categories, is to exclude the 'deviant' child. In doing so, the conceptual boundaries of childhood are strengthened. A graphic example of this can be seen by the response to the murder of James Bulger, where the two children who killed him were seen as outside the boundaries of 'child' – as monsters – rather than children (see James and Jenks, 1994; and Chapter 8, this volume).

The 'consumer' of professional care (mother)

The assumption made by professionals in a case conference dealing with a child's 'special educational needs' is that these needs are not being met elsewhere. This raises the implicit question of what areas of the child's environment have failed to address their need. There has been much work, in particular, by Walkerdine (1990) and Walkerdine and Lucey (1989) on the pathologisation of working-class mothers. It is also worth noting that a disproportionately large percentage of children identified as having moderate learning difficulties and emotional/behavioural problems are working class, male and black (Tomlinson, 1981). Clearly the dynamic of 'care' is racialised as well as gendered, such that black and Third World women and children have occasioned fantasies of both help and rescue that have served to reiterate and consolidate colonialism (Ware, 1992; Burman, 1994b). For reasons of space, we cannot extend this discussion further in relation to racism (but see Chapter 5). The discussion here will focus, more generally, on how mothers are either deemed extraneous to the proceedings or become the receptacle for blame.

First, however, it is important to indicate some of the ways in which professionals mystify the position of mothers as devalued or inconsequential participants within the meetings. One way of achieving the *appearance* of equitable collaboration with mothers is through the use of terminology. Oliver (1993) has identified a number of terms, including 'client', 'user' and 'consumer'. The term 'client' is often used to give the receiver of professional services a sense of status and dignity. Yet this seems to represent a 'very neat bit of professional sleight of speech, suggesting equivalence in choice and control' (Davis, 1993: 198). While the days when schools had notices at the gates saying 'no parents beyond this point' are long gone, educational professionals still seem to retain a great deal of power (despite their subjective experience of being powerless – which will be discussed below) over both pupils and parents. Certainly, the suggestion that the recipient of educational services has choice over the service they receive can be viewed with a measure of scepticism. Parents (and pupils) have far more chance of participating in decisions which affect them when they come to the attention of outside agencies such as social services than they have when working with schools (Whitney, 1993). New terms, designed to empower 'consumers' (a term which accords choice only in the selection of services rather than their structure), are misleading, since the change in terminology does not mark a shift in power. In addition, recipients are made vulnerable by virtue of the expectation that they exhibit gratitude.

If professional roles have been split into 'carers' and 'experts', it is important to have a symbolic marker identifying the converse of care and expertise. This category frequently seems to be occupied by mothers of case conference 'subjects'. The following analysis therefore explores some of the exchanges about mothers and between mothers and professionals. Specifically, the aim is to show that the way mothers are constituted by professional questions serves to position them as pathological, and to reinforce the status of professionals as carers.

Parents are often invited to attend case conferences, but do not always appear at them. In the majority of case conferences it is the mother rather than the father or any other carer who attends the meeting. (This absence of the father seems to mirror the masculine position within the discussion as being one which marks the boundaries around discourses on caring, rather than entering into discussions of care.) In the case conferences analysed, professionals set the agenda, despite operating under the assumption that it was important to give mothers 'a voice'. Where mothers did speak in the meetings, they adopted a deferential style. This took a variety of forms, some of which are elaborated in the analysis.

Three case conferences: the constitution of child, professional and parent

A recurrent way in which the child or young person was constituted in the meetings was as a passive victim. The underside of this category – bearing the image of an active and culpable actor – was resorted to at specific moments in the discussion, which will be elaborated below. This image of passivity was produced in a number of ways.

First, references to the 'subject' were made anonymously, by referring to 'the child' rather than by their name. Any image of a specific active 'subject' was expunged. By this, the child became a category, an object for intervention rather than a subject. In the vacuum created by reference to a particular grounded and inevitably complicated and divided subject, the meeting drew upon generalised discourses of a universal 'child'. Such discourses are rehearsed in the following account of Vivien's case.

Vivien's meeting was attended by the headteacher, maths teacher, team manager of social services, social worker from family services support unit, regional health officer, school nurse and research assistant (Deborah). In this meeting, all staff, with the exception of arguably the three most powerful participants (the two senior social workers and headteacher) were women. Nine-year-old Vivien was attending week-day residential school for children with emotional/behavioural difficulties. The focus of the meeting was a discussion of her future educational and residential provision. In the meeting, there was a dispute about whose responsibility it was to coordinate provision. The headteacher claimed that the social workers had acted too slowly in obtaining a court order which would provide Vivien with '24-hour residential care, with schooling on site' rather than her current placement at the week-day residential school. This alternative was felt necessary, first, because Vivien needed 'more containment' and second, because Vivien's mother was considered 'unpredictable and irresponsible'. Vivien's mother (who was not referred to by name) was absent from the meeting. She had, according to teachers, failed to pick Vivien up for the weekend, and had gone through alternate phases of wanting to see her child, and then 'disappearing'.

The tension in the meeting gradually mounted, as the teachers catalogued their concerns; that there had been a 'dereliction of duty' on the part of social workers in failing to secure appropriate provision for Vivien. Such accusations raised the temperature of the meeting. The teachers pressed the social workers to recognise the extent of Vivien's 'desperate plight'. However, after an initial strategy, on the part of social service personnel, to ward off attacks by attributing the slowness of any decision to 'delays by the courts', participants seemed to come together in agreement around the issue of Vivien's needs. At this point Vivien seemed to be positioned as a nameless victim. Teachers and social workers referred to her as '*the child* in limbo' and talked of '*the child* need[ing] supervision'. Reference to Vivien's needs seemed to soothe professional tensions and offer a space for agreement. The discussion of the child thus took on a more conciliatory tone. As Chapter 2 elaborates in relation to discussions of child sexual abuse, focus on the needs of a victim serves to position professionals as knowing and responsible, in relation to the vulnerable, powerless, innocent and passive child.

However, this generalised 'child' subject was transformed when professionals began to speak of Vivien's behaviour in particular contexts. It was necessary for the teachers to make the case that the need to remove Vivien from the school was urgent. In order to demonstrate that Vivien was 'uncontainable' in her current environment, she was presented as active. At these points, she tended to be referred to by professionals by her name, as in the following example; 'Vivien knows all the buttons to press.' Vivien's activity in relation to her mother was presented as provocative, difficult and destructive. Similarly, when accounts move to Vivien becoming involved in a fight with Charlotte she was no longer seen as a vulnerable and endearing girl. Rather, when viewed as being aggressive, her femininity is given an animal description as a 'wild cat'.

Once Vivien began to be positioned as active, the position of adults, and, in particular, her teachers was transformed. The teachers came to reposition themselves as helpless, as in the following extract:

Maths teacher: It's heartbreaking for us in the classroom. I honestly don't know how to answer her any more.
Social worker: I share your concerns, and um . . .
Maths teacher: I am going to walk out [of the classroom] because I would cry because I don't know how to answer her any more.

Here we have a picture of a teacher who was unable to alter the situation and is likely to be constrained by other demands, such as those made by other pupils. This leaves her feeling powerless and defeated. Her capacity to attend to needs was frustrated.

Several times in the meeting, when a highly emotional plea was made, the teacher was cut short by a change of focus on to action. Thus, the social worker says in response to the above extract:

Social worker (italicized text indicates emphasis in speech): She must have long-term stability and the only way that we can get that is to *quickly* and *surely* as possible, to move to either get a resolution . . .

At this point, discussion moves on to court dates and practical issues of placement. Further on, the end of the meeting is marked by generalised and summarising comments that compartmentalise activity into a series of administrative categories.

Headteacher: OK, well unfortunately, er, we were not the ones that made the decision that's . . . we're here to assess progress. Progress is being made slowly in general education. Social adjustment's a deterioration. Residence will continue here. Educational programme will continue. Access visits will continue as of present and the final court case is on December 12th or 13th. That's all I intend to put on the summary for our report.

Both these comments of the (male) social worker and headteacher seem to function as boundary markers, delineating the limits of the highly charged discussion of needs and care, activity and passivity, control and helplessness. The masculine position in the case conference seems to function as one of marking the perimeters of the meeting, and performing a linking function between the internal world of care and the external 'real' world. Thus, at the moment in the meeting when professionals are about to be overwhelmed by uncontainable feelings – both Vivien's and their own that she inspires – there is a return to structural categories that mark the paternal boundaries of the meeting.

The discursive functions of the masculine and feminine positions could thus be related to the functions which attachment theory marks out for the primary (maternal) object and the secondary (paternal) object (Holmes, 1993). These gendered positions seemed to operate in many of the meetings, although the masculine functions were not necessarily enacted by men. Where the headteachers were women, they often performed the function of setting limits on care. This highlights how what we are describing as masculine and feminine functions are cultural constructions which are not tied to particular sexed individuals.

We will now turn to another case conference, of Charlotte, to explore gendered conceptions of providing care, in relation to an active/passive child and a regulative authority. Charlotte was also a 9-year-old girl, attending the same 5-day residential school as Vivien. Her annual review was attended by her mother. The meeting began in a very different way from Vivien's, with invitations to her mother to speak and discussion of Charlotte's endearing qualities.

Teacher 1: I love watching her when she writes, the way that they, you know, she's got lovely hands, I think, and its so, the size.

Other comments are made about Charlotte's appearance and demeanour.

Teacher 2: She's had no tantrums.
Teacher 1: She's been very quiet [general murmuring of agreement].
Teacher 2: She's been lovely.

Here, Charlotte is presented as an archetypal child, feminised and passive. Yet as the meeting progresses, an incident is recounted by a teacher of a time when Charlotte 'refused to be silent'. A struggle ensued, in which Charlotte was portrayed as wilful and in need of physical restraint. In response to this active, struggling child, the teacher positions herself as passive.

Teacher: I just got her, *lightly*, by the wrist, so she started this battle of not being held [laughter] and my arm the next day was sore, just by holding her . . . because I've got weak wrists.

Moreover, the teacher effaces her own role in the struggle, by a variety of moves.

Teacher: As soon as its over, *you* sort of turn round and say, 'right Charlotte, are you going to stop wriggling?'

But referring to herself as 'you' the teacher generalises her activity. The teacher is thus only doing what anyone would do with a struggling child. The focus therefore remains on 'how to stop the struggling', not on the fact that there are two people involved in a relationship of struggle. Charlotte is not merely violating the boundary of what it means to be a good pupil, but also violating the boundary of the category of passive female child. Yet the next section repairs the damage done to Charlotte's position as archetypal girl-child. The struggle is explained in terms of Charlotte's craving for affection.

Key worker: She loves you to come up, you know, she wants to be with you and hold you.
Headteacher: mmm.
Key worker: She can look at you.
Headteacher: Those looks [general laughter].

The story of conflict and struggle was thus followed up with group protestations about Charlotte's charming, even beguiling nature. Emphasis here, is placed on Charlotte as malleable and loveable, a rag doll, who may collapse into a 'heap'. The headteacher describes a 'contretemps' he had with her:

Headteacher: She decided that she wasn't going to do anything so she flopped on the floor, and I decided that she was going to stand up,

> and I took her in and I held her in [laughing], with her feet on the floor [laughter is now loud].

To summarise then, Charlotte is positioned as both wilful, and lacking will, Vivien is both disruptive and a victim. Both children are, at different moments, positioned as active and resistant, and passive victims. Such variations in the portrayal of children at different moments in the meeting not only demonstrate that the children are not unitary subjects, but also that the rhetorical tasks which professionals are attempting to accomplish are ever changing. The conflictual nature of professional interactions with Charlotte are confounded and diminished by accounts which are characterised by humour and expressions of indulgent affection. In this way, the paternally inspired regulatory function of exerting physical constraint is desexualised so that it becomes acceptable for caring women professionals as well as authoritative males to enact such control.

So far, the position of gendered provision of care and expertise and needing have been marked out. Now it is important to examine the role of parents in case conferences. It seems to be the case that in the world of caring and expert professionals, those deemed neither providers nor recipients have little role in the discussion. This certainly seems to be the case with mothers in case conferences, who tend to be rendered pathological or irrelevant. In Vivien's case, the mother was absent, but highly censured by participants. In Charlotte's case, the mother was invited to join in debate about how sweet Charlotte was, prior to review of her progress. Then she was again offered a voice, at the end of the meeting. This invitation to make an intervention was thus restricted to giving the mother 'a voice' only at the margins of the meeting (see Marks, in press a). Where mothers do appear to make a substantial contribution to the review of educational progress, it tends to be made deferentially, as in William Higgins' case conference. Here, William's mother speaks through her son, when trying to convey a specific difficulty her son is experiencing in reading.

> *Mrs Higgins*: I said 'Oh you're reading the paper William', he said 'I can't read this', I said 'Of course you can so give it a go'. He said 'well', he said 'all the words are upside down'. He said 'everything is the wrong way round'.

The mother offers a story of a yet-to-be-categorised problem. She conveys a concern about her son's reading without usurping the teachers' professional authority to diagnose a problem. In doing this, she is able to maintain a deferential stance. The pattern of mothers telling stories and professionals accomplishing categorisations was typical of several of the case conferences. However, while such cooperation enables the mother to avoid being labelled as 'uncooperative', it simultaneously undermines the authority of the mother to challenge professional pronouncements.

Discussion

The constitution of 'difficult', 'culpable' children serves to posit responsibility for the failure of a school to meet their 'needs' in the hands of the child or the mother. By contrast, responsibility for rescuing the child is placed entirely in the hands of professionals. In order to avoid appearing hostile towards the child, a position which would threaten the child-centred stance that professionals adopted, discourses on 'difficult' children were followed up with discourses on 'lovely' children. In my research, discourses seemed to apply equally to girls and boys (Marks, 1993). Moreover, news about 'the negatives' are often conveyed by reports from people positioned as outside the meeting. Criticisms of the child are thus presented as unavoidable 'facts', which must, reluctantly, be faced by case conference participants. In this way, the split between needy 'special' children and caring professionals is sustained.

Professionals monopolise responsibility for decisions by attending to the needs of others. Their knowledge of the child is presented as offering a privileged overview, while the mothers' knowledge appears grounded, limited, local and subsequently less authoritative. While speaking in the voice of her child, the mother is further infantilised in relation to professionals. Women professionals, in these meetings, seemed to take responsibility for all care, by devaluing mothers and reinforcing passive needs rather than the rights of the child. The women professionals thus do not seem to identify with mothers as carers, but rather, to occupy the paternal position, colonising the provision of care within particular professional practices.

Emotionally charged discourses on care can raise anxiety levels. This is where omnipotent fears and social expectations come together to produce the caring woman professional. The masculine position of guardian of the boundary seems to constitute a meta-narrative for the discussion. Expressions of despair were regularly followed up by one headteacher with comments such as the following:

> Well right, we're here to assess progress. General education progress I can say is excellent.
>
> It's the old story isn't it. It's either an upward spiral or a downward spiral.

Such 'old stories' offer an authoritative backdrop, placing the particular events within a historical context.

Reality and discourse

While this chapter makes implicit criticism of professionals' practices in case conferences, my intention is certainly not to attribute blame to specific parties. One paradoxical consequence of the liberal humanist tendency to assert the good intentions of professionals and to expand further their regulatory activities, is that when things go wrong, professionals tend to get blamed. Professionals have all too often become scapegoats because they have been held responsible for problems associated with shortages of resources (Wilding, 1982). This is a particular danger when dealing with discourses on caring, which tend to be most frequently deployed by those who have greatest contact with the child such as care assistants and teachers. These professional groups, who tend to be overwhelmingly populated by women, really are emotionally involved in their charges; they really *do* care. Thus, an analysis of the caring discourse does not suggest that 'care' is self-consciously used by those positioned lower in the educational hierarchy to increase their influence over decision making. Rather, our account here is concerned with the way such emotional realities are overdetermined by structural, including patriarchal, relations.

Pejorative attacks are inappropriate. The point should be neither to make professionals responsible for all social ills, nor to deny that professional practices are ever useful for the production and maintenance of prevailing social structures. Criticism of professional practices should acknowledge patriarchal constraints. Caring discourses are not mustered solely for the purpose of cynically augmenting 'rights to speak'. Nor do they purely represent selfless acts of altruistic concern (although both of these elements may be present). Rather, they represent what Davies (1992) describes as a coping strategy. 'Coping management' looks inwards to the resources available. Rather than protesting at the impossibility of meeting all needs, the woman professional attempts (somewhat omnipotently) to monopolise care for pupils. Such a tactic avoids confrontation with those higher up in the educational authority. It produces the short-term effect of giving professionals the expected, highly valued and gendered status of being 'caring'. The long-term effect may be professional 'burnout' for those occupying such feminised roles. It addition, by taking responsibility for caring, a system which places heavy demands on women professionals to 'cope', is perpetuated. Professionals taking the masculine authoritative positions can continue to avoid responsibility for providing care or effecting change in a system which fails to meet the concerns of a number of pupils, professionals and parents.

Conclusion

This chapter has attempted to argue that the discourse of care is gendered, in such a way as to place heavy responsibility on women professionals to meet all needs. Mothers tend to emerge from case conferences bearing responsibility for any difficulties identified in their offspring.

Children appear overwhelmingly needy or wilful and male professionals police the boundaries of the meeting. Fathers remain outside the boundaries of debate, since, in the case conferences attended as part of this research (Marks, 1993), few attended. These positions become invested with powerful emotions of guilt and vulnerability.

Attributes traditionally associated with, and part of the social construction of, women such as caring for others, have undergone positive reappraisal from a number of feminist writers (Chodorow, 1978; Gilligan, 1982). However, in this chapter I have focused on some of the deleterious elements associated with the 'ethic of care', and some of the contradictions of the role of care in 'welfare' services. First, the professional provision of caring may render the mother invisible and limit her rights to speak. Those providing care seem to be operating *in loco parentis*. Second, the imperative to care may make the expression of negative feelings towards a difficult child inadmissible. Hence, I have discussed the swing from censuring a child to positioning them as innocent victims. Third, it places an overwhelming obligation on professionals to attend to all needs, rather than refuse to strive towards meeting unrealistic expectations. Notwithstanding its status as a traditionally (or perhaps arising from its) feminine characterisation, caring, in some contexts, may thus be positively detrimental to women.

chapter *eight*

'Fit to parent'? Developmental psychology and 'non-traditional' families

Pam Alldred

Does a child need to grow up with a mother and a father? Does a boy child need a 'father figure'? Do children have a right to know who their biological father is? Questions like these have structured the popular debates around recent changes in British social policy. Key stimuli for these debates in the early 1990s have included the 1989 Children Act, and the 1990 Human Embryology and Fertilisation Act. Particular political responses to these questions have dominated the expression of concerns about children, about the 'threat to the (nuclear) family' and about the perceived 'erosion of moral values'. Implicit in 'family' policy debates and rhetoric are anxieties about changing or changed gender relations. What is at issue here are women's changed expectations, as reflected in the power struggles between men and women around children, family and workplace. One site of contestation has been around who is 'fit to parent'.

Psychological arguments are championed in these debates through claims supported by research findings or through accepted 'common-sense' ideas about children. Psychological discourses occupy a particular, and a particularly powerful, position in such debates. Psychology's specific status as 'expert knowledge' is produced as a result of both its particular domain of interest: the human subject (here, children); and its authority as scientific knowledge (Rose, 1985; Billington, in press). The authority vested in psychology is evidenced in the practical consequences it has for the organisation of our everyday lives, not only through direct appeals to experts but also through the ways we (including feminists) come to think about and reflect on our own lives (Foucault, 1979; Rose, 1990).

This chapter is motivated by the way psychological discourses and ideas drawn from psychology function in popular discussions of 'non-traditional families'. The cultural context for some of the recent policy-related discussion of families includes the contemporary moral panics around children and around (certain categories of) mothers. The late 1980s and early 1990s witnessed renewed attacks on lesbian mothers, and scrutiny and ridicule of what the Conservative government called 'pretended families'.[1] Much debate in the early 1990s has been about 'lone mothers' and this chapter retains this focus. Arguments that growing up without a father is necessarily a bad thing have been associated most clearly with social commentators of the political right wing. These can be used to question whether 'children's needs' are met in either lone mother or lesbian households. This chapter considers some of the political implications of psychological theory, as a result of its deployment within both academic and popular culture spheres.

First, we describe the political context for these questions in 1990s Britain. Second, we consider how and why psychological discourses operate so powerfully in providing 'answers' to these questions, so that, third, we can discuss ways of making political interventions in these debates. We consider how, as feminists, we might respond to claims about lone mothers, lesbian mothers or other 'non-traditional families' that we find offensive or problematic, when such claims are backed up by academic research 'findings'. We suggest that these responses take the form of either 'using' or critiquing psychological research. We end by considering the political and academic dilemmas this poses for feminist engagement.

Monstrous mothers and selfish mothers

Making links between psychology and popular culture allows psychological research practice to be contextualised in the broader cultural and political issues of its time, and highlights the implications of psychological discourses as they operate in everyday life.

Marina Warner, in the 1994 Reith lectures, notes the co-occurrence of two cultural events in Britain in 1993–4. The first is the narrative of the massively successful Steven Spielberg film, *Jurassic Park,* in which the all-female population of dinosaurs (bred by a twentieth-century scientist from genetic material found in fossilised rock) develop the capacity to reproduce. The second is the moral panic from some sections of the British media's cultural commentators around (the numbers of) lone mothers having children, and having even more children (Warner, 1994). It seems that today's closest relatives of *Jurassic Park*'s self-progenitive female dinosaurs are lone mothers, lesbian mothers and women seeking donor insemination. They have received considerable media attention and psychological discourses have been mobilised in the discussions of the women and their children.

Warner aligned the recent 'moral panics' about mothers with fears that are expressed within myths of Medea, the Greek mother who, in some versions, kills her own children. The characterisation of the feminine as monstrous has been described in a variety of forms and cultural contexts, from the she-monsters of ancient mythology to the evocation of images of the all-devouring or toothed vagina in science-fiction and horror genres (Creed, 1987; 1993). Images of the *monstrous mother* have included the over-protective mother who refuses to relinquish the child and so smothers or subsumes them; the selfish and withholding mother; and the all-powerful and sadistic mother who threatens to castrate or emasculate men (Kaplan, 1992; Creed, 1987; 1993). Such narratives can be seen to reveal the intensity of fear about women's power over men and children, and the construction of mothers who deviate from the supposed ideal as dangerous. The fears evidenced in this particular cultural moment are about women bearing and rearing children without men, and the danger of these 'monstrous females' breeding 'monstrous children'. Hence these two sets of demonisations (of certain mothers and of children) are not purely coincidental.

Sophie Laws (1994) discusses some of the social policy suggestions that have rested on either discourses of lone mothers as bad mothers, or of single mothers as selfish teenagers who become pregnant in an attempt to jump the (long) queue for public housing. She laments the lack of feminist responses to the types of condemnation, vilification and scapegoating of mothers witnessed at and since the 1993 Conservative Party conference. Michael Howard, the Home Secretary, argued more recently that it would be a good thing if more single mothers gave their children up for adoption under the ambit of 'family values' and an editorial in the *Daily Mail* (19.1.94) argued that even if the proposed policies damage the real children of today, that this would be a kindness to children as yet unborn as people would be deterred from having more. This discourse of protecting the child's best interests is, of course, highly persuasive and is enshrined in the 1989 Children Act. Precisely what these interests might be and how they are to be assessed is seldom detailed though and indeed the whole discourse is problematic (Woodhead, 1990). This allusion to 'the best interests of the child', because it is so vague, can be used to draw moral backing for a wide range of arguments and it leaves unquestioned any 'common-sense' ideas invoked. The above can be seen as instances of intense counterposing of children's and women's rights.

While the pitch reached in condemning lone mothers in the mass media approached hysterical, the most venomous rhetorical attack was reserved for women deliberately choosing to have children without men. However, the distinction between the general category of lone mothers and this particular subset sometimes collapsed, and it was implied that all lone mothers chose to parent alone. In fact, of course, many had planned to parent with the child's father. The arguments about psychological development were applied to women in either situation. One particular media event in which the women in question were choosing to parent without known biological fathers was what came to be known as the Virgin Births Scandal.

The 'Storm over Virgin Births', as the *Daily Mail* headline put it on 11 March 1991, was when the British popular press sensationally revealed that 'virgins' were being helped to have babies by medical services. 'Virgins' was used to designate women who were not in relationships with men, and the media story was about three women who were being considered for provision of donor insemination by a Birmingham clinic. Three tabloid newspapers capitalised on the chance to have the word *virgin* across their front pages (the *Today* newspaper, the *Daily Mail* and the *Daily Mirror* (11.3.91)) and the journalists salaciously enjoyed this aspect of their stories. They seemed to relish the opportunity to scrutinise and put into doubt the sexual status of these women to whom they had applied the term virgin in the first place. Not only were these women single, but the heterosexism of hegemonic discourses of sexuality made not being progenitively sexually active with men, equivalent to 'not fully sexually active'. The term also provided the implicit and offensive suggestion of the women's immaturity or incomplete development. On the Radio 4 *Call Nick Ross* discussion programme that week (13.3.91) a British-trained clinical psychologist called up to say that, in his expert opinion, women who were not mature enough to be able to maintain relationships (by which he meant specifically heterosexual, long-term, monogamous and including penetrative sex) were evidently unfit, or perhaps if they were lucky, just *not yet fit*, to mother children.

The supposed 'selfishness' of these women was a key theme and the Archbishop of York, John Hapgood, was one of the 'moral authorities' the newspapers quoted making this accusation. His statement was about selfish or pathological motives for wanting a child and the danger this might pose to the child. This might not be controversial in itself, but given that he did not know these women, it functioned in this debate, not as a general background comment, but to condemn these women:

> A child wanted because the parent wants something to love, wanted as an act of defiance, wanted in extreme cases, as a kind of accessory, has to carry too much of the emotional burden of its parent's needs. It can be the victim of dangerous selfishness.
>
> (*The Guardian*, 12.3.91)

According to MP Dame Jill Knight (whose remarks in parliament were quoted widely in these articles), the deliberate bringing into the world of a child with only one parent was 'highly irresponsible and with no thought for the child' (*Daily Mail*, 11.3.91). Lack of forethought or regard for the needs of others are associated with a selfishness and irresponsibility that is popularly associated with immaturity. Hence, these comments undermine the women's developmental status and suggest immature recklessness. Yet there are inconsistencies in the condemnation of women who have chosen to parent alone, and conceive through donor insemination, since theirs has clearly been planned parenthood.

The leading sentence of the same article in the *Today* newspaper was 'A CAREER woman has chosen the colour of her unborn child's skin, hair and eyes in what will be Britain's first virgin birth' (original emphasis). The term 'career woman' functioned as a signifier of the selfish, demanding greediness of women actively choosing to have children outside traditionally gendered roles and division of labour, and fears about genetic selection were mobilised for dramatic effect, although these concerns might apply more to other clauses of the Human Embryology and Fertilisation Act (1990), such as those concerning regulations on embryo research.

While the suspicion might be that this preoccupation with selfishness relates to the concern about men's loss of (or denied) familial and sexual roles (Radford, 1991), this was not how it was expressed. Instead this was conveyed through implied negative effects for the child. Exactly how the child would be affected was not spelt out, but vague suggestions and unspecified crucial points managed to provide common-sense validity and the impression of consensus about these views. As Radford points out, the appeal to populist moralism remained powerful as long as the confused and partial nature of the assumptions was not revealed (Radford, 1991).

An opportunity for renewed 'popular' questioning of the fitness to parent of lesbian mothers arose in June 1994. This was when legal precedent was set under the Children Act (1989) by the granting of joint legal parenthood to a lesbian couple who had organised the conception of their child together. Articles in *The Guardian* and *Observer* on the 2nd and 3rd July 1994 reporting this case both drew on empirical research findings and expert testimonies to provide reasoned and reasonable arguments in support of their generally sympathetic positions. The *Observer*'s piece was called 'Why is it wrong to have two mums?' and its second header was 'As lesbians win the legal right to be joint parents, Lisa O'Kelly discovers that children can get on very well without a father figure.' It began by reporting some of the exclamations of outrage and disgust at the court's decision, which included statements by Conservative MPs Emma Nicholson and (again) Dame Jill Knight. Sir Nicholas Fairbairn (the former Scottish Solicitor-General) was quoted: 'It's ridiculous. We don't put children in the hands of the insane. Why should we put them in the hands of the perverted?' This comment, which questions the health or development of the women, was not given the credibility of being engaged with on its own terms. Instead the article discusses the development of children in lesbian or mother-only households.

These examples of representations of lone, lesbian and fertility-aided mothers when taken together illustrate the demonisation of women who mother (or wish to do so) outside of the conventional ideal mother image. The intensity of the popular condemnation has been startling. Such representation in the media cannot simply be dismissed as inconsequential popular 'small-talk' for, although the relationship is not straightforward or easy to formulate, the concepts popularised in them were addressed and developed in policy discussions.

Mothers in the popular representations described above are divided by a simple, well-worn good/bad distinction which maps on to the dominant discourse of marriage and motherhood as women's primary duty (Kaplan, 1992). The bad mothers in this schema are deviating doubly from their role: failing in their duty as mothers to provide an 'adequate family' (actually implied to be *the* adequate family), instead selfishly denying their children a father; and failing to be 'wifely' by selfishly denying men their rights to their children. Of course selfishness in a mother is supremely deviant; it is antithetical to representations of true motherliness (Woollett, 1991; Kaplan, 1992). In the 1970s feminists challenged the cultural discourses of traditional motherhood (Oakley, 1974; Dinnerstein, 1976). It is political opposition to this that is likely to underlie expressions of 'concern' that the 'selfish' generation of women that the 1970s spawned is responsible for the moral development of today's children.

Being seen as selfish in one's decision to have a child is applied with double standards, both between men and women, and between women. The category of absent father may have become one of moral condemnation at some points during news media discussions of the Child Support Act (1991) and Agency, but this category of father-who-is-lacking applies to a man who has moved out of co-residency with his children, has usually moved out of close contact with them and who no longer takes financial (or emotional) responsibility for them. Condemnation and a charge of being lacking or absent is levelled at mothers who have 'chosen' to go out to work full or part-time even while remaining primary emotional and financial support for their child(ren). A man's absence from his family might be considered a sort of weakness; a woman's absence is more likely to be met with disbelief and pathologisation. There are differences in the attribution of selfishness between women: if a woman is heterosexual but is not interested in having children (without evidence of psychopathology – although lack of interest may be evidence enough!); if a woman has chosen to have a career and has also chosen not to have children (though 'yet' can always be added to such a sentence). Yet paradoxically, if a woman is single and wants a child, or if she doesn't work and can therefore provide full motherly care, but then happens to be financially dependent on the state, she can be accused of selfishness. Therefore, women deemed fit to mother are considered 'selfish' for choosing not to have children, while women who want children, but who are not deemed suitable, are 'selfish' for wanting them. Women's desires to have or not to have children are thus an area of public comment and moral judgement.

The traditional family?

The Introduction describes how women 'carry the burden of gender', by being 'other' to the dominant category of male. Similarly, analyses of 'race' and ethnicity have described how the dominant 'race' is not used to having to think of itself as racialised (Minh-Ha, 1989; Collins, 1990; Davis, 1990). Yet it is those defined as different from this naturalised category that are seen as Other. In the dominant British culture, *black* is a commonly used descriptive term and a category of identity (but is sometimes used to include multiple categories), whereas *white* is used far less frequently because it is the default, the assumed. Similarly, the concept of the 'traditional family' requires no definition or justification. If you 'belong' to one you are not likely to be asked why. An analogous point has been made by lesbian and gay writers; one is not generally called to defend one's heterosexuality, or explain its cause. Heterosexuality is one of the key assumptions within common deployments of the term family.

The examples in this chapter happen to be the usual, recognisable 'non-traditional' family constellations (lone parent families and lesbian and gay families). They are minority, but clearly identifiable forms of family, but are only some of those that are made 'other' by the normative formulations of family. The label 'non-traditional' for families sets them outside the norm, and renders them oppositional to those seen as traditional. The term 'traditional' evokes a history, by virtue of which the object is then naturalised. This then confers a moral weight so that it becomes possible to argue that it *ought to be* simply because it *has been*.

As with many invocations of history and tradition, in the British context the image evoked is of white families; leaving black families already positioned as Other. The supposedly general concept of family is actually fairly narrow. Jo Van Every describes the way this construction of 'the family' takes as its central defining characteristic the existence of children, though rarely states this explicitly, and besides presuming heterosexual relations and marriage, the children are assumed to be the genetic children of the couple and to have been conceived 'naturally' (1991). British social policy replicates and reinforces this set of assumptions (Van Every, 1991). The relationship between discourses of family and class is complex; while ideas about 'proper' families and good parenting often contain particularly middle-class values and features, there can be a tendency to romanticise the family in discourses of working-class struggle. The meanings family has and its oppressive versus supportive nature relate to the broader social and political culture as it impacts on people at a specific location. As *bell hooks* describes, for black people in racist societies, family and homeplace has figured as an important site of resistance and strength (*hooks*, 1991).

These theoretical/political constructions as Other have real implications. People whose living arrangements do not resemble the conventional family are asked; why not? or, when will they change their situation? Non-conventional living arrangements are tolerated only because they are assumed to be temporary. Families that are defined as different are more likely to be considered problematic, and to be scrutinised by professional bodies (such as psychologists) as well as public discourse.

The monstrous children of monstrous mothers

Moral panics about children co-occur with those about mothers. Although often couched in terms of concern for *children*, the children in these narratives are gendered too. The concern has almost exclusively centred on boy children and follows in the wake of a series of panics about boys from joy-riding in the early 1990s, youth crime-rate concerns, and violent crime and murder more recently (see Campbell, 1993). The intense interest in child murderers witnessed in the British media in 1993 and 1994 is one example of how a phenomenon with a considerable history (Smith, 1994; Wilson, 1973) is presented as new, adding fuel to the moral panic. Deborah Marks describes how children whose actions do not fit in with the dominant cultural constructions of childhood as innocent and impotent are marked as deviant individuals, and outside of 'natural childhood' (Marks, in press b; and see Chapter 7, this volume). Each of these media 'stories' has been linked to the discourse of *concern* (though already confounded with *cause*) over the gendered development of boys growing up 'without a father figure' and so they can be implicitly invoked as 'outcomes' in discourses of lone mothers.

The fear of crime, and moral panic about kids who are seen as out of control, connects to fear of disorder 'from below' in the discourse of a dangerous and growing 'underclass' (Mann and Roseneil, 1994). This discourse has racialised as well as gendered associations, which arises both through the danger attributed to unbridled black masculinity, and to the 'unnatural' power wielded by black mothers in allegedly deteriorating family structures (Collins, 1992). Economic factors such as high rates of long-term unemployment and relative increases in the (usually part-time) employment of mothers, mean that the traditional expectations of gendered family roles, that is of men as breadwinners and women as full-time homemakers, are not necessarily possible. Changed gender expectations are drawn on to account for the sense of 'being adrift' that is observed in many young men today, compared with the increasing self-confidence and positive sense of identity it seems more girls display. However, structural factors are often missing from the analysis and, instead, the popular discourse of concern for the children of lone mothers manages to blame mothers for the conditions in which they raise their children. These are some of the key elements for contextualising the incidence of, and attention to, lone mothering.

Lone mothers and their children: scapegoats and scape-kids?

The writings of Hall *et al.* (1978) about the moral panic around 'mugging' in the early 1970s resonate with the construction of moral panics today. Just as the increasing crime rate in the early 1970s was proposed as an index of disintegration of the social order, so the rate of increase in lone parent families (which are mostly headed by women) is interpreted. The themes of 'race', crime and youth identified within the mugging crisis are also part of the contemporary discourse on the crisis of the family. Reports that there are a higher proportion of black mothers than white mothers who are single are 'easily' misinterpreted as suggesting that black mothers outnumber white mothers among the 'rising tides' of lone mothers, and this fuels popular racism. It resonates with the racist and xenophobic discourses of the 'swamping of "British culture" by "immigrants"' that has enjoyed various revivals since the 1950s. Chains of association run in both directions; 'youth' are out of control and engaging in crime because the now weakened family is unable to socialise them properly and inculcate in them 'family values'; and, because women have taken men's jobs and pushed them out of the family, men are left without their expected social roles and so, midst this despondency, grows a culture of social alienation and a disintegration of 'the family'. There is a parallel 'underclass' debate in the USA, which is heavily racialised and illustrates very similar themes. Maxine Baca Zinn describes how in one of the two models of the underclass in the US debate (which she calls the structural deficiency model) the cause of the swelling underclass is seen as a value system which is 'characterised by low aspirations, excessive masculinity, and the acceptance of female-headed families' (Zinn, 1992: 72).

The rhetoric of a moral panic can sometimes become melodramatic, as claims about the threat to 'the family' in the 'virgin births' debate illustrate. The *Daily Mail*'s opening sentence was: 'In a scheme which *strikes at the very heart of family life,* women who have never had sex are being helped to have a baby' (11.3.91, emphasis added). Emphasising the newness of a phenomenon, and any increase (better still, 'escalation') that can be associated with it, help to build the drama. The same article made this explicit as it continues with: *'and will seriously undermine the ideal of the family unit by encouraging more single mothers'*. It is interesting that the type of 'family unit' is not specified here. What is meant by 'the family' is so common-sensical as to not need specifying.

In these illustrations of how mothers are represented in popular culture, an implicit norm which is common to each is the 'natural mother'. In the 'virgin births' debate Dame Jill Knight's description of 'these women' (single women choosing to become mothers) who have 'none of the natural feelings about the matter' (*Daily Mail*, 11.3.91) constructs their motherhood as something *other* to the natural motherhood of 'ordinary', 'normal' women. Since motherhood is so naturalised for ('normal') women, it is still constructed as a woman's ultimate fulfilment (Marshall, 1991). So it is only women who fall outside of the category of 'natural' whose desire to be a mother is questioned. Anne Woollett describes this in relation to women using fertility services (Woollett, 1991). However, in the reasoning of Peery (1994), this 'natural desire' to be a mother, when held by 'unnatural' women (such as, in his view, women who are lesbians), makes them not 'more natural' but doubly deviant.

It seems that there need be no concern about the 'natural children' that are born to 'natural mothers', but that 'unnatural mothers' may breed monstrous children. The imperative to be conventionally gendered applies to children as well as mothers. The accusation that mothers are emasculating their sons and defeminising their daughters is a concern that 'natural', 'normal' boys and 'natural', 'normal' girls are raised. When children do things we find shocking or unnatural for a child, it appears that our anxiety is lessened once we have someone to blame. Placing the blame on the individual mothers deflects from a broader, cultural analysis of the problem.

Interestingly, concern for boys growing up without a father figure was not applied to mothers and grandmothers rearing children without men during war time. Although greater 'national interest' and personal worries may have prevented this from being a moral issue then, perhaps it did not constitute a threat to the traditional family because men were off doing 'manly' things. Although more women, especially from the middle classes, took paid work at this time, there was not a corresponding fear of loss of socially useful roles for men.

Our intention is not, of course, to deny or dismiss either the existence of social and economic problems or the anxieties that they generate. Rather, in analysing the emergence of moral panics about lone mothers and virgin births we can see how they function as a means for constructing an authoritarian backlash, and a sense of conservative consensus about the meanings or causes of 'social problems', both of which function to restrict women's freedom and autonomy around motherhood (Falludi, 1992). Hall *et al.* (1978) argue that, in moral panics, irrelevent or peripheral aspects are raised into sensational focus and that this serves to hide and mystify deeper causes. The preoccupation with women's relationship status and identity diverts attention from questions about the quality of the children's experiences of care and relationships. It supports an analysis in which the sphere of influence on a child extends no further than the household, where responsibility is therefore located, to the occlusion of broader social and economic analyses. Writers such as Campbell (1993) and Warner (1994) understand the social changes that have produced, or accompany, these moral panics as centring on masculinity, such that anxiety about the 'crisis in masculinity' is displaced or projected on to mothers as they provide a convenient scapegoat for social problems and political ills.

Psychological connections

Dominant western ways of thinking about knowledge attribute higher status to knowledge derived through scientific methods. Such knowledge therefore carries more weight (in almost every cultural context) than discourses whose claim to truth is not mediated by empirical methodology (such as discourses of experience that mothers might articulate). Thus, discourses of developmental psychology currently function powerfully both in political debates and at a personal level too. Our claim is not, for instance, that social policy is simply the operationalisation of discourses that academic psychology produces. Rather, the deployment of psychological ideas, with the truth claims that are accorded to them as 'scientific', increases the persuasiveness of a discourse for policy makers, as indeed it does generally. This is illustrated in the articles from *The Guardian* and the *Observer* mentioned earlier. The longer statements allowed professionals reflects the status they were attributed, and as Swaan (1990) describes they 'obligingly allow the last word to the appropriate expert'. However, the relationship between psychological theory and social policy does not become predictable, at least in part because the findings of research on a given question are multiple and contradictory. This is what sometimes enables opposing arguments each to be supported by 'what the experts say'.

Academic knowledge produced by psychology (and other disciplines) informs broader cultural representations of children, but the relationship between the two is not as straightforward as is suggested by the top–down model of 'truer' knowledge filtering down to non-professional people that academic discourses sometimes imply. Instead there is a much more reciprocal relationship whereby each informs the other and the two cannot be completely disentangled from each other (Riley, 1983). Academic research is stimulated by political questions (as is research funding) and it becomes productive both through supporting particular policy and legal interventions into children's lives and more generally through its popularisation (see Riley, 1988). Riley analyses processes of popularisation of psychological concepts and Chapter 7 (this volume) gives an example of the psychoanalytic concept of containment being used beyond the theoretical framework in which it is theorised. Convergences of scientific and popular moral rhetoric can be seen in the types of questions that academic psychologists ask, as well as the areas in which, or assumptions upon which, answers are sought. Because psychology produces knowledge about children and their needs, it has consequences for what parents, especially mothers, are required to be and do. Developmental psychology reinforces cultural gender roles and relations by constructing the limited range of gendered positions of man, woman (for adults) and boy, girl (for children) (Burman, 1991). Motherhood is increasingly defined in terms of psychological discourses of children's needs and potential. In particular, this leads to the production of the notion that certain kinds of women are 'fit to parent'. As well as informing and reinforcing normative policies and institutional practices, such discourses are productive through the anxieties generated by the apparent fragility of children's 'normal' and healthy development (Urwin, 1985; Woollett and Phoenix, 1991). In addition, there are specific locations at which (non-psychological) professionals employ psychological discourses on health, development and normality as they implement social policy. Examples of this include social workers' assessments of people for consideration as foster/adoptive parents, and medics' decisions in the case of access to fertility services.

The cultural construct of 'fitness to parent' is rarely explicated, but we understand what is 'normal' from the more frequent and more explicit representations of difference from the norm. The category is not defined directly, but its boundaries are maintained through the pathologisation of those who fall outside of it. Doubt is cast on parents who are seen as marginal. In the last few years we have seen the scrutiny of different categories of parent: those at the margins of typical age ranges; teenage mothers (see Phoenix, 1991), and older women who have been helped to conceive post-menopausally; as well as those described here whose household, relationship status or sexuality bring them into question.

Psychological discourses, because they can describe what is 'normal', have the power to define what is pathological. The fact that the 'virgin births scandal' subsequently gave its name to a 'syndrome' (Donovan, 1992) indicates that the desire to have a child when exhibited by women in this category is considered worthy of professional attention. It is designated an identifiably peculiar desire, something other than the norm: a category of pathology. The British organisation Families Need Fathers report how in the USA there is now public recognition for a syndrome, called Parental Alienation Syndrome (Palmer, 1988; Gardner, 1992), which describes mothers who are poisoning the minds of their children and maliciously turning them against their fathers.

We have already noted in this book how what is described as normal is often then constructed as natural. Discourses of what is natural are powerful across the cultural spectrum, but feminist critics have often challenged this notion since it has been used to over-ride women's reproductive decisions (Stanworth, 1987). The professionalisation of childrearing practices can be seen as the colonisation of an area of women's (mothers') knowledge by male-dominated professions (Ehrenreich and English, 1979; Margolis, 1984). It can also be seen as an instrument of colonisation in another sense. The cultural domination by western industrialised countries, and processes of commodification and globalisation, mean that the discourses of western experts also carry considerable authority in non-western ('non-developed') countries (see Burman, 1994c). The supposedly universal individual whose optimal development is the concern of western child psychology is, of course, the rational economic individualist subject that capitalism requires.

Discourses of development are common in the discussion of children's well-being, but in the 'virgin births' discussion the development of the mothers under scrutiny was at issue. A woman's relationship status was taken to be an indication of maturity (yet relationship was defined in the crudest of senses as whether she was planning to co-parent with her male sexual partner). The quality of any relationship was not the issue (apparently any relationship with a man would have removed the need to challenge her right to parent). No questions were asked about the emotional or practical support these women had. The unspoken underpinnings of such discourses are assumptions about development. It is implied that there is both a consensus about psychological criteria for, and a means of assessment of, a person's developmental status or maturity. In fact, there is neither. Rather, a tautological argument circulates whereby the 'normal' development of an individual to a certain point of 'maturity' indicates their fitness to parent. The parent's 'normality' is constructed as indicator of 'successful outcome' for themselves, and through the model of 'influence on the child', this is seen as the best predictor of successful/normal outcome in the child. It is paradoxical that in some discourses a woman who is not 'mature enough' should have her mothering prevented, while in other discourses being a mother is constructed as a, or the, route to maturity (Woollett, 1991).

Who is 'fit to parent'?

The term 'fit to *parent*' masks the fact that discourses of parents and parenting are profoundly gendered. Even when gender neutral terms are used, as they are in most social policy, and in discourses of parental involvement in schools, these usually do have gender-specific addresses and effects. Smart and Sevenhuijsen (1989) demonstrate how the gender neutral discourses of parents now used in legal decisions on child residency and care works to the advantage of men. Standing (1994) considers how 'parental involvement in the classroom' is (unpaid work) usually done by women (see also Chapter 4, this volume). The skill(s) of 'parentcraft' are discursively ungendered, yet the implications for women offered or seeking help are probably different from those for men. Assumptions about women's propensity for mothering mean that a woman requiring help for this could be seen as unnatural and deviant, and a possible danger to her children, whereas a man might more likely receive a (condescending) congratulatory pat on the back for being willing to try to learn to be nurturant. Chapter 7 discusses the different gendered positions produced by ideas about the care and education of children and the roles of (rhetorically ungendered) parents and professionals. Recent discussions of parents in the media have been highly gender specific; it is precisely a problem about *how* women are 'parenting' and usually *how little* men are 'parenting', or rather, being 'allowed' to take up their role as parent.

We have retained the term *parenting* for discussion of rhetoric that is auspiciously gender neutral (yet primarily functions to judge and regulate women), but support the use of the term *mothering* to discuss interaction between child and primary carer. The latter is common practice among some feminist social scientists since it acknowledges that most child-care work is in fact done by women. On the other hand, writing about parents in the abstract maintains the impression of a non-gender-essentialised caring adult. The possibilities and desirability of men doing more parenting in the future, given the existing relations of gender under which they themselves have been raised, is an issue on which feminists differ in opinion.

To summarise so far, women who fail to conform to dominant cultural sexual, reproductive and gender positions continue to be pathologised and marginalised in some of the misogynistic representations of women in popular culture. Some of the models employed in developmental psychological discourses support these through their assumptions and narrow focus. They construct only a narrow range of outcomes of development that are seen as normal, and an over-simplified and unitary pathway of development. Among the implications of this are that childbearing on the margins of the 'normal' category can render one's parenting suspect, or pathological, or can even prevent or deny it.

Responding to the arguments

How can feminists engage with and intervene in these debates which are bolstered by academic claims to know what is normal and natural? One response is to contest the claims 'from within' the framework, that is, to deploy psychological research findings to make counter-claims. The second is to take issue with the agendas that inform the appeal to psychology, or the conceptual framework of psychological 'answers'. Each strategy involves particular opportunities and limitations that we will now consider.

McCartney (1985) responded to the charge that single women choosing donor insemination (DI) are selfish by publishing an empirical study of women requesting medical services for DI from which she concludes that there was no support for describing these women's motivations as 'purely selfish'. This study was published in a gynaecology journal and so intervenes at the level of academic debate and professional practice. When children raised without a father are addressed in psychological literature the focus is on the child's gender identity, sex-typed behaviour, sexual orientation and experience of social stigma. This fourth issue, that children in mother-only or lesbian/gay families have additionally to cope with prejudice, is sometimes used in custody/residency cases as an argument against them, but since it is not the actual parents or parenting that is problematised it will not be considered here, except to note that this argument results in blaming the victim (of homophobic stigma or abuse) for 'their problem'. One can respond to each of these points with research findings that provide reassurance that these worries are not realised. Susan Golombok and colleagues have conducted research employing psychosexual and psychiatric assessments of the children of lesbian and single heterosexual mothers (Golombok *et al.*, 1983). All the children in the study (37 in lesbian households and 38 in heterosexual mother-only households) were deemed to have 'gender-role identities' or 'self-concepts', that corresponded to their physical sex. There were no differences in sex-role behaviour (behaviour deemed appropriate to their gender) between the two family types for either boys or girls, and, in fact, children in both types of family were shown to be 'rather traditional' in their choices of toys, activities, friendships. While it is noted that for school-aged children sexual orientation cannot be meaningfully assessed, the children mostly reported heterosexual 'crushes', with no differences according to family type.[2] By virtue of its direct response to the questions raised, its rhetorical style and the 'objectivity' of its appraisals, this is a powerful study which can be drawn on to inform policy discussions supporting lesbian mothers retaining 'care and control' of their children in individual legal cases. For campaigning and casework on legal and policy issues by organisations such as the Lesbian Custody Project,[3] this kind of study can be invaluable.

However, as Kitzinger (1987) notes, the crucial limitation of this approach is that the same agenda is preserved and there is no chance to challenge the terms of the debate. In this case, this means that tacit support is provided for the assumptions that a child's gender-identity needs always to correspond to their biological sex; that their behaviour needs to be that prescribed for their gender; and that their sexual preference should be heterosexual, if they are to be considered normally/naturally/healthily developing beings. Since, as feminists, we are critical of the dominant cultural formulations of gender and sexuality, and we reject the sexist, heterosexist and culturally imperialist assumptions of psychological models, the dilemma lies in the fact that as we intervene effectively in specific debates, we also reinforce the idea that complete, appropriate and normal outcomes require the production of 'proper' boys and 'proper' girls.

In their (1991) review article, Fiona Tasker and Susan Golombok criticise the assumptions that same-sex sexual orientation is a negative outcome, and that influence on the child is just seen in terms of the parents. They draw on theorists within psychology to support their argument that adults other than parents may be important influences. Hence, despite the fact that challenging the terms of the debate and responding within it are logically opposed, to a certain extent their review does both. It avoids compromising its effectivity as objective review by clearly prioritising one strategy; but by commenting on the assumptions which are embedded in the way research questions are framed, it offers some challenge to (particular aspects within) the terms of the debate.

We argue that both strands of response by feminists are valuable and would wish to preclude neither. Further to the division between 'using' and critiquing psychology, Prince and Hartnett (1993) argue that challenging psychology must involve interrogating both the 'content of psychology, that is psychological terminology and theories, methodological prescriptions and their applications' and its 'power, [and the] political, ideological and institutional structures within which the content of psychology is generated and applied' (1993: 219).

What does the call for feminists to maintain pluralist strategies of intervention mean in the context of the representations of 'deviant' mothers who are to blame for social problems? It means that it might be valuable to criticise both the structure of the discourse (for example, the misogynistic images, the limited analysis) and the ideological assumptions of psychological theories, yet simultaneously to present psychological research 'findings' that will support a preferred analysis in this case. These can be described as different strategies or approaches to intervention. Different strategies are effective in different ways, probably within different fora, such as public/mainstream media debates, academic and policy fora, and individual legal cases.

The challenge for feminism

Black and post-colonial writers have pointed out some of the exclusions produced by western feminism's invocation of the category of woman (Moraga and Anzaldua, 1981; CCCS, 1982; Spivak, 1988). The ethnocentric theorising of movements of predominantly white middle-class women replicates racist and class-biased structures. Resisting the construction of a singular feminist analysis is necessary in order to avoid repeating these or other exclusions. The final chapter of this book considers some of the difficulties we have in working with the differences between women and in theorising women's different power.

Adopting multiple and varied feminist positions or modes of response allows flexibility, and permits strategic decisions to be made about arguments and approach. It means that formulating political action requires consideration of the specific location. This avoids political positions becoming static and allows feminist arguments to be more responsive to the different contexts for issues to arise. Our interventions must be specific and tightly focused around the object of contestation. Acknowledging that our strategies are for the purpose of intervention at a specific point and time in the debate, and trying to attach this explicit qualifier, is the most we can do to limit the analysis and prevent generality. Not ruling out any approaches beforehand means that surprising and contradictory stances will sometimes be taken. For instance, it retains the possibility of deploying a discourse of 'the natural' in a situation in which it is felt this is the most effective strategy, as might be the case where it was useful to argue that a woman's 'natural' desire to parent ought not to be restricted because of her lesbianism. This is an example of what is described in the Introduction as strategic essentialism. The dilemmas of using this kind of argument can only be elaborated in very general ways in a piece of writing like this, since the advantages and disadvantages of a particular approach will relate to features of the specific location. While caution must be exercised, and an eye must be kept to the negative and unintended consequences of our discourses, particular discourses and tactics cannot be dismissed out of hand.

Refusing to assert that there can be a single feminist analysis and strategy, and hence advocating a plurality is not akin to saying 'each to her own'. This, like some arguments in post-modern discourses, would be to assume that different arguments compete on an equal footing. Since differences in power are not addressed, the same arguments or voices continue to be heard most loudly and the voices of Others are still not heard. Therefore existing power relations are likely to be replicated. Relating this back to discourses on lone mothers, this might mean that discourses backed by a claim to psychological knowledge continue to be more powerful than feminists' criticisms of these claims.

Feminist activism must be more than shouting for one's own causes. We must both call for support from other women, and be prepared to move to support the calls of other women. In addition, we need to work to enable hitherto silenced voices to be heard. This is an approach to politics in which agreements or coalitions can be formed on particular issues and approaches, which might then dissolve and reform to let people choose again where and how to act most effectively. Because uniting is temporary, these forms of feminist activity do not produce assumptions of homogeneity and suppressions of difference. Neither do they allow activism on the sole basis of personal identity (Spivak, 1988). This chapter has been about identifying and evaluating various avenues for feminists to respond critically to popular representations of mothers and children, and to social policy debates through which we or they are materially affected. We advocate maintaining, and continuing to enable, pluralist strategies of critical intervention, and urge ongoing reappraisal of those we decide to support.

Notes

1 Pretended Family Relationships were referred to in Section 29 (which had been 27 and 28) of the Local Government Act (1988). Clause 28, as it was most famously known, was developed in response to 'positive images' of lesbians and gay men being presented in schools and prohibited schools from 'promot[ing] homosexuality'. See Alderson (1988) and Cooper (1994) for critical discussions. In addition, this description informs Paragraph 16 of the Guidelines for the Implementation of the Children Act (1989) which states vaguely that some people's 'lifestyles' made them unsuitable to parent, and was campaigned against because of the way it could allow discrimination against lesbians and gay men who were applying to become foster or adoptive parents simply on account of their sexuality and before they had been assessed.
2 For useful reviews of the psychological literature on the children of lesbian mothers, see Pennington (1987), Steckel (1987) and Patterson (1992).

3 The Lesbian Custody Project is at Rights of Women, a London-based organisation offering legal advice to women. Rights of Women, 53/54 Featherstone Street, London, EC1.

chapter *nine*

Power in feminist organisations

Catherine Bewley

After ten years of paid and unpaid work in women's organisations and MSc research with a women's aid group, a rape crisis group and a women's centre, I have the opportunity in this chapter to address one of the issues which has challenged me most in those organisations: power between women. In relating to colleagues and clients, in the nature of the work, and in the life of the organisations, the expression of power between women was a daily issue.

At the time of my MSc in occupational psychology in 1990 I knew of some feminists writing about power between women, especially those who felt excluded from the dominant feminist models which had gained precedence during the 1970s and 1980s. These important texts noted differences of power usually in relation to race, ethnicity, culture, class and sexuality. However, at the time of completing my thesis I knew of very few women writing about power between women from an organisational perspective.

But my difficulty with power between women in women's organisations was also about my own fear. Individual women were immensely important in helping me believe in myself but the feminism I learned sometimes made me afraid to use any power that I had. The experience of doing my MSc research brought all this to a head. I found the psychology context in which I studied and researched alien and damaging; one in which I had to use indirect forms of power to survive. I received an outpouring of information from my MSc research participants about negative experiences of power in their organisations which I felt reluctant to address because it challenged the construction of feminism and feminist organisations in which I had invested time, energy and belief.

Now I want to revisit some of the debate which I largely avoided in 1990. I am choosing to focus on the negative and difficult aspects of power between women in some feminist organisations. I define feminist organisations as those run by and for women with an overtly feminist perspective. There are a variety of such organisations but when I refer to 'feminist organisations' in this chapter I am writing specifically about my experiences in rape crisis, women's aid and women's centre organisations. It is undoubtedly the case that such organisations have been important in the development of feminist theory and practice around changing relations of power between men and women. It is also true that women in these organisations have helped change attitudes to rape, domestic violence and sexual abuse, among other things, and have done extremely valuable work with individual women. However, in this chapter I will not be considering these positive dimensions of power because what I needed in 1990 was some clear writing, from an organisational perspective, about the abuses and muddles around power between women and it was specifically this debate which I could not find.

This chapter, then, focuses on feminist analyses of power and the experience of power between women in feminist organisations, primarily within a framework of feminist theory but also in relation to organisational theory.

The process of writing this chapter and the subsequent discussion of these issues with my co-authors has been an interesting one. There were a variety of reactions to my chapter from my co-authors, from 'Thank goodness someone's written this' and 'This is just like my experience' to 'The chapter seems to be against feminist organisations', 'Maybe there's not enough context in it ' and 'Is it anti-lesbian?' Whatever our individual responses, the issue of power between women in feminist organisations roused us to vigorous and stimulating debate. Despite our differences of opinion, I am grateful for the support of my co-authors for what is perhaps the most deliberately polemical chapter in this book.

Writing this chapter was an opportunity to express and discuss some of my views and experiences about power in feminist organisations within the context of other critiques. Part of my motivation to write comes from anger and frustration at the way in which power is sometimes abused and denied in feminist organisations. I also want to express an end point to a period of my life: at the time of writing I am no longer involved in either psychology or feminist organisations.

Although I describe a variety of feminist critiques about power, I locate myself quite clearly in this chapter as a political strategy to explicate my perspective. Some co-authors strongly identify with what I have written and would like the 'I' to be a 'we' at times. In support of the difference I discuss in the following pages, I offer this chapter as a specific addition to a vigorous debate between women about power and organisations.

Some background about my MSc

My MSc research took place over a period of six months with a women's aid group, a rape crisis group and a women's centre in the same town. All three organisations explicitly referred to feminist ideas in their aims and working practices, although they were structured and run very differently.

The research methodology consisted of three cycles of qualitative information-gathering and analysis using individual and group interviews, documents and observation. A brief analysis of the information was made at the end of each cycle, discussed with the organisation's members, and used to inform the next cycle. At the end of the process I wrote a confidential report for each organisation. In one case, this report brought out into open criticisms of the way in which the organisation was being run, particularly relating to the poor performance of the management committee. A difficult internal process of conflict was brought to a head as a result of my intervention and I was asked by the paid workers to work with the organisation for some months to follow this process through. Thus, in both content and process, issues of power came to the fore in the research.

I experienced a further dimension of power in relation to the department I studied in and the course I was doing. I had not felt comfortable with the content and style of the MSc course for the first six months of teaching. When I had to choose my research project I came into more conflict with the course leaders. I found it difficult to find appropriate supervision and, when I did, my two supervisors were themselves marginal in the department (a new male research assistant and a female PhD student). This had consequences at a later stage when there were arguments about whether or not my thesis was adequate since the supervisors had less power to argue my case.

In the end, the process of writing-up became, for me, a battle between myself and the course assessors over the style and content of my thesis, a battle which lasted more than three times as long as the research itself and involved me in three formal submissions. I was eventually awarded my MSc two-and-a-half years after I started the one-year course. By this time I was well and truly fed up with psychology and left to work elsewhere. I have not been tempted to go back since this experience.

Feminism and power

> On the one hand, many women tend to regard power ambivalently, as something to be avoided, something that corrupts, and something that is always used over and against others. On the other hand, many women who have been subjected to the perversities of patriarchal

> power have risen up in resistance against it and seized power for their Selves and other women. Women have had a dual relation to power.
>
> (Raymond, 1986: 193)

In the 1970s and 1980s some (usually white middle-class) feminist writing from an essentialist perspective developed the notion that 'women's power' was different to 'men's power'. It follows from this premiss that women's organising would be different from how men organised their groups and institutions. In this analysis, power became linked to hierarchy, status, money, exploitation and oppression. If feminists are not supposed to exploit and oppress, they must therefore be against hierarchy, against status and against money. Consistent with this challenge to what were seen as patriarchal structures and ways of organising was the linking of collective organising to feminist practice. The analysis went something like: if women are supposed to be different from men; if power is inherently 'male'; and if power equals exploitation and oppression, then women must not have power.

However, this critique of feminist theorising about power is, of course, too simplistic. First, the re-thinking of organisational structures and processes was a genuine attempt to challenge the strongly established structures of male dominated power in organisations. This challenge also came from the socialist collective movement in the 1970s. Second, despite Raymond's evocation of a collective 'women', not all women had problems with power. There were many women whose lives reflected a more complex pattern of power positions (including those between women); who had 'good' models of powerful women; who saw this shunning of power as a privilege of, on the whole, white middle-class educated women.

> When feminists write about 'women' in ways that it's very clear only certain women fit into, they are assuming a single meaning for the identity 'women' that excludes most of its potential members. There is a power move that requires the security of being the 'normal' centre.
>
> (Kahaleole Chang Hall, 1993: 221)

Many women have challenged the terms of the discussion about women and power prevalent in 1970s/early 1980s feminism. This dominant discussion relied on a unitary identity of 'woman' and an emphasis on male/female power relations as more significant than other power relations, such as those around race, colour, ethnicity, sexuality, disability, age, class, income, education and so on. I will now briefly draw attention to some challenges to this dominant feminist perspective.

Black feminists have highlighted the un-theorised and unrecognised white-centredness of much feminist theory and practice, thus changing the framework within which power is analysed.

> One of the effects of postmodernist deconstruction on feminism has been the realization that 'everyone is different'. The first ones who were struggling to break the assumed homogeneity and the necessary commonality of interests among women within feminism have been Black feminists like bell hooks who claimed 'The vision of sisterhood evoked by women's liberation was based on the idea of common oppression . . . a false and corrupt platform disguising and mystifying the true nature of women's varied and complex social reality'.
>
> (Yuval-Davis, 1993: 3)

This challenge is not simply to a discussion of power but also to a definition of feminism itself:

> The movement [1960s/70s feminism] was dominated by White women who seemed to think that all the problems women experience are caused by patriarchy, ignoring racism. In the 1980s Black women in Britain reclaimed the term feminist and redefined feminism to include issues of race, class, gender, sexuality and imperialism. They acknowledged the efforts of the long line of Black women before them who had negotiated their way through White western culture . . . In our countries of origin there are long traditions of feminists who have struggled against different forms of patriarchy. So the term feminist will mean different things to women of different backgrounds.
>
> (Mason-John and Khambatta, 1993: 42)

To include all women in a feminist analysis of power between women demands both that the dominant perspective (white, middle-class, non-disabled and so on) is acknowledged and analysed (charles, 1992); and that individual identity is not assumed. Likewise, it seems essential that feminist organisations recognise and accommodate different and self-defined identities (and lifestyles) before it is possible to address adequately issues of power between women in these organisations.

Heterosexual and bisexual women, and many lesbians who have strong relationships with men, have been alienated by a prescriptive type of feminism which implicitly or explicitly says 'men are bad', 'men can't be anti-sexist' and, by implication, that lesbianism (but only of a certain sort) is more aligned with feminist principles (Smyth, 1992; Wolf, 1993). An illustration that this latter view is still held by some feminists today, despite the developments in identity politics over the late 1980s and 1990s, can be found in Sheila Jeffreys work:

> The radical political potential of lesbianism rests upon precisely lesbian love of women. It is only lesbians in hetero-relational culture who can value women unequivocally and on this basis fight for the

> liberation of those they love and value. Heterosexual feminists too have seen the importance of loving and valuing women but they reserve their most important emotional and sexual energies for men.
> (Jeffreys, 1994: 146)

Views such as this, when they become dominant in feminist organisational ideology can lead, I believe, to many women, including lesbians, turning their backs on feminist organisations in favour of other movements. Cherry Smyth uses the attraction of queer political activities as an example:

> The attraction of queer for some lesbians is flavoured by the rebellion against a prescriptive feminism that had led them to feel disenfranchised by the lesbian feminist movement.
> (Smyth, 1992: 26)

Similarly, a singular focus on male/female relations in a discussion of women and power ignores the complexities of power for disabled women. Disabled feminists, such as Jenny Morris, have challenged the dominant non-disabled perspective in feminist theory and the priorities for action in feminist practice which arise from this.

> Disability and old age are aspects of identity with which gender is very much entwined but they are identities which have been almost entirely ignored by feminists.
> (Morris, 1991: 7)

What is common to all these critiques of dominant feminist thinking is the call to recognise the variety of dynamics through which women experience power, not simply those of patriarchy, and to acknowledge that the battle ground for these dynamics is just as likely to be between women as to be between women and men. Women's experience of power is multi-dimensional and must be addressed as such. An imperative for 'sameness' demands that individual women in feminist organisations pass the 'rigorous litmus tests of feminism' (Wolf, 1993: 143). And yet, as Jenny Morris writes, the essential core of liberation movements is 'the right to be both different and equal' (Morris, 1993: 189). The analysis of power which exists in some feminist organisations does not permit these differences of view, experience or lifestyle.

I believe that the linking of specific values, beliefs, politics and lifestyle to feminism *per se* has done the fight against sexism a great dis-service. My experience mirrors that quoted from Smyth above: many women have given up on feminism, feeling that it has nothing to do with them and their lives. They find some feminist prescriptions, particularly about power, as oppressive as sexist ones. These women leave feminist organisations to find other ways to express their desire for equality and other movements and allegiances within which to work.

Organisational theories of power

Power within organisational settings has been addressed by various organisational psychologists, theories and concepts tending to illustrate current fashions in organisational theory. For example, the concept of organisational culture which was developed in the 1980s linked concepts of power to those of organisational ideology and customs. This link, as I explain below, offers more to an understanding of power in feminist organisations than some earlier organisational theories which described power in terms of formal hierarchies, structures and bureaucracies. In this section I will not provide a detailed critique of all organisational theories of power, many of which I found from my MSc research to be of limited value in understanding feminist organisations. Instead, I will briefly reference some key issues and theoretical perspectives which I did find useful.

Within the theoretical frameworks of organisational psychology, there are two main concepts of power: relational (one person or group has more of something than another person or group) and absolute, a 'thing' one possesses.

> In recent years organization and management theorists have become increasingly aware of the need to recognise the importance of power in explaining organizational affairs. However, no really clear and consistent definition of power has emerged. While some view power as a resource, ie. as something one possesses, others view it as a social relation characterized by some sort of dependency, as an influence over something or someone.
>
> (Morgan, 1986: 158)

Often there is implicit in definitions of power the assumption that if someone has power they will use it against or over someone else; for example, the 'ability to get another person to do something that he or she would not otherwise have done' (Morgan, 1986: 158). Implicit in much organisational theory, as in much feminist theory, is the view that power is 'bad', something which needs to be limited and controlled.

Gareth Morgan has written about power, politics and ideology in organisational life in a way that is helpful for an analysis of feminist organisations. For example, he describes how the 'informal organisation' of friends and networks is used to gain power and manipulate decision-making. 'The coalitions, alliances, and networks built through these processes may remain highly informal and to a degree invisible' (Morgan, 1986: 174). Morgan also describes 'boundary management' as another way in which individuals and groups maintain power in an organisation. Boundary management is the control of information; the control of the contact between the organisation's members; and the control of the interpretation, the 'reality', of organisational events and relationships.

> Power accrues to the person who is able to structure attention to issues in a way that in effect defines the reality of the decision-making process. This draws attention to the key importance of knowledge and information as sources of power. By controlling these key resources a person can systematically influence the definition of organisational situations and can create patterns of dependency.
>
> (Morgan, 1986: 167)

I found that informal organisation and boundary management were key ways in which power was gained and maintained in the feminist organisations I studied.

In addition, Morgan usefully notes that members of organisations become powerful through access to or control of information, knowledge, longevity in the organisations, ability to articulate views or more status on, for example, the 'I'm having a hard time' or 'I'm a martyr for the cause' ladders. This illustrates some of the ways in which power exists without the need for formal structures or processes in organisations.

The perpetuation of destructive power dynamics in feminist organisations is sometimes maintained in the process of selecting new members for the organisation. These tacit processes can exist alongside formal selection procedures. Schein (1985; 1990) has described the unspoken behaviours, beliefs and organisational habits which can be described as 'organisational culture'. Organisational culture is, he writes, the 'pattern of basic assumptions, invented, discovered or developed by a given group as it learns to cope with its problems' (Schein, 1990: 111). If this coping works, it is taught to new members and perpetuated as 'the correct way to perceive, think, and feel' (1990: 111).

A number participants in my MSc research noted that feminist organisations, like other radical voluntary organisations, went through a time when the organisational culture required untidy and shabby premises; disorganised procedures; burnt-out workers and volunteers; and allegiance to whatever lifestyles and opinions were in favour at the time. Of course, most feminist organisations survive in a hostile environment with very few resources. Nevertheless, the chaos seemed at times to be justified as an expression of the organisation's ideological perspective, rather than simply its lack of resources.

As I have demonstrated, organisational theorists such as Morgan and Schein have developed concepts about power of relevance to feminist organisations. However, much organisational psychology reduces power to the level of individual pathology or organisational structure and process. There is little reference to the nature of power relations outside organisations which affect what happens within them. As an illustration of this, my MSc course in occupational psychology had, over a period of six months, one session on women and work, and no other reference to social inequality and its impact on organisational experience. It was as if unequal power relations around race, ethnicity, class, disability, sexuality, age and gender had no relevance to work and that students who would go on to become managers, personnel officers and organisational consultants had no need to give the slightest consideration to these issues. In addition, we were not offered an opportunity to consider how voluntary organisations functioned. It is not surprising, then, that I concluded in my MSc thesis that, on the whole, organisational theory appears irrelevant or impossible to apply to an analysis of feminist organisations.

Power in feminist organisations

In this section I will look more specifically at the experience of power in feminist organisations, using examples from my research and from the experience of other women interviewed for this chapter. I will consider what sorts of power women have in feminist organisations, and how this power is expressed and managed.

Using the feminist organisations which were participants in my MSc research as examples, it can be concluded that there are often few formal hierarchies and role divisions which assign explicit power to members of such organisations. However, there can be differences of power between paid and unpaid workers, and between workers and management committees. Power in these examples comes from the individual's position in the organisation and information or knowledge. Sometimes these positions of power feel uncomfortable to the women concerned because they appear to clash with the feminist framework within which the women work.

For example, in one feminist organisation I studied, there was a significant debate about the title of the organisation's leader, focusing on the use of the word 'manager'. The leader said:

> The decision to make my job 'manager' still doesn't sit comfortably with me because I don't think it reflects the community side of the work we do. I'd be much happier with 'coordinator' but the committee decided it should be 'manager'. Unfortunately it's a sign of the times we're living in. For me it is still a big contradiction. We're a women's centre but we're using very male language and defining jobs in very male terms. So I'm not personally very happy with that.
>
> (MSc research participant)

Another worker at the women's centre echoed this view: 'When the coordinator leaves and the job is advertised as "manager" I don't know what kind of woman that's going to attract. The kind of woman I'd want to see working here would be, might be, put off by that' (MSc research participant). Implicit in these worries about using the word 'manager' are a number of beliefs: that male managers behave in certain ways (aggressive, exploitative, hierarchical) and that becoming a 'manager' means taking on these characteristics; that a woman manager should not be like a male manager; that a woman manager could not define 'manager' behaviour to be other than aggressive and exploitative. The word manager suggests a formal position of power, in this case exercised by one woman over others. Again, this seems to be very uncomfortable for some women in feminist organisations.

Power often relates to ways in which networks and sub-groups develop and are used. These sub-groups can be those closest to the 'core' of the organisation or related to something specific the members have in common. They can be formally or informally set up and acknowledged in the organisation. Power is also gained through longevity in the organisation and its accompanying information, knowledge and 'wisdom'. This can be a particularly effective form of power when administrative procedures are poor and knowledge is carried almost solely 'in someone's head'. The 'wisdom' factor associated with longevity can reinforce the views of those who have been around the longest and are more familiar with the spoken and unspoken rules of the organisation, sometimes silencing newer members. 'The women that have been around longer have the power to make what they want happen' (MSc research participant). The power conferred through 'wisdom' is also sometimes related to notions of 'charisma'. A popular image used to describe this, and one I heard in some feminist organisations, was 'queen bee'. Sometimes this charisma comes from 'wisdom' and experience, knowing 'how we did it last time'. Sometimes it is the consequence of direct or indirect manipulation.

Members with this power can influence who joins and leaves the organisation, who 'fits in' with how things are done. During the course of my research a number of power battle stories were described to me by participants. These stories always ended with the person furthest from the core, the newcomer and those less networked within the organisation leaving.

In one feminist organisation I belonged to, a whole group of new recruits had left just before I joined because, as I was told, they were 'not feminist enough'. Of course, organisations might legitimately dismiss members who are so at odds with the organisation's values or approach that they are detrimental to its work. Whether this was the case in this example or not, I don't know. However, what I want to highlight is the unvoiced message I received as a new recruit: I had to be 'feminist enough' to be allowed to stay. I took the views of the 'core' group, which I saw as most powerful in the organisation, as the definition of what constituted 'good enough feminism'. It seemed to be the case that those who agreed with these views stayed and those who clashed with them or felt excluded eventually left.

This is where organisation and ideology interact, the point at which one cannot understand feminist organisations without an appreciation of feminism itself. In some ways groups of women are consistently excluded from feminist perspectives, as described above, and power between women in feminist organisations is a taboo subject. In other ways, feminist organisations have indeed attempted to address issues of oppression for a range of women. Sometimes, however, this brings with it not only a series of views to which members must subscribe but, more significantly in organisational terms, ways of behaving and relating in the organisation which can restrict discussion and development, and even sometimes threaten the life of the organisation.

An example which illustrates the connection between day-to-day organisational processes and wider experiences and analyses of oppression comes from the experience of a member of a rape crisis group in which an argument between two black workers escalated to the level that the group brought in an outside consultant to resolve the organisational issues. The organisation had a black workers sub-group which decided to deal with the argument itself and refused to discuss it outside the sub-group because it did not trust the remainder of the mostly white collective to handle the issue appropriately. However, the argument was not resolved easily and gradually the remaining collective and the sub-group came into direct confrontation. The sub-group felt that the collective could not handle the issue effectively and the collective felt they were denied the chance to help resolve the argument. In the frustrating impasse that developed, many members left and the service offered by the organisation had to be so drastically reduced that it nearly folded.

In this example, organisational issues of conflict-resolution and information-exchange were inextricably linked to wider experiences of inequality and oppression. As I noted above in reference to the teaching on my MSc course, these wider issues are invariably present in organisations but usually those with most power in society have most power in organisations to ignore them. At a level of general feminist theory, these issues are often explicitly acknowledged in feminist organisations but women are not necessarily skilled at resolving conflict or building coalitions around shared aims in the day-to-day life of the organisation. To do this effectively, it appears that feminist organisations need to develop ways of relating to, and managing, power differences, of whatever sort, in their organisational processes. Silencing discussion and information-exchange, for organisations in which information-exchange is crucial to effectiveness and survival, can threaten the very existence of the organisation. As Nira Yuval-Davis writes:

> It is vital in any form of coalition and solidarity politics to keep one's own perspective on things while empathizing and respecting the others as well as being open to change and growth as a result of the encounter . . . In the same way that there are diverse positions and points of view among people who are similarly rooted, so there are among members of the other group. The transversal coming together should not be with the members of the other group 'en bloc', but with those who, in their different rootings, share compatible values and goals to one's own.
>
> (Yuval-Davis, 1993: 9)

This information exchange can take place in meetings, which some feminist organisations use as the main collective site for information-exchange and decision-making. Those who attend meetings, set agendas and keep minutes have the power to influence the nature and flow of information in an organisation. Information exchange can also take place in informal gatherings of friends or cliques, often off the premises. Likewise, physical space is sometimes important in assigning and controlling power, for example in the location of offices, who has the keys, who sits in which chair at which desk and so on.

So how is power expressed in feminist organisations? On the surface, the answer might often be 'nicely and indirectly'. 'We must all get on. We must all be sisterly.' These beliefs influence how difference and disagreement are expressed and dealt with in feminist organisations. Perhaps this reinforces sexist ideas about 'how women should behave': be quiet; take everyone's feelings into account; avoid conflict at all costs; use your power covertly and manipulatively. As a consequence, hostility, conflict and the abuse of power can bubble just below the surface of sisterhood.

Most members of feminist organisations have some power but some have more power than others. In addition to the complex dynamics around social inequalities, power also accrues to those closest to the central networks of the organisation; those controlling information, decision making and 'reality setting'; those with expertise, knowledge, skills and experience; those with positions of leadership; and those seen as part of the tradition of the organisation. Where the overt recognition and use of power is taboo, it can be mis-used and abused, making it more difficult and frustrating to challenge.

> Trying to be the most powerless/innocent is a morality play whose only use is for personal redemption. It prevents making connections with others, first because it involves having to hide the often messy facts of our lives, and second because it usually involves making others guilty. Seeing power as inherently bad means having to deny and thus waste the power we have access to.
>
> (Kahaleole Chang Hall, 1993: 226)

In attempting to challenge structural power, feminist organisations may as a consequence encourage the denial of power. This seems a contradiction given that an aim of feminist organisations is to change women's relations to power in both individual and collective ways.

Why then does power between women in organisations become a problem? Feminist organisations do not exist outside the social, cultural and historical contexts of the society they are part of. To some extent, therefore, power inequalities and battles in society are brought into organisational life. Perhaps some women do feel an ambivalence about power which is then replicated in feminist theory and practice. For example, Naomi Wolf suggests that the feminist analysis which permanently places all women as victims of all-powerful men creates an ideology by which 'a woman seeks power through an identity of powerlessness' (Wolf, 1993: 147). This, she argues, has an important consequence for feminist organisations because it 'implies that real feminists must renounce power and pleasure in favour of the ideological requirements of a collective identity' (Wolf, 1993: 71).

Perhaps the experience of power between women in feminist organisations is not that different to the dynamics of power between people in any organisation or wherever there is inequality. The difficulty might arise because some dominant strands of feminist theory which have informed feminist practice assume the experience of power will be different in feminist organisations and thus women feel unprepared, hurt and disappointed when it isn't.

Concluding comments

One woman I interviewed for this chapter, who has many years experience with a number of feminist organisations, said she thought power took on such an emotive and fraught nature because feminist organisations become 'life, the universe and everything' for many of the women in them. The strength of some women's belief in the organisation and its values creates high stakes if they seem to rock the boat. Women have so much invested in the ideology of feminist organisations that rocking the organisational boat means rocking their personal boat as well.

In my experience, feminist organisations offer some alternative concepts of power to those prevailing in the mainstream of organisational theory and practice. These alternatives are, and have been, important in changing individual lives, social attitudes and the practice of other organisations. However, I believe we need much better ways of conceptualising and managing difference before power between women in organisations can be effectively discussed. Paradoxically, it sometimes seems that feminist organisations give an anti-power message which reinforces sexism, denies the responsible expression of power, prevents empowerment and creates a vacuum in which power can be abused. Surely feminists should be strengthening individual and collective responsibility for the positions of power we occupy and challenging those who use their power oppressively, rather than equating power itself with something bad.

In critiquing particular dominant strands of feminism in this chapter I have been reminded that feminism's difficulties with power and feminism's difficulties with identity and difference are interconnected. I believe there cannot be an effective discussion about power between women until there is a real acceptance of difference and self-determination of identity and lifestyle. My conclusion is that without an honest and positive engagement with the complexity of power and difference between women, there can be no real chance of coalitions, of solidarity and perhaps even of liberation.

> We must reclaim feminism as that which makes women stronger in ways which each woman is entitled to define for herself. Ironically, this 'letting go' of the rigorous litmus tests of feminism will not make us lose the power of consensus we already have, the common feminist fear; it will expand and enrich what we have and draw in millions more women.
>
> (Wolf, 1993: 143)

Endnote: Psychology's exclusions, feminist possibilities?

This book has covered a wide range of topics and issues. This final section is divided into two main sections. In the first part we return to some of the guiding themes of the book as a commentary on where its nine substantive chapters have brought us, as Challenging Women. In the second part, we discuss aspects of the process of developing and producing this book, and how we, whether wittingly or inadvertently, enacted some of the very exclusions and possibilities that form its topic. We write this Endnote, not to draw together or complete this book into a tidy finished whole. Such an enterprise would run counter to the set of philosophical positions we have been elaborating. Rather, our account here comments on the interventions mobilised by the stories told in individual chapters, and then – avoiding the conventional privileging and separation of content over process – analyses these interventions in relation to the contexts of the book's production.

I

Challenging subjects and objects

The title of this book, *Challenging Women*, addresses everyone as a subject of psychology, as a psychological and gendered subject brought into being through discourses and practices of modern western psychology. Its particular focus is on the impact of these practices on the representation and regulation of women's experiences, whether in medical (Chapter 4), psychiatric (Chapter 1) or legal arenas (Chapters 2 and 8). In this book we challenge how women are positioned by psychology's alleged expertise, and consider some of the consequences of the devaluation and marginalisation of women. While we offer criticisms of the production of 'woman' through the gaze of 'the psychological complex', we speak from inside psychology as well as reaching outside its domain. Using our experiences as students, researchers, teachers and practitioners, we offer a range of insider accounts that we hope will be useful for those theorists, practitioners and activists less involved in psychology, and therefore perhaps less confident about critiquing its knowledge base and effects.

Yet while we repudiate psychology's objectification of women's experiences, we have attempted to do this without reinstating an alternative homogenising narrative of 'what women are like'. The last section of this Endnote addresses our difficulties with maintaining this as a group of women writers. Here we can note that, while broadly feminist in orientation, and committed to furthering feminist debates, the chapters in this book put into question some of the central presuppositions of second wave feminism, and refuse to offer a stable, singular account of 'woman' or 'women'. In particular, the analysis of discourses of sexual abuse in Chapter 2 reverses the traditional ordering of gender and sexuality to take gender as instituted by practices of sexuality (in this case sexual abuse) rather than the basis for them. Chapter 5 explores the complex relations between race and gender both in research relationships and impact on the credibility accorded the study. The experiences and analyses presented in this book both testify to the diversity of, and to the conflicts between, women's positions and perspectives, and highlight the possibilities for alliance and coalition.

Using versus intervening in psychology

As a particular instance of the double nature of our positions as Challenging Women, various chapters address the dilemmas for feminists in either drawing upon or acting to counter psychology's prescriptions for women. While this is perhaps most clearly developed in Chapter 8 in relation to representations of lone parent and lesbian families, other chapters avoid absolute injunctions either to use or to refuse psychology. We have already suggested that such refusal would, in any case, be impossible owing to our saturation in psychological notions through contemporary cultural as well as technical practices.

However, beyond this, some women writing here speak as professionals operating from institutional contexts within psychology. These women would want to claim that, alongside the processes of compromise and collusion documented in Chapter 4, such positions remain an important site of intervention. In the latter, the process of recognising how her topic and explicit feminist identification became transformed in funding proposals made it possible to distinguish strategic involvement from mere recuperation. Such reflexive evaluation therefore does not obviate the importance of making interventions in services to provide a space for women to discuss their concerns about their bodies or gynaecological procedures. Similarly, Chapter 1 offers a critical perspective on psychological and psychiatric analyses of women's problems around food and also on feminist psychotherapeutic frameworks. Nevertheless, it still retains a place for feminist psychotherapeutic work. Chapter 9 calls for organisational psychology to inform understanding of the functioning of feminist organisations, as well as highlighting its male-oriented hierarchical presuppositions.

Theorising the silences

An analytical strategy informing this book is that of the value of identifying and commenting on those topics and processes that are commonly undisclosed or suppressed. We treat such silences as indicating something of the structure of institutional relations governing us. Perhaps the most graphic examples of this are Chapters 5 and 6 where experiences of racial and sexual harassment in research are discussed. The point here is not simply to give voice to those excluded experiences (though this is also of value), but also to consider how such exclusions function in maintaining the oppressive structure of psychology. While questions of racism and personal safety are far from specific to psychological research, these chapters explore how central unexamined presuppositions – about notions of empowerment arising from feminist critiques of research, and how 'no data' means 'no research' in positivist psychology – render them uncontestable. These accounts contribute to the growing body of feminist commentaries on research processes that take reflexive attention as a vital tool for challenging dominant notions of the production and definition of knowledge, and in particular whose definitions prevail.

Chapter 5 also articulates what has, until recently, been an area of silence within feminism and women's studies, that is questions of the racialisation of gender and the complexity of the positions and experiences of black women. The limits of theorising identities as separate and additive are painfully exemplified in this account, since all four positions (as black, woman, researcher, parent) were jointly mobilised in different ways within different moments and relations of this research project to frustrate it. Moreover, rather than treating the relations between 'race' and gender as rendered visible through the account written by a black woman, all the chapters have considered the racialisation of the positions from which they are written, thus attempting to address the significance of (the varieties) of whiteness, alongside other relations of difference and power, in our group process and product.

Beyond these, this book provides other instances of theorising silenced experiences. Chapter 3 revisits (and subverts) undergraduate experiences of studying psychology and being subjected to racist and misogynist theories and exploitative (and bizarre) research procedures. The study of feminist organisations discussed in Chapter 9 occasioned a long and unforseen struggle over the legitimacy of qualitative methods in gaining a higher degree. Perhaps this explains why there is so little work conducted from within psychology on this topic. As already indicated, Chapters 1 and 4 highlight something of the structure of professionalisation which feminists both have investments in and struggle to resist. Finally, Chapter 7 takes up questions of the institutionalisation of gender and divisions between women by addressing the disempowering effects of professional caring for both the women professionals, and the mothers and children they avowedly support.

Undisciplined resources

As Challenging Women we have aimed to comment on specific intersections between feminist debate and psychological practice. However, in line with our efforts to avoid closed and essentialised understandings of gender, we maintain a robust suspicion of the Psychology of Women and feminist psychology. This is not to say that we (or some of us at least) would not count ourselves feminist psychologists. Rather, we wish to ward off institutional efforts to contain feminist critiques within particular labelled arenas, and to maintain a vigilance over the dynamic of investment and recuperation that we, inevitably (and the more so for publishing this book), get caught up in. More than this, the category of feminism has itself been put in question, both theoretically in terms of the topics of chapters, and practically in our identifications and interpretations. So the chapters in this book in different ways challenge dominant psychological frameworks and perspectives, and invite feminists to take up an equivalent set of questions. While we do not offer alternatives to the psychological and feminist theories that form the focus for our critiques, we do offer some possible strategies for intervention. Chapters 2 and 8 perhaps most clearly voice the call for partial and strategic alliances and organisations to disrupt current legal-technical hegemonies that psychology partakes of and to which it contributes. But at a more affective – though no less politicised – level Chapter 3 treats humour as a means to shrug off and resist some of psychology's pernicious and offensive practices.

If we do not locate ourselves theoretically within psychology, we would not position ourselves anywhere else either. Rather we draw on a range of current theory and practical political experiences to inform the perspectives presented in this book. While, individually, some of us incline towards particular theoretical perspectives, these are not uncritical dogmas but are deployed and evaluated according to their usefulness in disturbing the current psychological ordering of women. The theoretical resources we draw on here include: poststructuralist ideas, psychoanalysis (Chapters 3 and 7), organisational theory (Chapter 9) and feminist psychotherapy (Chapter 1). Apart from these relatively discrete arenas of theory, the chapters are all informed by, and by our discussions of, black feminist critiques and queer theory. These last, perhaps by virtue of the histories of exclusion and struggle that they highlight, have proved very helpful in challenging orthodoxies around both psychology and feminism.

Writing as a political strategy

This book is a collection of accounts of individually written chapters, developed and discussed through a group process. We present them as a record of our engagement with critiques of psychology, and as such to express our particular contribution to, and commitment to, a strengthened feminist practice which addresses all women's positions. That is, a practice that not only acknowledges its own classed, raced and heterosexist histories, but that in knowing this, reconfigures a feminist politics so that differences between women are not merely a matter for toleration but are understood as power relations demanding redress. Much of the rationale for this book arises from our resolve to make public our dissent, to create a forum for our criticisms – of feminism as well as psychology. Central to this is an assumption that publicising such accounts may speak to the experiences of others, and more than this, can function as a means of joint and individual reflection on our work around feminist and psychological arenas. It is relevant to note that for some of the women writing this book this was a first opportunity to record their experiences, and for the rest of us, new perspectives emerged both in our writing process and during our discussions. As stated in the Introduction, a jointly written book of this kind is profoundly challenging to notions of single, separate authorship, and therefore by definition is subversive of the rational, unitary, masculine subject of psychology. It has also exercised, and thus displayed, dominant criteria used by publishers.

As such, with its publication this book can already claim a history of challenge. However, we would not wish to treat writing or academic intervention as a privileged or sole arena for intervention. The chapters in this book all address areas of practice, of institutional locations where psychological knowledges and gendered assumptions combine in powerful ways. While we offer analytical perspectives on these intersections here, our political practice neither arises from, nor stops at, the academy. Your reading of this does not stop here either.

II

In this section, we want to document and reflect on both the processes of co-authoring and the themes which have arisen in writing. Although this book is co-authored, motivation to work on the project and to write for publication did not come just from our commitment to feminist theories. Nor did it simply spring from a collective interest in the subject of psychology – indeed, one of us has never studied the subject. Neither was it solely motivated by our academic interests. For some of us, it's been a way of ending our ambivalent relationships with psychology and moving on to other disciplines or institutions. For some of us, it's been a process of exploring what inclusions different kinds of feminisms and psychologies could take on board; that is, we want to continue to work with the debates, within the institutions. One aim of the book was to have an academic text that included writings from women who might not get published; that is women who may be marginalised for reasons made explicit in the different chapters. This project also brought us together in order to learn from each other through, rather than despite, our differences. While the introduction and the book itself obviously illustrates some of these differences, there were other differences which emerged in relation to co-authoring which we felt were useful to highlight both in the context of women working together and in the context of the subject matter of our text.

In calling this book *Challenging women: Psychology's exclusions, feminist possibilities,* we hope that both the title and the contents provoke readers to question not only the issues we have raised, but also the ideas we generate. In choosing to write as co-authors, we too have been provoked and challenged by issues: perhaps first and foremost by our particular topics, but also by each other and by participating in the process of working together. Discussions about the book as a whole highlighted three major themes: our use of 'I' and 'we', reproducing debates as opposed to subverting them, and being both inside and outside psychology *and* feminism. Discussions also led us to think reflexively about the course of our project and how much we were subject as a group, to challenge, exclusion and possibility.

Our varied use of 'I' and 'we' have been made clear throughout the book, in the context of not just the subject 'woman', but also in relation to particular topics. We spoke to our audiences in varied ways, just as our chapters sometimes 'spoke to us'. We questioned the unity of orthodoxy in relation to woman, psychology and feminism. However, in terms of writing, we came together as different women. Operating as both 'I' and 'we' have meant challenge, exclusion and possibility within the group as a whole. As individuals, we took responsibility for producing and contributing, for revising and finishing. Nevertheless, these stages involved collaborating with others. Mostly, this meant sending our work to others for feedback and meeting in subgroups as well as the whole group, to discuss its progress. This inevitably involved a process in which each of us also related to an imaginary group of others who might respond in ways we hoped or feared. This imaginary group was with us as we worked alone and in the group. Meetings with the group did challenge each of us in various ways and on different levels, leading us to feel both – at different times – included and excluded, with possibilities both opened up and closed down.

We've posited feminist theories as challenges to psychology, by drawing on critiques of the ungendered nature of the discipline and how attending to gender highlights the limitations of psychology. We also discussed within the group how the various commitments we had as women might affect our ability to produce chapters; for instance, how hard it might be as women, to write or to go public. However, it wasn't until the final meeting that we fully realised the gendered process of our writing. Our understandings of 'caring' influenced the way we dealt with each other's difficulties. Some of us were able to trust individual others with our emotional vulnerabilities in terms of the project, while at other times we critiqued from an academic or stylistic point of view. We have reproduced feminism's 'tyranny of structurelessness' in that we didn't formally chair meetings. Thus, by the end of the writing process we became aware how some marginalised voices within the group had not been heard. In understanding this, we have had to remind ourselves of differing theories of feminism and feminisms. For instance, it was sometimes easier to focus on the critical audience 'out there' than it was to focus on how we colluded in silencing and being silenced within the group and also in writing; that is how, as women, we scrutinise each other as well as ourselves. Our multiple, fluctuating positions in relation to feminism, psychology, our special interests, and each other, have been active in this work. Sometimes this has made it very difficult to pin down or locate ourselves in terms of our topics, sometimes it has added to the richness of our writing as we learn from each other, sometimes it has complicated what we think as we learn more and are exposed to more in-depth analyses.

Although we challenge the orthodoxy of psychology, we have structured the book in a way that reflects our subscription to some of psychology's disciplines. For example, the three sections of this book, despite our efforts, could still be read as reflecting traditional false separations of the academic tradition. Still, in this final section we have resisted the temptation to conclude. Instead, we call for more discussion, more speculation. Thus, though we wish to highlight psychology's exclusions, we are both included within and including of psychology – literally and politically. We replicated the hierarchy of academia within the group; for some of us who had never written anything other than essays, the 'masters' (*sic*) and 'doctors' were seen as more powerful. We have had to struggle not to replicate psychology's tendency to polarise differences, as good and bad, better or worse. So, our different starting points in terms of academic achievements has meant that we have both contributed, and drawn on, various strengths.

While our project is unique, in that working together has meant we have generated particular constellations of ideas, it would be false to say that these ideas 'belong' to us. We have drawn on a multiplicity of ideas from feminists, psychologists, philosophers, sociologists, writers of literature and others. While we can claim 'expertise' in some areas, we are always constructing our understandings with communal building blocks – and now we want to share what we have built, with others. We see feminism as plural, as feminisms that have stable enough foundations to deal with difference, conflict and challenge. This means that collective projects such as ours can offer a variety of feminist critiques, each of which has something to contribute to the project of women, rather than woman. But in this instance, we are not saying, 'different but equal', as we do have a commitment to poststructuralist critiques of both feminisms and psychologies. While we argue that 'the personal is political', we also deconstruct the personal as opposed to seeing it as an overarching concept that embraces all women. Moreover, the 'personal' can be both left and right of the political spectrum, and so we have tried to grapple with how we as women, in differing ways, reproduce the very debates in which we want to intervene. This means intervening by positioning ourselves within and out of current feminist debates. So, as challenging women, we operate as both adjective and verb.

References

Acker, J. (1991) Hierarchies, jobs, bodies: a theory of gendered organisations, in J. Lorber and S. A. Farrell (eds) *The Social Organisation of Gender*. London: Sage, in cooperation with Sociology for Women Society.

Afshar, H. and Maynard, M. (eds) (1994) *The Dynamics of Race and Gender*. London: Taylor and Francis.

Ahmed, I. U. W. and Sheldon, T. A. (1991) Race and statistics, *Radical Statistics*, 48 (spring): 27–33.

Alderson, L. (1988) Clause 29: radical feminist perspectives, *Trouble and Strife*, 13: 3–9.

Alper, J. S. (1985) Sex differences in brain asymmetry: a critical analysis, *Feminist Studies*, 11 (1) (spring): 7–37.

American Psychiatric Association (1987) *Diagnostic and Statistical Manual of Mental Disorders*, 3rd edn. Washington DC: American Psychiatric Association.

Angelou, M. (1984) *I Know Why the Caged Bird Sings*. London: Virago.

Anthias, F. and Yuval-Davis, N. (1992) *Racialised Boundaries*. London: Routledge.

Araji, S. and Finkelhor, D. (1986) Abusers: a review of the research, in D. Finkelhor, S. Araji, L. Baron, A. Brown, S. Doyle Peters and G. E. Wyatt, *A Sourcebook on Child Sexual Abuse*. London: Sage.

Areskog-Wijma, B. (1987) The gynaecological examination: women's experiences and preferences and the role of the gynaecologist, *Journal of Psychosomatic Obstetrics and Gynaecology*, 6: 59–69.

Aziz, R. (1992) Feminism and the challenge of racism: deviance or difference?, in H. Crowley and S. Himmelweit (eds) *Knowing Women: Feminism and Knowledge*. Cambridge: Polity Press.

Baker Miller, J. (1976) *Toward a Theory of Women's Psychological Development*. Harmondsworth: Penguin.

Banister, P., Burman, E., Parker, I., Taylor, M. and Tindall, C. (1994) *Qualitative Methods in Psychology: A Research Guide*. Milton Keynes: Open University Press.

Banton, R., Clifford, P., Frosh, S., Lousada, J. and Rosenthall, J. (1985) *The Politics of Mental Health*. London: Macmillan.

Barlow, D. and McPherson, A. (1988) Menstrual problems, in A. McPherson (ed.) *Women's Problems in General Practice*. Oxford: Oxford University Press.

Bartky, S. Lee (1988) Foucault, femininity, and the modernization of patriarchal power, in I. Diamond and L. Quinby (eds) *Feminism and Foucault: Reflections on Resistance*. Boston, MA: Northeastern University Press.

Bell, V. (1993) *Interrogating Incest: Feminism, Foucault and the Law*. London: Routledge.

Bennathon, M. (1989) Multiprofessional work, *Maladjustment and Therapeutic Education*, 6 (2): 82–92.

Bentovim, A. (1987) Physical and sexual abuse of children: the role of the family therapist, *Journal of Family Therapy*, 9 (4): 383–8.

Bewley, C. (1992) 'Creating a space: for a feminist discussion of psychological theory and research into women's organisations in the voluntary sector and a case study of three such organisations', unpublished thesis. University of Sheffield.

Bhavnani, K. K. (1988) Empowerment and social research: some comments, *Text: an Interdisciplinary Journal for the Study of Discourse. Special Issue Discourse, Racism and Ideology*, 8 (1–2): 41–50.

Bhavnani, K. K. (1993) Tracing the contours: feminist research and feminist objectivity, *Women's Studies International Forum*, 16 (2): 95–104.

Bhavnani, K. K. and Phoenix, A. (eds) (1994) *Shifting Identities, Shifting Racisms*. London: Sage.

Billig, M. (1982) *Ideology and Social Psychology*. Oxford: Basil Blackwell.

Billington, T. (in press) Pathologising children: psychology in education and acts of government, in E. Burman (ed.) *Psychology, Discourse and Social Practice: From Regulation to Resistance*. London: Taylor and Francis.

Birke, L. and Best, S. (1980) The tyrannical womb: menstruation and menopause, in Brighton Women and Science Group, *Alice Through the Microscope: The Power of Science Over Women's Lives*. London: Virago.

Bleier, R. (1986) Lab coat: robe of innocence or klansman's sheet? in T. de Lauretis (ed.) *Feminist Studies/Critical Studies*. London: Macmillan Press.

Bleier, R. (1988) Sex differences research: science or belief?, in R. Bleier (ed.) *Feminist Approaches to Science*. Oxford: Pergamon Press.

Bordo, S. (1988) Anorexia nervosa: psychopathology as the crystallization of culture, in I. Diamond and L. Quinby (eds) *Feminism and Foucault: Reflections on Resistance*. Boston, MA: Northeastern University Press.

Bordo, S. (1993) Feminism, Foucault and the politics of the body, in C. Ramazanoglu (ed.) *Up Against Foucault: Explorations of Some Tensions Between Foucault and Feminism*. London: Routledge.

Boskind-White, M. and White, W. C. Jr (1987) *Bulimarexia – The Binge/Purge Cycle*, 2nd edn. New York: W. W. Norton and Co.

Bovey, S. (1989) *Being Fat is Not a Sin*. London: Pandora.

Bozett, F. W. (1987) Children of gay fathers, in F. W. Bozett (ed.) *Gay and Lesbian Parents*. New York: Praeger.

Brah, A. (1992) Difference, diversity and differentiation, in J. Donald and A. Rattansi (eds) *Race, Culture and Difference*. London: Sage.

Bray, G. A. (1976) The obese patient, in L. H. Smith Jr (ed.) *Major Problems in Internal Medicine*, vol. 10. Philadelphia, PA: W. B. Saunders Co.

Breakwell, G. M. (1995) Interviewing, in G. M. Breakwell, S. Hammond and C. Fife-Schaw (eds) *Research Methods in Psychology*. London: Sage.

Brennan, T. (ed.) (1989) *Between Feminism and Psychoanalysis*. London, Routledge.

British Psychological Society Scientific Affairs Board (1988) The future of the psychological sciences, Report of the Working Party from the Harrogate Conference. Leicester: British Psychological Society.

British Psychological Society Scientific Affairs Board (1994) Report of the Working Party on Psychology of Women Courses. Leicester: British Psychological Society.

Broughton, J. (1988) The masculine authority of the cognitive, in B. Inhelder (ed.) *Piaget Today*. London: Erlbaum.

Broverman, I., Broverman, D., Clarkson, F., Rosenkranz, P. and Vogel, S. (1970) Sex role stereotypes and clinical judgements of mental health, *Journal of Consulting and Clinical Psychology*, 34: 1–7.

Brown, L. S. (1989) Fat-oppressive attitudes and the feminist therapist: directions for change, in *Women and Therapy: A Feminist Quarterly, Special Issue*, 8 (3): 19–30.

Brownmiller, S. (1975) *Against Our Will: Men, Women and Rape*. London: Secker and Warburg.

Bruch, H. (1957) *The Importance of Obesity*. New York: W. W. Norton.

Bruch, H. (1974) *Eating Disorders: Obesity, Anorexia Nervosa and the Person Within*. London: Routledge and Kegan Paul.

Bruch, H. (1978) *The Golden Cage: The Enigma of Anorexia Nervosa*. London: Open Books.

Burman, E. (ed.) (1990) *Feminists and Psychological Practice*. London: Sage.

Burman, E. (1991) Power, gender and developmental psychology, *Feminism and Psychology*, 1 (1): 141–55.

Burman, E. (1992a) Identification and power in feminist psychotherapy: a reflexive history of a discourse analysis, *Women's Studies International Forum*, 14 (4): 487–98.

Burman, E. (1992b) Feminism and discourse in developmental psychology: psychology, power and subjectivity, *Feminism and Psychology*, 2 (1): 45–59.

Burman, E. (1994a) Identities, experiences and alliances: Jewish feminism and feminist psychology, *Feminism and Psychology*, 4 (1): 155–78.

Burman, E. (1994b) Innocents abroad: intrapsychic investments and political limits of child imagery, special issue of *Disasters: The Journal of Disaster Studies and Management*, 18 (3): 238–53.

Burman, E. (1994c) Poor children: charity appeals and ideologies of childhood, *Changes: International Journal of Psychology and Psychotherapy*, 12 (1): 29–36.

Burman, E. (1995) What is it? Masculinity and femininity in the cultural representation of childhood, in C. Kitzinger and S. Wilkinson (eds) *Feminism and Discourse*. London: Sage.

Burman, E. and Parker, I. (eds) (1993) *Discourse Analytic Research*. London: Routledge.

Burns, J. and Wilkinson, S. (1990) Women organising in psychology, in E. Burman (ed.) *Feminists and Psychological Practice*. London: Sage.

Burstow, B. (1992) Troubled eating, in B. Burstow, *Radical Feminist Therapy*. New York: Sage.

Butler, J. (1990a) *Gender trouble: feminism and the subversion of identity*. London: Routledge.

Butler, J. (1990b) Gender trouble, feminist theory and psychoanalytic discourse, in L. Nicholson (ed.) *Feminism and Postmodernism*. London: Routledge.

Butler, J. (1993) *Bodies That Matter*. London: Routledge.

Byrne, P. (1984) Psychiatric morbidity in a gynaecology clinic: an epidemiological survey, *British Journal of Psychiatry*, 144: 28–43.

Califa, P. (1988) *Macho Sluts*. Boston, MA: Alyson Publications.

Campbell, B. (1993) *Goliath: Britain's Dangerous Places*. London: Methuen.

Carby, H. (1987) Black feminism and the boundaries of sisterhood, in M. Arnot and G. Weiner (eds) *Gender and the Politics of Schooling*. London: Hutchinson.

CCCS (Centre for Contemporary Cultural Studies) (1982) *The Empire Strikes Back: Race and Racism in 70s Britain*. London: Hutchinson.

Carol, A. (1993) Porn, perversion and sexual ethics, in V. Harwood, D. Oswell, K. Parkinson and A. Ward (eds) *Pleasure Principles: Politics, Sexuality and Ethics*. London: Lawrence and Wishart.

Carrigan, T., Connell, B. and Lee, J. (1987) The 'sex role' framework and the sociology of masculinity, in G. Weiner and M. Arnot (eds) *Gender Under Scrutiny*. London: Hutchinson.

Carter, B. and Williams, J. (1987) Attacking racism in education, in B. Troyna (ed.) *Racial Inequality in Education*. London: Tavistock Publications.

charles, H. (1992) Whiteness – the relevance of politically colouring the 'non', in H. Hinds, A. Phoenix, and J. Stacey (eds) *Working Out: New Directions in Women's Studies*. London: Falmer Press.

Chase, A. (1975) *The Legacy of Malthus: The Social Costs of the New Scientific Racism*. New York: Alfred A. Knopf.

Chernin, K. (1981) *Womansize: The Tyranny of Slenderness*. London: Virago Press.

Chernin, K. (1985) *The Hungry Self: Women, Eating and Identity*. London: Virago Press.

Chodorow, N. (1978) *The Reproduction of Mothering: Psychoanalysis and the Sociology of Gender*. Berkeley, CA: The University of California Press.

Chodorow, N. (1989) *Feminism and Psychoanalytic Theory*. New Haven, CT: Yale University Press.

Choi, P. and Nicolson, P. (1994) *Female Sexuality: Psychology, Biology and Social Context*. Hemel Hempstead: Harvester Wheatsheaf.

Coleman, G. (1991) *Investigating Organisations: A Feminist Approach*. Bristol: SAUS (School for Advanced Urban Studies), University of Bristol.

Collins, P. Hill (1990) *Black Feminist Thought: Knowledge, Consciousness, and the Politics of Empowerment, vol.* 2. Cambridge, MA: Unwin Hyman.

Collins, P. Hill (1992) Black women and motherhood, in B. Thorne and M. Yalom (eds) *Rethinking the Family: Some Feminist Questions*. Boston, MA: Northeastern University Press.

Cooper, D. (1994) *Sexing the City: Lesbian and Gay Politics Within the Activist State*. London: Rivers Oram Press.

Cornwell, N. (1989) Who directs power in talking to clients? *Social Work Today*, 28 September.

Coulter, A., Bradlow, J., Agass, M., Martin-Bates, C. and Tulloch, A. (1991) Outcomes of referrals to gynaecology outpatient clinics for menstrual problems: an audit of general practice records, *British Journal of Obstetrics and Gynaecology*, 98: 789–96.

Coulter, A., Peto, V. and Doll, H. (1994) Patients' preferences and general practitioners' decisions in the treatment of menstrual disorders, *Family Practice*, 11: 67–74.

Coward, R. (1984) *Female Desire: Women's Sexuality Today*. London: Paladin Books.

Cowie, E. (1978) Women as Sign, *M/F*, 1: 42–50.

Creed, B. (1987) Horror and the monstrous-feminine: an imaginary abjection, *Screen*, 27 (1): 63–89.

Creed, B. (1993) *The Monstrous Feminine: Film, Feminism, Psychoanalysis*. London: Routledge.

Crisp, A. H. (1980) *Anorexia Nervosa: Let Me Be*. London: Academic Press.

Dalley, G. (1988) *Ideologies of Caring: Rethinking Community and Collectivism*. London: Macmillan Educational.

Dally, P. (1969) *Anorexia Nervosa*. London: William Heinemann Medical Books.

Dally, P. and Gomez, J. (1979) *Anorexia Nervosa*. London: William Heinemann Medical Books.

Dana, M. and Lawrence, M. (1988) *Women's Secret Disorder: A New Understanding of Bulimia*. London: Grafton Books.

Danica, E. (1989) *Don't: A Woman's Word*. London: Women's Press.

David, M. E. (1989) Education, in M. McCarthy (eds) *The New Politics of Welfare: An Agenda for the 1990s?* Basingstoke: Macmillan.

Davies, C. (1992) Gender, history and management style in nursing: towards a theoretical synthesis, in M. Savage and A. Witz (eds) *Gender and Bureaucracy*. Oxford: Blackwell.

Davis, A. Y. (1990) *Women, Culture, Politics*. London: Women's Press.

Davis, K. (1993) The crafting of good clients, in J. Swain, V. Finkelstein, S. French and M. Oliver (eds) (1993) *Disabling Barriers – Enabling Environments*. London: Sage.

Deem, B., Brehoney, J. K. and Hemmings, S. (1992) Social justice, social divisions and the governing of schools, in D. Gill, B. Mayor and M. Blair (eds) *Racism and Education, Structures and Strategies*. London: Sage.

Dinnerstein, D. (1976) *The Rocking of the Cradle and the Ruling of the World*. London: Women's Press.

Dolan, B. (1991) Cross-cultural aspects of anorexia nervosa and bulimia: a review, *International Journal of Eating Disorders*, 10 (1): 67–78.

Dolan, B. and Gitzinger, I. (1991) *Why Women? Gender Issues and Eating Disorders*. London: European Council on Eating Disorders.

Domar, A. D. (1986) Psychological aspects of the pelvic exam: individual needs and physician involvement, *Women and Health*, 10: 75–90.

Donovan, C. (1992) Keeping it in the Family: An Analysis of Doctors' Decision-making about Access in the Provision of Donor Insemination, unpublished PhD thesis. Edinburgh University.

Dorn, A. and Hibbert, P. (1987) A comedy of errors: Section 11 funding and education, in B. Troyna (ed.) *Racial Inequality in Education*. London: Tavistock.

Draijer, N. (1989) Long-term psychosomatic consequences of child sexual abuse, in E. V. van Hall and W. Everaerd (eds) *The Free Woman: Women's Health in the 1990s*. London: Parthenon Publishing Group.

Dwyer, T. (1991) Humor, power and change in organisations, *Human Relations*, 44 (1): 1–19.

Edwards, R. (1990) Connecting method and epistemology: a white woman interviewing black women, *Women's Studies International Forum*, 13 (5): 477–90.

Ehrenreich, B. and English, D. (1979) *For Her Own Good: 150 Years of Experts' Advice to Women*. London: Pluto Press.

Eichenbaum, L. and Orbach, S. (1982) *Outside In, Inside Out*. Harmondsworth: Penguin.

Eichenbaum, L. and Orbach, S. (1983) *What Do Women Want?* London: Fontana.

Ernst, S. (1989) Gender and the phantasy of omnipotence: case study of an organisation, in B. Richards (ed.) *Crises of the Self and Further Essays on Psychoanalysis and Politics*. London: Free Association Books.

Ernst, S. and Maguire, S. (eds) (1987) *Living With the Sphinx: Papers From the Women's Therapy Centre*. London: Women's Press.

Evans, M. (1990) The problem of gender for women's studies, *Women's Studies International Forum*, 13 (5): 457–63.

Evans, M. (1994) *The Woman Question*. London: Sage.

Faderman, L. (1985) *Surpassing the Love of Men: Romantic Friendship and Love Between Women from the Renaissance to the Present*. London: Women's Press.

Fairburn, C. and Cooper, P. (1989) Eating disorders, in K. Horton, P. Salkovskis, J. Kirk and David M. Clark (eds) *Cognitive Behavioural Therapy for Psychiatric Problems*. Oxford: Oxford Medical Publications.

Falludi, S. (1992) *Backlash*. London: Vintage.

Featherstone, M. (1991) The body in consumer culture, in M. Featherstone, M. Hepworth and B. S. Turner (eds) *The Body: Social Process and Cultural Theory*. London: Sage.

Fichter, M. (ed.) (1990) *Bulimia Nervosa: Basic Research, Diagnosis and Therapy*. Chichester: John Wiley.

Finkelhor, D. (1990) Early and long-term effects of child sexual abuse, *Professional Psychology: Research and Practice*, 21 (5): 325–30.

Flax, J. (1990) *Thinking Fragments: Psychoanalysis, Feminism, and Postmodernism in the Contemporary West*. Berkeley, CA: University of California Press.

Ford, J., Mongon, D. and Whelan, M. (1982) *Special Education and Social Control: Invisible Disasters*. London: Routledge and Kegan Paul.

Foucault, M. (1976) *The History of Sexuality: Volume 1: An Introduction*. Harmondsworth: Penguin.

Foucault, M. (1977) *Discipline and Punish: The Birth of the Prison*. London: Penguin.

Foucault, M. (1979) On governmentality, *I & C*, 6: 5–22.

Frankenberg, R. (1993) *White Women, Race Matters*. London: Routledge.

Freeman, J. (1970) *The Tyranny of Structurelessness*. USA: Women's Liberation Movement.

Freud, S. (1905/1976) *Jokes and their Relation to the Unconscious*. London: Pelican.

Freud, S. (1905/1977) *On Sexuality: Three Essays on Sexuality and Other Works*. London: Penguin Books.

Frude, N. (1989) Sexual abuse: an overview, *Educational and Child Psychology*, 6 (1): 34–41.

Frude, N. (1992) The sexual nature of sexual abuse: a review of the literature, *Child Abuse and Neglect*, 6: 221–3.

Gagnier, R. (1988) Between women: a cross-class analysis of status and anarchic humor, in R. Barreca (ed.) *Last Laughs*. London: Gordon and Breach.

Gardner, R. A. (1992) *Parental Alienation Syndrome*. Cresskill, NJ: Creative Therapeutics.

Garner, D. M. and Garfinkel, P. E. (eds) (1985) *Handbook of Psychotherapy for Anorexia Nervosa and Bulimia*. New York: Guilford Press.

Gibson, D. (1987) Hearing and listening: a case study of the 'consultation' process undertaken by a local education department and black groups, in B. Troyna (ed.) *Racial Inequality in Education*. London: Tavistock.

Gilligan, C. (1982) *In a Different Voice: Psychological Theory and Women's Development*. Cambridge, MA: Harvard University Press.

Golby, M. and Brigley, S. (with the Exeter Society for Curriculum Studies Research Group) (1989) *Parents as School Governors*. Tavistock: Fairway Publications.

Goldberg, B. (in press) Come to the Carnival: women's humour as transgression and resistance, in E. Burman (ed.) *Psychology, Discourse and Social Practice: From Regulation to Resistance*. London: Taylor and Francis.

Golding, S. (1993) Sexual manners, in V. Harwood, D. Oswell, K. Parkinson and A. Ward (eds) *Pleasure Principles: Politics, Sexuality and Ethics*. London: Lawrence and Wishhart.

Goldner, V., Penn, P., Sheinberg, M. and Walker, G. (1990) Love and violence: gender paradoxes in volatile attachments, *Family Process*, 29 (4): 343–64.

Golombok, S., Spencer, A. and Rutter, M. (1983) Children in lesbian and single-parent households: psychosexual and psychiatric appraisal, *Journal of Child Psychology and Psychiatry*, 24: 551–72.

Green, R. (1978) Sexual identity of 37 children raised by homosexual and transsexual parents, *American Journal of Psychiatry*, 135 (6): 493–502.

Greenberg, M. (1983) The meaning of menorrhagia: an investigation into the association between the complaint of menorrhagia and depression, *Journal of Psychosomatic Research*, 27: 209–14.

Griffin, C., Henwood, K. and Phoenix, A. (eds) (in press) *Standpoints and Differences: Essays in the Practice of Feminist Psychology*. London: Sage.

Grosz, E. (1992) What is feminist theory?, in H. Cowley and S. Himmelweit (eds) *Knowing Women: Feminism and Knowledge*. Oxford: Polity/Blackwell.

Hall, E. I. (1991) *The Moon and the Virgin: A Voyage Towards Self-Discovery and Healing*. London: Women's Press.

Hall, S., Critcher, C., Jefferson, T., Clarke, J. and Roberts, B. (1978) *Policing the Crisis: Mugging, the State and Law and Order*. London: Macmillan Press.

Hallam, J. and Marshall, A. (1993) Layers of difference: the significance of a self-reflexive research practice for a feminist epistomological project, in M. Kennedy, C. Lubelska and V. Walsh (eds) *Making Connections: Women's Studies, Women's Movements, Women's Lives*. London: Taylor and Francis.

Hamburg, P. (1989) Bulimia: the construction of a symptom, *Journal of the American Academy of Psychoanalysis*, 17 (1): 131–40.

Hanko, G. (1991) Breaking down professional barriers – the 1990 David Wills lecture, *Maladjustment and Therapeutic Education*, 9 (1) (spring): 3–15.

Harasym, S. (ed.) (1990) *The Post-Colonial Critic*. London: Routledge.

Haraway, D. (1991) *Simians, Cyborgs and Women*. London: Verso.

Harding, S. (ed.) (1986) *Feminism and Methodology*. Milton Keynes: Open University Press.

Harwood, V., Oswell, D., Parkinson, K. and Ward, A. (1993) *Pleasure Principles: Politics, Sexuality and Ethics*. London: Lawrence and Wishart.

Hatcher, R. (1987) Race and education: two perspectives for change, in B. Troyna (ed.) *Racial Inequality in Education*. London: Tavistock.

Haug, F. (1992) *Beyond Female Masochism, Memory Work and Politics*. London: Verso.

Heenan, M. C. (1983) Discuss the sociological factors underlying eating disorders amongst women and the validity of conventional medical approaches, unpublished undergraduate dissertation. University of Leeds.

Heenan, M. C. (1995) Feminist psychotherapy – a contradiction in terms?, *Feminism and Psychology*, 5 (1): 112–17.

Hekman, S. J. (1990) *Gender and Knowledge: Elements of a Postmodern Feminism*. Cambridge: Polity Press.

Henriques, J., Hollway, W., Urwin, C., Venn, C. and Walkerdine, V. (1984) *Changing the Subject: Psychology, Social Regulation and Subjectivity*. London: Methuen.

Henwood, K. and Pidgeon, N. (1995) Remaking the link: qualitative research and feminist standpoint theory, *Feminism and Psychology*, 5 (1): 7–30.

Hesse-Biber, S. (1991) Women, weight and eating disorders – a socio-cultural and political-economic analysis, *Women's Studies International Forum*, 14 (3): 173–91.

Hollway, W. (1989) *Subjectivity and Method in Psychology*. London: Sage.

Holmes, J. (1993) *John Bowlby and Attachment Theory*. London: Routledge.

hooks, bell (1991) *Yearning: Race, Gender and Cultural Politics*. London: Turnaround.

Hsu, L. K. George (1989) The gender gap in eating disorders: why are the eating disorders more common among women?, *Clinical Psychology Review*, 9: 393–407.

Hubbard, R. (1982) Have only men evolved?, in R. Hubbard, M. S. Henifin and B. Fried (eds) *Biological Woman – The Convenient Myth*. Rochester, VT: Schenkman.

Hufnagel, V. (1990) *No More Hysterectomies*. London: Thorsons.

Iles, S. and Gath, D. (1989) Psychological problems and uterine bleeding, in J. O. Drife (ed.) *Dysfunctional Uterine Bleeding and Menorrhagia*. Bailliere's Clinical Obstetrics and Gynaecology, Bailliere Tindall.

Jackson, C. (1985) Fast food feminism, *Trouble and Strife*, 7 (winter): 39–44.

James, A. and Jenks, C. (1994) Public perceptions of childhood criminality, *Childhood and Criminality Seminar, ESRC Seminar Series – Childhood and Society*. Keele University, 15 April.

James, A. and Prout, A. (1990) *Constructing and Reconstructing Childhood*. London: Falmer Press.

James, K. and MacKinnon, L. (1990) The 'incestuous family' revisited: a critical analysis of family therapy myths, *Journal of Marital and Family Therapy*, 16 (1): 71–88.

Jeffreys, S. (1994) *The Lesbian Heresy: A Feminist Perspective on the Lesbian Sexual Revolution*. London: Women's Press.

Jehu, D. (1988) *Beyond Sexual Abuse: Therapy with Women who were Childhood Victims*. Chichester: John Wiley.

Johnson, D. (1990) *Parental Choice in Education*. London: Unwin Hyman.

Kahaleole Chang Hall, L. (1993) Bitches in solitude: identity politics and lesbian community, in A. Stein (ed.) *Sisters, Sexperts, Queers: Beyond the Lesbian Nation*. Harmondsworth: Plume.

Kaplan, E. A. (1992) *Motherhood and Representation: The Mother in Popular Culture and Melodrama*. London: Routledge.

Kempe, R. and Kempe, C. H. (1984) *The Common Secret: Sexual Abuse of Children and Adolescents*. New York: W. H. Freeman.

Kendall-Tackett, K. A., Meyer Williams, L. and Finkelhor, D. (1993) Impact of sexual abuse on children: a review and synthesis of recent empirical studies, *Psychological Bulletin*, 113 (1): 164–80.

Kennedy, M., Lubelska, C. and Walsh, V. (eds) (1993) *Making Connections: Women's Studies, Women's Movements, Women's Lives*. London: Taylor and Francis.

Kimball, M. M. (1981) Women and science: a critique of biological theories, *International Journal of Women's Studies*, 4: 318–38.

Kitzinger, C. (1987) *The Social Construction of Lesbianism*. London: Sage.

Kitzinger, C. and Wilkinson, S. (eds) (1992) *Heterosexuality: A Feminism and Psychology Reader*. London: Sage.

Kitzinger, C. and Wilkinson, S. (eds) (1995) *Feminism and Discourse*. London: Sage.

Kitzinger, C., Wilkinson, S. and Perkins, R. (1992) Theorizing heterosexuality, *Feminism and Psychology*, 2 (3): 293–324.

Kitzinger, J. (1992) Sexual violence and compulsory heterosexuality, *Feminism and Psychology*, 2 (3): 399–418.

Kremer, M. (1990) On saying no: keeping feminism for ourselves, *Women's Studies International Forum*, 13 (5): 463–8.

Kristeva, J. (1981) Women's time, *Signs*, 7 (1): 13–35.

Lachowsky, M. (1989) Gynecological practice as a violence or . . . What are we doing to our patients? in E. V. van Hall and W. Everaerd (eds) *The Free Woman: Women's Health in the 1990s*. London: Parthenon Publishing Group.

Lawrence, M. (1984) *The Anorexic Experience*. London: Women's Press.

Lawrence, M. (ed.) (1987) *Fed Up and Hungry: Women, Oppression and Food*. London: Women's Press.

Laws, S. (1990) *Issues of Blood: the Politics of Menstruation*. London: Macmillan.

Laws, S. (1992) 'It's just the monthlies, she'll get over it': menstrual problems and men's attitudes, *Journal of Reproductive and Infant Psychology*, 10: 117–28.

Laws, S. (1994) Un-valued families, *Trouble and Strife*, 28 (spring): 5–11.

Layland, J. (1990) On the conflicts of doing feminist research into masculinity, in L. Stanley (ed.) *Feminist Praxis*. London: Routledge.

Lee, R. M. and Renzetti, C. M. (1993) The problems of researching sensitive topics, in C. M. Renzetti and M. L. Raymond (eds) *Researching Sensitive Topics*. London: Sage.

Lees, S. (1986) *Losing Out: Sexuality and Adolescent Girls*. London: Hutchinson.

Lewis, H. (1994) *House Rules*. London: Secker and Warburg.

Lieven, E. (1981) If it's natural, we can't change it, in The Cambridge Women's Studies Group, *Women in Society*. London: Virago.

Lorde, A. (1984) The transformation of silence into language and action, in *Sister Outsider*. New York: Crossing Press.

Lumsden, M. A. (1990) Menorrhagia – the cost and scope of treatment, in R. W. Shaw (ed.) *Dysfunctional Uterine Bleeding*, Progress in Obstetrics and Gynaecology Series. Edinburgh: Churchill Livingstone.

Lyne de Ver, J. (1994) Research and development: a leading role for clinical psychologists, *Clinical Psychology Forum*, 11–13 May.

MacCannell, D. and MacCannell, J. K. (1993). Violence, power and pleasure: a revisionists reading of Foucault from the victim perspective, in C. Ramazanoglu (ed.) *Up Against Foucault: Explorations of Some Tensions Between Foucault and Feminism*. London: Routledge.

Mahoney, T. (1988) *Governing Schools: Powers and Issues and Practice*. London: Macmillan.

Mann, K. and Roseneil, S. (1994) 'Some mothers do 'ave 'em': backlash and the gender politics of the underclass debate. Paper presented at the Good Enough Mothering?: Feminist Perspectives on Lone Motherhood Conference, Leeds, 6 June.

Margolis, M. L. (1984) *Mothers and Such: Views of American Women and Why They Changed*. Berkeley, CA: University of California Press.

Marks, D. (1993) 'Discourse analysis and education case conferences', unpublished Ph.D. dissertation. Manchester Metropolitan University, May.

Marks, D. (in press a) Working together: defending against anxiety and conflict in education case conferences, *Journal of Therapeutic Education and Care*.

Marks, D. (in press b) Accounting for exclusion: giving a voice and producing a 'subject', in Burman, E. (ed.) *Psychology, Discourse and Social Practice: From Regulation to Resistance*. London: Taylor and Francis.

Marks, D., Burman, E., Burman, L. and Parker, I. (1995) Collaborative research into education case conferences, *Educational Psychology in Practice*, 11 (1): 94–101.

Marshall, H. (1991) The social construction of motherhood: an analysis of childcare and parenting manuals, in A. Phoenix, A. Woollett and E. Lloyd (eds) *Motherhood: Meanings, Practices and Ideologies*. London: Sage.

Mason-John, V. and Khambatta, A. (1993) *Lesbians Talk: Making Black Waves*. London: Scarlet Press.

Maynard, M. (1993) Violence against women, in D. Richardson and V. Robinson (eds) *Introducing Women's Studies*. London: Sage.

Maynard, M. (1994) Race, gender and the concept of 'difference' in feminist thought, in H. Afshar and M. Maynard (eds) *The Dynamics of 'Race' and Gender: Some Feminist Interventions*. London: Taylor and Francis.

McCartney, C. F. (1985) Decision by single women to conceive by artificial donor insemination, *Journal of Psychosomatic Obstetrics and Gynaecology*, 4: 321–8.

McFarland, B. and Baker-Baumann, T. (1990) *Shame and Body Image – Culture and the Compulsive Eater*. Deerfield Beach, FL: Health Communications.

McIntosh, M. (1993) Queer theory and the war of the sexes, in J. Bristow and A. Wilson (eds) *Activating Theory: Lesbian, Gay and Bisexual Politics*. London: Lawrence and Wishart.

McKee, L. and O'Brien, M. (1983) Interviewing Men: 'Taking Gender Seriously', in E. Gamarnikow, D. Morgan, J. Purvis and D. Taylorson (eds) *The Public and the Private*. London: Heinemann.

McLeod, E. (1994) *Women's Experiences of Feminist Therapy and Counselling*. Buckingham: Open University Press.

McNay, L. (1992) *Feminism and Foucault*. Oxford: Polity/Blackwell.

McRae, S. (1991) *Maternity Rights in Britain: The PSI Report on the Experience of Women and Employers*. London: Policy Studies Institute.

Melkie, J. (1994) Half of pupils 'lacking in motivation', *Guardian*, 23 August.

Mercer, K. and Julien, I. (1988) Race, sexual politics and black masculinity: a dossier, in R. Chapman and J. Rutherford (eds) *Male Order: Unwrapping Masculinity*. London: Lawrence and Wishart.

Middlemist, R. D. and Knowles, E. S. (1976) Personal space invasions in the lavatory: suggestive evidence for arousal, *Journal of Personality and Social Psychology*, 33 (5): 541–6.

Minh-Ha, T. (1989) *Woman, Native, Other*. Bloomingham, IN: Indiana University Press.

Mitchell, J. (1974) *Psychoanalysis and Feminism: A Radical Reassessment of Freudian Psychoanalysis*. London: Penguin.

Moore, S. (1988) Getting a bit of the other: the pimps of postmodernism, in R. Chapman and J. Rutherford (eds) *Male Order: Unwrapping Masculinity*. London: Lawrence and Wishart.

Moraga, C. and Anzaldua, G. (eds) (1981) *This Bridge Called My Back: Writings by Radical Women of Colour*. New York: Kitchen Table, Women of Color Press.

Morgan, G. (1986) *Images of Organization*. London: Sage.

Morris, J. (1991) *Pride against Prejudice: Transforming Attitudes to Disability*. London: Women's Press.

Morris, J. (1993) *Independent Lives? Disabled People and Community Care*. Harlow: Longman.

Morrison, T. (1981) *The Bluest Eye*. London: Triad Grafton Books.

Morrison, T. (1987) *Beloved*. London: Picador.

Mulvey, L. (1975) Visual pleasure and narrative cinema, *Screen*. 16 (6): 6–18.

Nelson, S. (1987) *Incest: Fact and Myth*. Edinburgh: Stramullion.

Oakley, A. (1974) *Housewife*. Harmondsworth: Penguin.

Oakley, A. (1979) *Becoming a Mother*. Oxford: Martin Robertson.

Oakley, A. (1981) Interviewing women: a contradiction in terms, in H. Roberts (ed.) *Doing Feminist Research*. London: Routledge and Kegan Paul.

Oliver, M. (1993) Disability and dependence: a creation of industrial societies?, in Swain *et al.* (eds) *Disabling Barriers – Enabling Environments*. London: Sage.

Omand, L. (1993) Food for thought: an exploration of some symbolic functions of food and eating, in British Psychological Society, *Psychotherapy Section Newsletter*, 14 (December): 44–54.

Orbach, S. (1978) *Fat is a Feminist Issue*. London: Paddington Press.

Orbach, S. (1982) *Fat is a Feminist Issue . . . II*. London: Hamlyn Paperbacks.

Orbach, S. (1985) Accepting the symptom: a feminist psychoanalytic treatment of anorexia nervosa, in D. M. Garner and P. E. Garfinkel (eds) *Handbook of Psychotherapy for Anorexia Nervosa and Bulimia*. New York: Guilford Press.

Orbach, S. (1986) *Hunger Strike*. London: Faber and Faber.

Orbach, S. (1990) Gender and dependency in psychotherapy, *Journal of Social Work Practice*, 4 (314), 1–15.

Palmer, N. R. (1988) The legal recognition of parental alienation syndrome, *American Journal of Family Therapy*, 16 (4): 361–3.

Parker, I. (1992) *Discourse Dynamics*. London: Routledge.

Patterson, C. (1992) Children of lesbian and gay parents, *Child Development*, 63: 1025–42.

Peckham, M. (1991) Research and development in the National Health Service, *The Lancet*, 228: 367–71.

Peery, J. C. (1994) Should sexual orientation be a consideration in custody proceedings? Yes, in M. A. Mason and E. Gambill (eds) *Debating Children's Lives: Current Controversies on Children and Adolescents*. London: Sage.

Pennington, S. Bisnovich (1987) Children of lesbian mothers, in F. W. Bozett (ed.) *Gay and Lesbian Parents*. New York: Praeger.

Phoenix, A. (1991) *Young Mothers?* Cambridge: Polity.

Phoenix, A. (1994) Practising feminist research: the intersection of gender and 'race' in the research process, in M. Maynard and J. Purvis (eds) *Researching Women's Lives from a Feminist Perspective*. London: Taylor and Francis.

Prince, J. and Hartnett, O. (1993) From 'psychology constructs the female' to 'fe/males construct psychology', *Feminism and Psychology*, 3 (2): 219–25.

Pringle, R. (1989) Bureaucracies, rationality and sexuality: the case of secretaries, in J. Hearn, D. Sheppard, P. Tancred-Sherif and G. Burrell, *The Sexuality of Organisation*. London: Sage.

Psyclit (1974–) Electronic database on CD Rom, American Psychological Association.

Radford, J. (1991) Immaculate conceptions, *Trouble and Strife*, 21 (summer): 8–12.

Ramazanoglu, C. (ed.) (1993) *Up Against Foucault*. London: Routledge.

Ramazanoglu, C. and Holland, J. (1993) Women's sexuality and men's appropriation of desire, in C. Ramazanoglu (ed.) *Up Against Foucault: Explorations of Some Tensions Between Foucault and Feminism*. London: Routledge.

Raymond, J. (1986) *A Passion for Friends: Towards a Philosophy of Female Affection*. London: Women's Press.

Reynolds, G. (1993) 'And Gill came tumbling after': gender, emotions and a research dilemma, in M. Kennedy, C. Lubelska and V. Walsh (eds) *Making Connections: Women's Studies, Women's Movements, Women's Lives*. London: Taylor and Francis.

Ribbens, J. (1989) Interviewing – an 'unnatural situation'?, *Women's Studies International Forum*, 12 (6): 579–92.

Rich, A. (1984) Compulsory heterosexuality and lesbian existence, in A. Snitow, C. Stamsell and S. Thompson (eds) *Desire: The Politics of Sexuality*. London: Virago.

Riley, D. (1983) *War in the Nursery: Theories of the Child and Mother*. London: Virago.

Riley, D. (1988) *'Am I That Name?': Feminism and the Category of Women in History*. Oxford: Polity/Blackwell.

Ritenbaugh, C. (1982) Obesity as a culture-bound syndrome, *Culture, Medicine and Psychiatry*, 6: 347–61.

Roberts, H. (1992) Answering back: the role of respondents in women's health research, in H. Roberts (ed.) *Women's Health Matters*. London: Routledge.

Rose, N. (1985) *The Psychological Complex: Psychology, Politics and Society in England, 1869–1939*. London: Routledge and Kegan Paul.

Rose, N. (1990) *Governing the Soul: The Shaping of the Private Self*. London: Routledge.

Rothblum, E. D. (1992) The stigma of women's weight: social and economic realities, *Feminism and Psychology*, 2 (1): 61–73.

Rothblum, E. D. (1994) 'I'll die for the revolution but don't ask me not to diet': feminism and the continuing stigmatization of obesity, in P. Fallon, M. Katzman and

S. Wooley (eds) *Feminist Perspectives on Eating Disorders*. New York: Guilford Press.
Rowth, G. (1982) *Feeding the Hungry Heart: The Experience of Compulsive Eating*. Scarborough, Ontario: Signet Books.
Rushton, J. P. (1988) Race differences in behaviour: a review and evolutionary analysis, *Personality and Individual Differences*, 9: 1009–24.
Rushton, J. P. (1990) Race differences r/K theory and a reply to Flynn, *The Psychologist*, 5: 195–8.
Ryan, J. (1983) *Feminism and Therapy*. London: Polytechnic of North London.
Saghal, G. and Yuval-Davis, N. (eds) (1992) *Refusing Holy Orders: Women and Fundamentalism in Britain*. London: Virago.
Sahlins, M. (1976) *Culture and Practical Reason*. London: The University of Chicago Press.
Sarup, M. (1991) *Education and the Ideologies of Racism*. London: Trentham Books.
Sayers, J. (1980) Psychological sex differences, in Brighton Women and Science Group, *Alice Through the Microscope: The Power of Science Over Women's Lives*. London: Virago.
Schein, E. (1985) *Organisational Culture and Leadership*. Oxford: Jossey-Bass.
Schein, E. (1990) Organizational culture, *American Psychologist*, 45 (2): 109–19.
Schoenfielder, L. and Wieser, B. (eds) (1983) *Shadow on a Tightrope: Writings by Women on Fat Oppression*. San Francisco, CA: Spinsters/aunt lute.
Scott, S. (1985) Feminist research and qualitative methods: a discussion of some of the issues, in R. G. Burgess (ed.) *Issues in Educational Research: Qualitative Methods*. London: Falmer Press.
Segal, L. (1990) *Slow Motion*. London: Virago.
Selltiz, C., Jahoda, M., Deutsch, M. and Cook, S. W. (1965) *Research Methods in Social Relations*. London: Methuen.
Seu, I. Bruna (1995) Psychoanalytic and feminist readings of women and shame, unpublished Ph.D. thesis. University College London.
Sherif, C. W. (1987) Bias in psychology, in S. Harding (ed.) *Feminism and Methodology*. Milton Keynes: Open University Press.
Showalter, E. (1987) *The Female Malady*. London: Virago.
Simon, W. T. and Schouten, P. G. W. (1991) Plethsmography in the assessment and treatment of sexual deviance: an overview, *Archives of Sexual Behaviour*, 20 (1): 75–91.
Sivanandan, A. (1990) *Communities of Resistance: Writings on Black Struggles for Socialism*. London: Verso.
Slade, P. and Jenner, F. A. (1980) Attitudes to female roles, aspects of menstruation and complaining of menstrual symptoms, *British Journal of Social and Clinical Psychology*, 19: 109–13.
Slade, R. J., Ahmed, A. I. H. and Gillmer, M. D. G. (1991) Problems with endometrial resection, *Lancet*, 337: 1473.
Smart, C. and Sevenhuijsen, S. (1989) *Child Custody and the Politics of Gender*. London: Routledge.
Smith, D. J. (1994) *The Sleep of Reason: The James Bulger Case*. London: Century.
Smyth, C. (1992) *Lesbians Talk: Queer Notions*. London: Scarlet Press.
Soothill, K. and Walby, S. (1991) *Sex Crimes in the News*. London: Routledge.
Spelman, E. V. (1988) *Inessential Woman: Problems of Exclusion in Feminist Thought*. London: Women's Press.
Spivak, C. G. (1988) *In Other Worlds: Essays in Cultural Politics*. New York: Routledge.

Spivak, C. (1990) The intervention interview, in S. Harasym (ed.) *The Post-Colonial Critic*. London: Routledge.
Spring, J. (1987) *Cry Hard and Swim*. London: Virago.
Squire, C. (1989) *Significant Differences: Feminism in Psychology*. London: Routledge.
Squire, C. (1990) Feminism as antipsychology, in E. Burman (ed.) *Feminists and Psychological Practice*. London: Sage.
Standing, K. (1994) *Lone Mothers' Unpaid Schoolwork as a Household Issue*. Paper for the Gender Perspectives on Household Issues Conference, Reading, April 1995.
Stanley, L. (ed.) (1990) *Feminist Praxis*. London: Routledge.
Stanley, L. and Wise, S. (1990) Method, methodology and epistemology in feminist research, in L. Stanley (ed.) *Feminist Praxis*. London: Routledge.
Stanley, L. and Wise, S. (1993) *Breaking Out Again: Feminist Ontology and Epistemology*. London: Routledge.
Stanworth, M. (ed.) (1987) *Reproductive Technologies: Gender, Motherhood and Medicine*. Cambridge: Polity Press.
Steckel, A. (1987) Psychosocial development of children of lesbian mothers, in F. W. Bozett (ed.) *Gay and Lesbian Parents*. New York: Praeger.
Stein, A. (ed.) (1993) *Sisters, Sexperts, Queers: Beyond the Lesbian Nation*. Harmondsworth: Plume.
Swaan, A. de (1990) *The Management of Normality: Critical Essays in Health and Welfare*. London: Routledge.
Swain, J., Finkelstein, V., French, S. and Oliver, M. (eds) (1993) *Disabling Barriers – Enabling Environments*. London: Sage publications, in association with the Open University.
Swartz, L. (1985a) Is thin a feminist issue?, *Women's Studies International Forum*, 8 (5): 429–37.
Swartz, L. (1985b) Anorexia nervosa as a culture-bound syndrome, *British Journal of Medical Psychology*, 20 (7): 725–30.
Szekeley, E. A. (1989) From eating disorders to women's situations: extending the boundaries of psychological inquiry, *Counselling Psychology Quarterly*, 2 (2): 167–84.
Tasker, F. and Golombok, S. (1991) Children raised by lesbian mothers: the empirical evidence, *Family Law*, May: 184–7.
Taylor, K. (1995) 'Family friendly policies in practice – home and work perspectives', unpublished MPhil thesis. Manchester Metropolitan University.
Tickner, L. (1987) *The Spectacle of Women: Imagery of the Suffrage Campaign 1907–14*. London: Chatto and Windus.
Tindall, V. R. (1987) *Jeffcoate's Principles of Gynaecology*, 5th edn. Butterworth.
Tomlinson, S. (1981) *Educational Subnormality: A Study in Decision-Making*. London: Routledge and Kegan Paul.
Troyna, B. (1988) The career of an antiracist education school policy: some observations on the mismanagement of change, in A. Green and S. Ball (eds) *Progress and Inequality in Comprehensive Education*. London: Routledge.
Unger, R. K. (1979) *Female and Male*. London: Harper and Row.
Urwin, C. (1985) Constructing motherhood: the persuasion of normal development, in C. Steedman, C. Urwin and V. Walkerdine (eds) *Language, Gender and Childhood*. London: Routledge and Kegan Paul.

Ussher, J. (1989) *The Psychology of the Female Body*. London: Routledge.
Ussher, J. (1990) Choosing psychology or not throwing the baby out with the bath water, in E. Burman (ed.) *Feminists and Psychological Practice*. London: Sage.
Ussher, J. (1991) *Women's Madness: Misogyny or Mental Illness?* Hemel Hempstead: Harvester Wheatsheaf.
Van Every, J. (1991) Who is 'the family'? The assumptions of British social policy, *Critical Social Policy*, 33 (Winter 1991/1992): 62–76.
von Foerster, H. (1991) Through the eyes of the other, in F. Steier (ed.) *Research and Reflexivity*. London: Sage Publications.
Walkerdine, V. (1990) Sex, power and pedagogy, in *School Girl Fictions*. London: Verso.
Walkerdine, V. and Lucey, H. (1989) *Democracy in the Kitchen: Regulating Mothers and Socialising Daughters*. London: Virago.
Walsh, B. T. (1992) Diagnostic criteria for eating disorders in DSM-IV: work in progress, *International Journal of Eating Disorders*, 11 (4): 301–4.
Ward, E. (1984) *Father–Daughter Rape*. London: Women's Press.
Ware, V. (1992) *Beyond the Pale: White Women, Racism and History*. London: Verso.
Warner, M. (1994) *Managing Monsters: Six Myths of Our Time, the 1994 Reith Lectures*. London: Vintage.
Warner, P. (1994) Preferences regarding treatments for period problems: relationship to menstrual and demographic factors, *Journal of Psychosomatic Obstetrics and Gynaecology*, 15: 93–110.
Weedon, C. (1987) *Feminist Practice and Poststructuralist Theory*. Oxford: Basil Blackwell.
Weijts, W., Widdershoven, G. and Kok, G. (1991) Anxiety-scenarios in communication during gynaecological consultations, *Patient Education and Counselling*, 18: 149–63.
White, J. H. (1991) Feminism, eating, and mental health, *Advanced Nursing Science*, 13 (3): 68–80.
Whitney, B. (1993) *The Children Act and Schools*. London: Kogan Page.
Wijma, K. and Areskog-Wijma, B. (1987) Women's experiences of their genitals as an important aspect of their meetings with gynaecologists, *Journal of Psychosomatic Obstetrics and Gynaecology*, 6: 133–41.
Wilding, P. (1982) *Professional Power and Social Welfare*. London: Routledge and Kegan Paul.
Wilkinson, S. (ed.) (1986) *Feminist Social Psychology*. Milton Keynes: Open University Press.
Wilkinson, S. (1988) The role of reflexivity in feminist psychology, *Women's Studies International Forum*, 11 (5): 493–502.
Wilson, M. (1993) *Crossing the Boundary: Black Women Survive Incest*. London: Virago.
Wilson, P. (1973) *Children Who Kill*. London: Michael Joseph.
Wilton, T. (1993) Queer subjects: lesbians, heterosexual women and the academy, in M. Kennedy, C. Lubelska and V. Walsh (eds) *Making Connections: Women's Studies, Women's Movements and Women's Lives*. London: Taylor and Francis.
Winkel, M. (1993) Autonomic differentiation of temporal components of sexist humor, *Humor – International Journal of Humor Research*, 6 (1): 27–42.
Wolf, N. (1993) *Fire with Fire: The New Female Power and How It Will Change the 21st Century*. London: Chatto and Windus.

Woodhead, M. (1990) Psychology and the cultural construction of children's needs, in A. James and A. Prout (eds) *Constructing and Reconstructing Childhood*. London: Falmer Press.

Wooley, S. C. and Wooley, O. W. (1979a) Obesity and women – I. A closer look at the facts, *Women's Studies International Quarterly*, 2: 69–79.

Wooley, S. C. and Wooley, O. W. (1979b) Obesity and women – II. A neglected feminist topic, *Women's Studies International Quarterly*, 2: 81–92.

Woollett, A. (1991) Having children: accounts of childless women and women with reproductive problems, in A. Phoenix, A. Woollett and E. Lloyd (eds) *Motherhood: Meanings, Practices and Ideologies*. London: Sage.

Woollett, A. and Phoenix, A. (1991) Psychological views of mothering, in A. Phoenix, A. Woollett and E. Lloyd (eds) *Motherhood: Meanings, Practices and Ideologies*. London: Sage.

Yuval-Davis, N. (1993) Beyond difference: women and coalition politics, in M. Kennedy, C. Lubelska and V. Walsh (eds) *Making Connections: Women's Studies, Women's Movements, Women's Lives*. London: Taylor and Francis.

Zinn, M. Baca (1992) Family, race, and poverty in the eighties, in B. Thorne and M. Yalom (eds) *Rethinking the Family: Some Feminist Questions*. Boston, MA: Northeastern University Press.

Zmroczek, C. and Duchen, C. (1989) Women's studies and feminist research in the UK, *Women's Studies International Forum*, 12 (6): 603–10.

Zukerman, M. and Brody, N. (1988) Oysters, rabbits and people: a critique of 'Race Differences in Behaviour' by J. P. Rushton, *Personality and Individual Differences*, 9: 1025–33.

Index

QUALITATIVE METHODS IN PSYCHOLOGY
A RESEARCH GUIDE

Peter Banister, Erica Burman, Ian Parker, Maye Taylor and Carol Tindall

This book is a collaborative production, based on the experiences of the co-authors in presenting a course in qualitative methods over many years to MSc students. This is not an edited book, the authors have drafted particular chapters, but the team has collectively discussed, reworked and rewritten the text to produce a coherent review and guide to the area. This research guide is designed to be an introductory text to qualitative methods, intended for advanced undergraduate and postgraduate students. As well as furnishing an understanding of the assumptions underlying such research methods, the book is intended to present a practical guide as to how to carry out qualitative investigations, and in addition to provide the basis for a critical evaluation of these methods.

Contents

192pp   0 335 19181 9 (Paperback)   0 335 19182 7 (Hardback)

POWER IN STRUGGLE
FEMINISM, SEXUALITY AND THE STATE

Davina Cooper

What is power? And how are social change strategies shaped by the ways in which we conceptualize it? Drawing on feminist, poststructuralist, and marxist theory, Davina Cooper develops an innovative framework for understanding power relations within fields as diverse as queer activism, municipal politics, and the regulation of lesbian reproduction. *Power in Struggle* explores the relationship between power, sexuality, and the state and, in the process, provides a radical rethinking of these concepts and their interactions. The book concludes with an important and original discussion of how an ethics of empowerment can inform political strategy.

Special features:

- brings together central aspects of current radical, political theory in an innovative way
- offers a new way of conceptualizing the state, power and sexuality

Contents

192pp 0 335 19211 4 (Paperback) 0 335 19212 2 (Hardback)

GENDERED WORK
SEXUALITY, FAMILY AND THE LABOUR MARKET

Lisa Adkins

Gendered Work contributes to current debates on the labour market via an exploration of the significance of sexual and family relations in structuring employment. Through detailed studies of conditions of work in the British tourist industry, it shows how men and women are constituted as different kinds of 'workers' in the labour market not only when segregated in different occupations but also even when they are nominally located in the same jobs.

This differentiation is shown to be connected to two key processes: the sexualization of women workers which locates women as sexual as well as 'economic' workers, and the operation of family work relations within the sphere of employment when women work as wives rather than waged-labourers in the context of the contemporary labour market. These two processes are then drawn together to show the ways in which labour market production is gendered. This book therefore makes an important contribution to the growing feminist literature which is exposing the deep embeddedness of gender within labour market processes and practices.

Special features:

- New empirical material on the terms and conditions of typical contemporary jobs for women.
- New ways of understanding the gendered structure of the labour market.
- Reviews a range of analyses (feminist and sociological) in a constructively critical way to throw light on change and continuity in employment in the consumer society.

Contents

Introduction – Sexuality and the labour market – Family production and the labour market – Sexual servicing and women's employment – The condition of women's work – Bibliography – Index.

192pp 0 335 19296 3 (Paperback) 0 335 19297 1 (Hardback)